No ....,...............

Author ....

Title ....

D0997955

Adrian Vaughan, foremost railway historian, discovered Brunel's Great Western Railway in 1946, when he passed under the line daily on his way to school. He worked on the railways until 1975, since when he has written twenty-five books on the subject, most recently *The Heart of the Great Western* (1994), *Railwaymen, Politics and Money: The Great Age of Railways in Britain* (John Murray, 1997) and *Tracks to Disaster* (2000).

ADRIAN VAUGHAN

Isambard Kingdom
BRUNEL

Engineering Knight-Errant

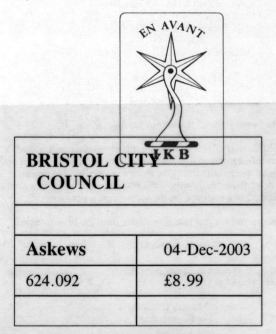

EN AVANT

IKB

John Murray

© Adrian Vaughan 1991

First published in 1991 by John Murray (Publishers)
A division of Hodder Headline

Paperback edition 1993
Reissued 1997
Reprinted 2000, 2001, 2002, 2003

This paperback edition 2003

1 3 5 7 9 10 8 6 4 2

A CIP catalogue record for this title is available from the British Library

ISBN 0-7195-5748 8

Typeset in Times New Roman
Printed and bound in Great Britain by Clays Ltd, St Ives plc

John Murray (Publishers)
338 Euston Road
London
NW1 3BH

To my dearest Susan
to whom I owe everything

Contents

Illustrations

ACKNOWLEDGEMENTS

1 Bristol Museum and Gallery; 2, 3 from Richard Beamish, *Memoir of Sir Marc Isambard Brunel*; 4, 13 Public Record Office; 5, 6, 7, 8, 18, 20, 21, 22 British Rail; 9, 10, 11, 12 Science Museum, reproduced by permission of the Trustees; 14 Felton Bequest 1932, reproduced by permission of the National Gallery of Victoria, Melbourne; 15 Bristol University Library; 16, 17, 19 Author; 23, 24, 25, 26, 27, 28 Brunel University Library. Illustrations in the text are taken from Isambard Brunel, *Life of Isambard Kingdom Brunel*.

Preface

The Isambard Kingdom Brunel I 'knew' was the one introduced to me by L.T.C. Rolt in the biography he published in 1957. I never thought to query his view until 1984 when I re-read that book. I thought that the following passage, to be found on p. 138, was a very sweeping statement: 'No strikes or labour disputes marred the building of the Great Western. Every man from Brunel down to the navvy . . . was inspired with a determination to see the job through. . . .' The passage continues at length in increasingly cosy, romantic tones.

Considering that the railway was 118 miles long and that it had taken many thousands of men six years to build it, I wondered if this absolute statement concerning strikes was true. I also questioned whether a strike necessarily 'mars' a job of work. I consulted *The Times* for the second quarter of 1838 and at once discovered a strike of navvies. In May 1838 the hard-working men had not been paid for two weeks so they were right to strike work and it was their employer, not the workmen, who was marring the job.

I realised that Rolt's view of Brunellian history was distorted by an uncritical hero-worship of his subject and his book was written to support his preconceived ideas. He gives only Brunel's account of events while his statements concerning John Scott Russell denigrate an outstanding Victorian engineer and naval architect. I realised that a more objective story of Isambard Kingdom Brunel still remained to be written and looked forward to the opportunity to do my own research.

I spent hundreds of hours reading Isambard's own words, at the end of which time I felt I could hear his different tones of voice and feel his moods. This was good but after a short time I realised that the Brunel collection of books and papers in London and Bristol contained very little *from* others *to* Brunel. There was no record of the other side of the argument, only thousands of letters *to* the others *from* Brunel. Because of this I read Isambard's letters with extra care and after a while I became alarmed at the unconventional picture (unconventional if one has grown up on the 'Roltian' view) that was taking shape. Sometimes he seemed not a very pleasant person. Was I constructing a false picture of the man?

I was reassured when I discovered a book on John Scott Russell by George Emmerson, marine engineer and Professor of Engineering Science at the University of Western Ontario. This meticulously researched book is essential reading for anyone who wants to know the full story of Brunel, John Scott Russell and the SS *Great Eastern*. Emmerson published letters from the Hollingworth Collection at Bath University – material which escaped the attempt by the Brunels to sanitise – or sanctify – the family archive after the death of Isambard. These letters, from Russell and John Yates (Company Secretary to the Eastern Steam Navigation Co., for whom Isambard was Engineer), give us that very valuable other side to the argument. The chapters in this book that deal with the SS *Great Eastern* draw heavily on Professor Emmerson's fine research.

Charles Hadfield's book *Atmospheric Railways* also contains a rare letter, replying to Brunel and giving the other side of the argument. I was encouraged by this, and felt that I had correctly seen through the edited archive to the real man Brunel, a normal human being, and so pressed on with the work – two years in all. Brought up as I was on the conventional, heroic story, the discovery of the real I.K. Brunel was a considerable surprise to me but I think I have arrived at my conclusions fairly and honestly.

I have drawn my information, as far as possible, from original papers, rather than published books. The largest collection of Brunel papers is held at Bristol University Library and I spent several weeks there reading Isambard's letters and private diaries – from which two pages concerning his adolescent love affairs have been removed, presumably by his wife, after his death. I must thank the past and present curators of the Brunel Collection at Bristol University

Library, George Mayby and Nick Lee respectively, for their kindness, patience and very helpful assistance. I read the Bristol local papers 1831–43 for information on Bristol Corporation, the riots and the SS *Great Britain* at Bristol City Reference Library; at Norwich Public Library I consulted contemporary issues of *The Times*; and at Cambridge University Library I read the *Observer* for November 1854. I also used the House of Lords Record Office and the Library of the Institution of Civil Engineers, which among many important papers has obituaries for several of Isambard's chief assistants, thus throwing light on hitherto shadowy people and allowing me to show the cavalier way Isambard treated men of intellect equal to his own. I must thank the staff of these libraries for their kind assistance. G.C. Tudor of Torquay, the expert on Brunel's estate at Watcombe, was generous in supplying information in this regard, and the Headmaster of Harrow School, Ian Beer, was very helpful with facts concerning the school career of Isambard Brunel junior.

I also spent many days in British Rail's private warehouse at Royal Oak near Paddington, reading legal documents relating to the Brunel/McIntosh litigation, the Brunel/Mudge-Marchant arbitration and the Birmingham Snow Hill tunnel fiasco. These are not yet in the public domain and I must thank British Rail for giving me access to them.

I have to thank my friends Kalla Bishop and Angus Low for advice regarding Italian history and place names, and Hattie Low both for her painstaking decipherment of Marc Brunel's handwriting and for her translations from the French of his letters to Breguet and others. My friend Kenneth Leech gave me the true story concerning the legend of sunrise and Box tunnel, meticulously researched and proved by his friend Donald Stuart. For his account of the structure of Brunel's hospital in the Crimea, published in the *Ove Arup Journal* of July 1981, I am indebted to David Toppin.

I want to thank those kind friends who gave me the free quarter which enabled me to spend weeks away from home on research, Paul and Sue Dye in Bristol, Ron and Jo Price and my sister Frances in London. I would also like to thank Duncan McAra for his continuing kindness and editorial expertise and Grant McIntyre, my editor at John Murray. And I thank, of course, my wife Susan for her loyal support.

I

Apprentice to Marc

1

Invention and Insecurity

Isambard Kingdom Brunel was born on 9 April 1806 in a terrace house in Britain Street, Portsea, Portsmouth, a brother for five-year-old Sophia and two-year-old Emma. Their father was Marc Brunel, a French *émigré* who, though a Royalist at the time of the Revolution, had escaped the guillotine and, after attempting to make his fortune in the State of New York, had come to England to assist the war effort against Napoleonic France.

Marc had arrived in March 1799 in London, where he had married Sophia Kingdom that November. They had met in 1792, during the Terror, and after his abrupt flight abroad she had been imprisoned by the Jacobins and had escaped execution only after the urgent intercessions of the townsfolk of Rouen, where she had been sent to learn the language. She was a Plymouth girl, granddaughter of the great English clockmaker, Thomas Mudge.

Sophia was loyal, warm-hearted, patient and brave and to her Marc attributed all his success. Marc was a musician, artist, inventor and practical engineer. He had given up the Catholicism he inherited at birth and seems to have cared little for any established religion, although he prayed privately, as diary entries show. He cared not at all for money – except in so far as it was needed to meet domestic commitments or pay workmen. Above all else he wanted to invent and construct.

So Isambard was born into a loving, unassuming and near-penniless family, living on credit for most of the time, their collateral Marc's new-fangled machines – for which he hoped one day the

Government would pay him – and the prospect of more inventions to come.

Marc was probably one of the most inventive engineers in Europe at that time. Between 1799 and 1825 he was granted seventeen patents for machines that were seminal for the development of the mechanised nineteenth century. He was alert to identify a need and enterprising enough to create a product which would meet that need. This was evident during the period when Britain was at war with France and two examples illustrate his initiative: one was the mass-production of blocks for the Royal Navy; the other was a plant for turning out sturdy boots for the British Army. Unhappily, his hopes of making a fortune from these projects were never realised because the Government of the day, though ready to take advantage of his inventions, was slow and niggardly to reward him.

Resilient in the face of frustration, disappointments and financial reverses, he had moved the family home from Portsea to Chelsea to set up his own sawmill and boot-making factory at Battersea and, with a partner, a heavy-machinery plant at Chatham Dockyard for processing timber for naval ships.

Marc Brunel's new home was at 4 Lindsey Row, corresponding now to 98 Cheyne Row, and this was where young Isambard spent his early boyhood. An active, lively lad, he learned to swim in the Thames at the end of the garden. As the water was not much better than sewage in 1813 and as he must have swallowed the odd mouthful it is possible that he weakened his health in this way. It is certain that, even as a boy, he suffered intermittent but fairly lengthy bouts of illness. Nevertheless he would bounce back to vigorous health and, living on the river bank, also learned to handle a rowing boat. He enjoyed making up plays and acting in them with his sisters just as he enjoyed, and showed early promise at, drawing and painting. The artistic side of his nature, though, was not deliberately developed.

Marc wanted his son to be an engineering genius and planned quite deliberately to turn him into one. Marc was determined to give him all the things that he himself had had to fight so hard for when he was a boy. He decided the boy's future as an engineer in exactly the same way as his own father had decided he was going to be a priest. Isambard's education began at home, at the age of four, under his father who taught him the rudiments of arithmetic and geometry – Marc's own boyhood enthusiasms – and showed him how to draw, free-hand, perfect circles. When Isambard was eight, in 1814, he was sent for a short time to a school in Chelsea run by the Revd Weedon Butler and continued with his very modern education – arithmetic and some geometry as well as Greek and Latin – and showed an aptitude for figures. It is incorrect though to state, as Rolt has stated, that Isambard had 'mastered Euclid' by the time he was six. He did not start studying Euclid until he was eleven.

In April 1814 the Emperor Napoleon was forced to abdicate and to go into exile. The long war then being over, the British Government did not want any more army boots. This was a serious blow to the Brunels because they had not yet recouped the money they had invested in the boot-making machines and they were left with thousands of boots which the Government now would not buy from them. However, they still had their sawmill, which was very busy, so they could afford to send Isambard, now aged eight, to Dr Morell's boarding school in Hove. His father had chosen the school very carefully. Dr Morell was a Unitarian clergyman, of fairly advanced views on education – for instance he preached sermons on the advisability of a formal education for girls – and specifically did not allow bullying, fagging, flogging or any other of the horrors which typified the leading public schools of that time. He also taught modern languages as well as Greek and Latin and included geography and mathematics in the curriculum. Dogmatic religious faith – as perceived by the Established Church – was not taught. It was a progressive academy and its choice says much about Marc.

Disaster struck the Brunels on the night of 30 August 1814 when Marc's Battersea sawmill was burned down. In the ensuing stock-taking he found that instead of the expected £10,000 he had £865 in the bank. His partner had been cheating him. Marc did not despair but scraped together some more money and rebuilt the mill with improved machinery. The family fortunes rose when army boots were again in demand after Napoleon's escape from Elba in March 1815, but after the Emperor's defeat at Waterloo in June the Government once more promptly cancelled their orders for boots leaving Marc with a large surplus of boots and a larger deficit of money. Since Marc had built his boot-making plant at the Government's request he had a good case for compensation, but he had not been paid when his boots were vital to the British war effort so there was no likelihood at all that he would be paid once the crisis was over.

Marc often prefixed his designs 'Great' when the vogue word was

'Grand'. He designed a 'Great Saw' and in 1818 he planned a 'Great Bridge' over the Neva using an 880-ft arch of laminated wood. This did not answer the case so he designed a cylindrical tunnelling device but the Russians then dropped the project. These hopes and disappointments are characteristic of the way the Brunels lived on the edge of ruin. They were supported by a friendly banker and by actual receipts from the sawmill. Marc had developed new concepts in mass-production but he could not keep accounts. When he called in his banker friend Sansom to unravel his accounts, Sansom reported: 'It is such an extraordinary jumble which, had you understood it, I would not have been more surprised than if one of your saws had walked into Town.'

Still, so long as Marc's bankers honoured his cheques, he and his family continued to eat and to enjoy a quiet social life. They were particular friends of the Hawes family, soap manufacturers of Lambeth. William Hawes was Isambard's age and Benjamin Hawes was six years older, just the right age for Isambard's sister, Sophia. Benjamin and Sophia were married in 1819 or 1820. She was then clear of the Brunellian ship, foundering in its sea of debt.

Isambard was aware of his father's inventiveness and the good it had done the British war effort. He was also aware of the wealth of his father's admirers and acutely aware of his father's lack of financial reward, which amounted to his being cheated.

The bright, cheerful, often rumbustious little boy was tutored, channelled and trained for a career in which great results were expected. It was more than merely sending Isambard to school, he was groomed for stardom. He was told he could be a great man only if he worked hard.

But a lively lad of eleven is not the sort of creature who will easily forsake boyhood for ambition, and Marc had to work hard to direct the boy along the 'straight and narrow'. It was to this end that in September 1817, Isambard, not yet twelve, was taken away from Hove and sent to Marc's nephew somewhere in France. The identity of this nephew is not known but during this stay it is known that Isambard was introduced to Louis Breguet, famous for the chronometers he made in his workshop in Paris.

Marc wrote to his nephew:

I entrust my little boy to you as he needs a Mentor. I don't believe I could make a better choice than in imploring you to moderate the impetuosity of his youth. He is a good little boy but he doesn't care for books except mathematics for which he has a liking. He has started Euclid. Use it as much as you can. . . . You must not let him sit an excessive or immoderate examination as he often becomes exhausted. . . . As he is not always in the best of health he sometimes needs to take a small dose of rhubarb which he carries with him. He must not be allowed to drink cider.

Isambard later returned to Dr Morell's school in Hove, a reformed character. His French mentor had turned him into an enthusiast for Latin in addition to mathematics. In 1819, aged thirteen, he wrote a report on himself to his mother:

I am at present reading Terence and Horace. *I like Horace very much but not as much as Virgil*. I have been making half a dozen boats recently till I have worn my hands to pieces. I have also taken a plan of Hove which is a very amusing job. I should be much obliged if you would ask Papa (I hope he is well and hearty) whether he would lend me his long measure . . . for I want a more exact plan. I have also been drawing a little. I intend to take a view of all (about five) the principal houses in that great town – Hove.

It is, I think, significant of Isambard's attitude towards his father that he addressed requests to him through his mother. Marc was full of love for Isambard but desired above all that he should achieve great things. So he, Marc, was also the stern father whom Isambard viewed as a kindly but none the less Olympian figure to be approached with circumspection. To imitate him would be to become as clever and as highly admired as he was. It was not a large step to go from imitation to rivalry.

In April 1820, Isambard was sent to Caen College. Only in France could he find an advanced mathematical education. From there he went to the Lycée Henri IV in Paris. The Lycée existed to prepare boys for the entrance examination to the world's only university of science and engineering – the École Polytechnique – which trained all French civil and military engineers. There is a fine irony in the fact that the college was set up under the progressive rule of Napoleon for whose downfall Marc Brunel had so assiduously worked.

Marc also arranged that, during this second period in France, Isambard should take tuition in the workshops of Louis Breguet, and indeed he lived with the Breguet family. For such a great and meticulous craftsman as Breguet to take a personal interest in a youth of fourteen says much for the craftsmanship of the boy – and for the potential which Breguet perceived in him. On 28 November 1820, Marc Brunel wrote to Breguet:

> I would have liked to have come to Paris . . . but I was occupied . . . with a new process of stereotype which Isambard will be able to explain to you with the greatest precision as he has now been my collaborator for several months. I have found him not only very useful but of still greater, unflinching, perseverance. He never gets tired even though we work till past midnight. As a draughtsman he surpasses me . . . not only by his exactitude with which he copies but also by his rare frame of mind. He loves work . . . which holds his attention and involves his hands. He cannot find a better way of occupying himself than working with you and is persuaded that he will be recognised by it.

This is the earliest indication of Isambard's ambition for public recognition.

Early in 1821, Marc's bankers, Sykes & Co., failed. Marc's credit was no longer sound and on 14 May 1821 he was committed to the prison of King's Bench for debt. Sophia insisted on going to gaol with him. Isambard was in Paris at the time and distance may have cushioned him from the shame all the family would undoubtedly have felt.

Isambard's education continued even after the imprisonment of his parents and one supposes that some benefactor was footing the bill. While Isambard was busy with quill pen, quadratic equations, lathe and file, his father and mother were sitting in a prison cell, she darning his socks, he working on drawings for new ideas. Marc wrote to Lord Spencer: 'My affectionate wife and I are sinking under it. If my enemies were at work to effect the ruin of mind and body they could not do so more effectually.' But no one in England could move the Chancellor to pay Marc what he was owed, so he played his trump card. He let it be known that he had written to Tsar Alexander, asking 'to work under the protection of a sovereign whose enlightenment and liberality seems to shine forth doubly in contrast with the callousness of the government at home'. At this the Exchequer granted him £5000 on condition that he did not later go to Russia, a condition Marc accepted. He and Sophia were released early in August 1821 and returned home free of debt but otherwise penniless.

2

Without a Penny

Marc at once set to work to regain his fortune. His office at 29 Poultry, in the City close to the Bank of England, was staffed only by a clerk, and Marc asked Breguet whether Isambard should remain with him continuing his education or whether it would be reasonable to call him home to help in the office. Breguet replied on 21 November 1821: 'I feel it is important to cultivate in him his happy, inventive disposition that he owes to nature or to education; it would be a pity to see it lost.' Isambard stayed with Breguet, living with the family, working as a clock- and instrument-maker. He wrote to his parents dutifully every week, and on 19 February 1822 Marc was moved to write the following to Louis Breguet:

> He has his admission to the École Polytechnique next August and he will not be put off under any circumstances. I look forward impatiently to what could be a successful examination whilst he must be scared stiff of the result. If he has the good luck to acquit himself well he will not only be more sure of himself and the future but it will also decide his future.

It is interesting to read Marc's reference to Isambard's surprising lack of confidence in himself, an aspect that I shall return to later. He failed the entrance examination to the École although that need not reflect upon his ability – there were 600 French boys chasing fewer than 100 places. Indeed, it might be a measure of his distress at events at home that he failed the exam. In any case, he returned to his family on 21 August, carrying with him a priceless experience, the personal friendship of Louis Breguet and the only title which he was really proud to own: 'Élève de Breguet'.

Isambard was not the only person blessed with boundless energy in the Brunel household. His father was working at several important projects. In June 1822 he had patented 'certain improvements to steam-engines'. These included expanding rings around pistons to keep them steam-tight and a boiler so designed that no matter how a ship rolled the fire-tubes were never uncovered and burned. Steam in this boiler was collected in a large dome, the first time a dome had been applied to a boiler. For good measure, it was fired by a mechanical stoker.

These improvements were applied to a 'V twin' steam engine which was installed in the Thames paddle-steamer, *Regent*, plying between London and Margate. Marc suggested to the Admiralty that his machinery could be fitted in a steam-tug which could haul their sail-driven warships in and out of port. Their Lordships were appalled at the thought of all that soot falling on the clean, white sails of British men o' war and replied sternly, considering it their 'bounden duty to discourage the employment of steam vessels as they consider the introduction of steam is calculated to strike a fatal blow at the naval supremacy of the Empire'.

At this time Marc was also designing two 131-ft-span suspension bridges for the French Government at the Ile de Bourbon, two more to cross a canal in Huddersfield, yet another over the Thames at Kingston, the Bermondsey Dock for the Grand Surrey Canal, a floating pier for Liverpool Dock, a stone bridge with a very flat arch over the Dart at Totnes, a survey for a canal from Fowey to Padstow and a sawmill for the British Government in British Guiana. Isambard could not have had a better training in civil engineering design than in his father's office and it is interesting to see that the germ of much of what he was later to undertake in his own career already existed in his father's works or on his drawings.

Between August 1822 and the start of the Thames Tunnel in 1825, Isambard's life was, relatively speaking, relaxed. He was busy on many small jobs for his father and continued his manual engineering experience in the shops of the machine-tool craftsman Henry Maudslay, while his entertainment took the form of visiting his sister Sophia and his brother-in-law Benjamin Hawes, with whom he grew to be very close, and walking or rowing with Benjamin's younger brother William.

Marc never ceased to urge Isambard to grasp every opportunity to improve himself. He was encouraged, if not actually forced, to skip adolescence and go straight to maturity. On his seventeenth birthday in 1823, Isambard went away for a few days and, from the following letter, it would seem that not even Marc knew where he had gone. By way of birthday greeting Marc sent him this exhortation:

> I hope, dear child, that you are using your time wisely. If you are at Bowling it is there you must study the true composition of iron, from the mineral to the finished product. How much coal, how much lime, mineral, how much coke, in a word, every process, with all the precision of a chemist. They will refuse you no opportunities there and when you know your facts you will be able to speak with manufacturers whom you will see later.

A delightful birthday message for Isambard! Although only a solitary letter, all that is available to researchers, it is probably representative of the whole tenor of Isambard's upbringing. Having urged upon the boy the necessity for iron facts on his birthday, Marc tried to sweeten the lesson with a dollop of gruesomely patronising sentimentality – and even then he could not resist just one more exhortation to grab at vaulting ambition. He wrote: '17 years old today! What a man! Years do not matter to the noble soul! You have a career open to you from which you must seize every opportunity. . . .' Poor Marc. He was no doubt only trying to be as loving and encouraging as his own father had been brutal and dismissive.

Did Isambard never feel the oppressive patronage? Did the constant urgings to collect facts and work, work, work to become famous never make him feel rebellious? During 1823 he wrote in his diary – in shorthand French – 'A dispute with my father. He threatened to give me a clout. This I will not stand.'

In January 1823, I.W. Tate, a Director of the moribund Thames Archway Company which had tried and failed, with various contractors, to drive a tunnel beneath the Thames, discovered Marc Brunel and the tunnelling shield he had invented. The shield would support an excavation while a brick tube was built behind it – a brilliant idea and exactly what was required. Tate offered Marc the post of Engineer of the Thames Tunnel Company with a salary of £1000 a year with an immediate royalty of £5000 for the use of his shield and a further £5000 when the job was complete. Marc accepted and

Marc Brunel's tunnelling shield

a Board of Directors was formed including G.H. Wollaston, an eminent scientist and close friend of Marc's, as Deputy Chairman, and Ben Hawes and Brian Donkin, an engineer and owner of a manufactory, as Directors. The Chairman was William Smith, MP for Norwich, a pompous know-all famous for his ability to support totally incompatible causes – being simultaneously Parliamentary spokesman for various Christian groups and also for the slave-trading lobby.

Marc designed a single, rectangular excavation, 1200 ft long, which would be filled with twin brick archways each 17 ft tall and 14 ft wide, dipping from the foot of the shaft at Cow Court, Rotherhithe, to midstream and then rising to another shaft near Wapping High Street. During 1823 the Brunel family moved from Chelsea to 30 Bridge Street, Blackfriars, about two miles from the tunnel site and Marc began to plan its detail design while also pursuing other engineering jobs.

In the spring of 1823, at a meeting of the Royal Society, of which he was a Fellow, Marc heard Sir Humphry Davy read a paper describing Michael Faraday's work on the liquefaction of gases. Faraday showed that when sulphuric acid and carbonate of ammonia were brought together a gas was produced. When the vessel containing the gas was immersed in very cold water an extremely light, colourless fluid was produced which, at 0°C, exerted a pressure of 450 lb per square inch. At 50°C the pressure rose to 975 lb psi. Marc wanted to use this pressure differential as a power source – although he would have to find a metal which could withstand 975 lb psi when 50 lb psi was considered exceedingly dangerous. Probably because the Gaz engine promised power without a lot of black smoke, the ultra-conservative Lords of Admiralty thought it a splendid idea and gave Marc £200 towards his development costs – which up to July 1825 amounted to £1250.

Isambard's diary gives a good indication of the brisk, but far from overwhelming, pace of his life. A particularly picturesque entry is the one for 1 May 1825:

Went to Town to catch 8 a.m. stage-coach to Kingston from Gracechurch St. The only morning stage – the Guildford – had gone. They said, however, that if I made haste I could catch up with it at Elephant & Castle. [He made haste and caught it, for the entry continues:] Got on the outside and then measured Kingston Bridge with the help of a young man whom

I got to help me. Dined at Lion tavern. Next day moored boat under arch and took a sketch of the river both above and below [the bridge]. Walked along the towing path to Richmond and returned by steamboat.

He spent many days, over a period of weeks, making drawings for his father's suspension bridge at this site.

While Marc decided to re-design his tunnelling shield, Isambard worked hard to bring the Gaz engine to an operational state, and also made the definitive drawings of the brick shaft from the bottom of which the tunnel would be driven under the Thames. He may also have had a hand in its design but all the diary entry for 1 July 1824 states is: 'Began a drawing of the ironwork of the circular shaft' and this entry is repeated over several days. He also undertook various experiments with different kinds of cement to discover the best type for quick-setting, underwater work. He carried out the negotiations to buy the land on which the shaft would be sunk and designed the heraldic device which, as a steel signet, formed the official Seal of the Company.

Besides these activities he spent some time designing a treadmill for a gaol and a mausoleum for his father's projected Cemetery Company. In connection with the latter, it is fascinating to read the diary entry for 29 March 1825: 'A Mr Pugin, an architectural draughtsman, called today about the necropolis of which he is to make a bird's-eye view.' In his spare time, Isambard rowed, walked, visited exhibitions of water-colour painting with William Hawes, attended early morning lectures at the Royal Society and listened carefully to sermons on Sunday. On at least one occasion he and William Hawes walked from Blackfriars to a Nonconformist chapel in York Street, Marylebone, when Dr Morell came from Hove to preach. He always drove himself hard and on 10 September he recorded laconically in his diary: 'Illness and idleness.'

Meanwhile the family's finances continued in poor state. On 21 December 1824 he rowed from Blackfriars to Chelsea carrying to the Brunels' banker, Hollingworth, a cheque for £100 together with a note from Marc asking Hollingworth to sign it. The banker was not in so Isambard left the cheque and rowed home. Next day he rowed back only to find the cheque still unsigned. Furious, the eighteen-year-old Isambard left this note: 'Mr Brunel desires Mr Hollingworth will have the goodness to sign the enclosed cheque immediately as Mr Brunel is waiting for it.'

Isambard then rowed home and continued his work on the Gaz engine. On 24 December a note arrived from Hollingworth conveying his regrets but pointing out that as an earlier cheque for £200 had been dishonoured he could not sign one for £100. Work continued all that day in the workshop and on Christmas Day Isambard and his parents went to church at Bridewell and returned to, I suppose, a rather spartan Christmas dinner.

On 2 March 1825 a ceremony, presided over by William Smith MP, was held to mark the construction and sinking of a 50-ft-diameter, 40-ft-deep, brick shaft from the bottom of which the Thames tunnel would be driven.

A ring-shaped iron plate or curb, 3 ft wide and 50 ft in diameter, with a sharp cutting edge on the underside, was laid on a ring of piles. On this bricklayers, each laying 1000 bricks a day, began to raise a tower. Forty-eight vertical iron tie-rods, bolted to the underside of the curb, rose through the bricks and were eventually bolted through an iron capping ring. In three weeks the tower's full height was reached, putting 910 tons on the iron curb.

A further three weeks were allowed for the cement to set, whereupon a steam engine was placed on top of the tube to operate a continuous chain of buckets to the ground. The piles were removed and workmen inside the tower excavated the soil into the bucket elevator so that the building sank under its own weight to the desired depth. Marc wanted to dig a sump below the shaft and dig a drain below the tunnel into the sump which would be constantly pumped out. The meanness of the Company Chairman, William Smith, prevented this obvious safety precaution and as a result several workmen were later drowned.

Two years had elapsed since the Tunnel Company was formed and Marc's £5000 advance had long since been spent on research. On 9 March 1825, Isambard, irked by lack of money, confided his impatient thoughts to his diary:

I am preparing plans for South London (Bermondsey) docks in case my father should be named Engineer. I am very busily engaged on the Gaz engine and a project is made for a canal across the Panama. Surely one of these may take place? It may be curious at some future date to read the state we are in at present. *I am most terribly pinched for money.* Should barely receive enough to pay my debts and am this moment without a penny. *We keep neither carriage nor footman and only two maidservants.* I am looking forward with great anxiety to this Gaz engine – building castles in the air about steam boats that go 15 mph . . . making a large fortune, building a house for myself. How much more likely that all this will turn to nothing. The Gaz engine, if it is good for anything, will only be tolerably good and perhaps will make us spend a great deal of money; that I should pass through life as most people and that I should forget my castles in the air, live in a small house and at most keep my gig.'

His father, who never felt the need either for public acclaim or a lavish style of living, had constantly urged him to look for fame and fortune and the urgings had found fertile ground in the theatrical side of Isambard's nature. He had it in him to be an actor but his father had directed him towards engineering with all the determination that his own father Jean-Charles had tried to force him, Marc, into the church. The two strands of Isambard's nature, the mathematical and the artistic, were entwined and his actor's desire to be centre-stage would show itself in his great engineering works designed with a dramatic flair which, while second nature to him, was also calculated to gain the public admiration he so ardently desired.

Isambard wanted not only to be successful but to show his success to the world. He wanted a large house, many servants, and several carriages. At the age of nineteen, he was invited to dinner at Lord Spencer's house and was impressed with the grand style of the place: 'Met Lord Bessborough, Mr Ponsonby and Dr Wollaston. . . . The etiquette is very great. The servants are all in gloves and many other things peculiar to houses of this kind.' With his young head full of impatience and pretension, Isambard could not have been pleased when his father chose as Resident Engineer of the tunnel John Armstrong, a fifty-year-old Northumbrian engineer of much practical experience, while Isambard was paid merely as Armstrong's assistant at £4 a week.

Marc's re-designed shield was rectangular, not cylindrical, as shown on the drawings for the 1818 Patent (and also on the wall of the present-day passageway between the British Rail and Circle line stations at Paddington). The original 'cellular' principle was retained but the rectangular shape, Marc thought, gave better support to the excavation. The 80-ton shield was made in twelve cast-iron sections at Maudslay's works.

The shield began its painstaking march on 28 November 1825 and it was hoped that the work would be completed in three years. That was rather too optimistic. Conditions in the tunnel were vile beyond words. It was little better than tunnelling through sewage; the air was foul, the soil was putrid and among its many unhealthy properties was the very painful one of rotting away the men's finger nails. Sickness and drunkenness were rife. In April 1826 Marc went sick with pleurisy, followed very shortly by John Armstrong, leaving Isambard, aged barely twenty, the Resident Engineer although to his undoubted annoyance he did not receive the title or increased pay to match his new responsibilities.

Nevertheless he flung himself into the 'big one' with all the enthusiasm of a pent-up longing to show what he could do. A sensitive, imaginative young man, he was none the less eager to work in the candle-lit, water-logged, stinking hell-hole to show the uncaring world what he could achieve, given the chance. Indeed, he could not tear himself away and worked for thirty-six hours without sleep before snatching a couple of hours' rest on straw bales on the bricklayers' platform behind the shield.

The men were ill trained, ill disciplined and frequently drunk. Armstrong had not been able to improve matters but Isambard sacked the drunks, taught the men how to use the tunnelling gear without breaking it and had them on parade prior to going below to start work. At first Marc and Sophia were proud of Isambard's capabilities, but after he had worked night and day for a fortnight with barely a break they became fearful for his health and were sure he would make himself so ill he would die. But his enthusiasm kept disease at bay and for three months, until Marc was sufficiently well to take over one shift, Isambard ran the entire operation. Armstrong, who had no personal stake in the tunnel, resigned in August 1826.

Marc was too old and too prone to pleurisy to spend long in a stinking, cold and wet environment so Isambard was given three assistants. The first to arrive was the gentlemanly Anglo-Irishman from County Cork, Richard Beamish, an ex-officer in the Coldstream Guards, who began work as an unpaid volunteer on 7 August 1826. Next, on 15 August, came William Gravatt, almost exactly the same age as Isambard, the son of the Inspector-General of the Woolwich Military Academy, the training school for artillery officers. Gravatt was a born scientist, mathematician and engineer, easily Isambard's intellectual equal, though lacking any of the drawing room etiquette Isambard prized so highly and not in the least bit interested in acquiring any. Gravatt was proud and very touchy. He would take offence easily but conceal his resentment until it all burst out to the general astonishment of everyone. Years later Gravatt was to become a successful bridge engineer and to be deeply involved with the mathematics of mechanical computers. Charles Babbage stated, 'Without him there would have been no Difference Engine.'

The third assistant was a Mr Riley, aged twenty-four, who came in November 1826 and, after contracting 'tunnel fever' in January 1827, died on 5 February. Besides the powerful trinity of Isambard, Gravatt and Beamish, the other important men in the tunnel were Michael Lane, a dark-haired, 6-ft-tall, foreman bricklayer, three years older than Isambard, and two miners of great courage: Collins and Ball. Michael Lane became one of Isambard's most trusted assistants and was appointed Chief Engineer of the GWR after Isambard's death.

Isambard always recognised a good workman. When his father sent him a recruit who wished to be taken on as an assistant, Isambard summed him up at once and that night wrote in his diary: 'A Mr Smith came down bringing with him a note from my father. He is an aspirant but was quite unfit – old – totally ignorant of engineering or machinery – unaccustomed to command men – and *not a Gentleman*.' Isambard, throughout his career, expected his assistants to be 'gentlemen' and, indeed, the Great Western Railway was still glowing from this influence in 1947. Isambard was quite sure, at twenty, that he could 'command men', as indeed he could. He was a born officer, at his best in a crisis. Indeed he positively enjoyed crises. But the best officer needs good sergeants and he relied on such brave men as Michael Lane and other loyal workmen as an army officer depends on his sergeants and sergeant-majors to keep the ranks steady in times of crisis. And in the tunnel, driving through sandy, waterlogged ground, the crisis was continuous.

Isambard made it quite clear that he was solely responsible, to his father, for the tunnel. He worked harder than any man on the site, he was enthusiastic and he was brave. The men were cheered by his presence at the working face and looked to him for leadership; which is not to say that he was 'one of the boys'. He was never that, but there was a camaraderie between 'officers' and 'sergeants' down in the tunnel. On Old Year's Night 1826, Isambard, Gravatt, Beamish, Lane and six other trusted workmen sat down to dinner in the short length of completed tunnel and saw in the New Year together.

He was to all practical purposes in charge of a great work, perhaps the most audacious engineering work in the world at that time – but he was still a subordinate. He remained impatient for the great destiny his father had told him to look for. When would his career receive the necessary boost?

3

Isambard the Indestructible

On 3 January 1827, Isambard was at last given the title Resident Engineer, with a salary of £200 a year. Gravatt and Riley also had pay rises. To fund these advances the workmen's wages were reduced and the men, unaware of the true circumstances, asked the much respected young Isambard to try to have their old wages restored. He wrote of this incident in his diary: 'I thought it time to exercise some authority and ordered those on duty to return to work and those not on duty to leave the works. I was obeyed by both.' Which must have given him a nice feeling. Next day the men went on strike and Isambard employed a new crew. Three days later the old crew returned and asked for their jobs back. He re-employed twelve.

The Chairman, William Smith, was very impatient of the slow progress of the shield, refused to see the difficulties and tried to force the pace of tunnelling. In February 1827, to earn some money, he turned the tunnel into a peep-show and any idler with a shilling to spare was allowed to watch, from behind a barrier, as the brave workmen pressed on with the job. In spite of the foul air and water which brought the workmen fever, hallucinations and even death, hundreds of visitors thronged the arches each day. 'Not all of them gentlemen,' wrote Isambard disapprovingly. Marc protested to Smith that if the tunnel collapsed when it was full of visitors the loss of life would be considerable, but the visitors were still encouraged to come in and risk their lives for a shilling. The work was hazardous in the extreme. Marc wrote in his diary for 6 April 1827: 'We have no alternative but trusting the shield. The roof is nothing but loose sand. Awful!'

On his twenty-first birthday in April 1827 Isambard spent the day sacking workmen and generally maintaining discipline in the tunnel.

My birthday. Two steam pumps working hard but pressure will not stop up. When the afternoon shift came on they did not go below but remained on top grumbling about last week's wages. [Isambard had docked a day's pay as a 'punishment' for what he considered to be slow work – this on top of the official pay cut the men had suffered.] It seemed that their Ganger, Nelson, had not informed them of my intention to make it up to them next Saturday. Pride, who was drunk and seemed very much the cause of it ['it' was not Isambard's fault!], I immediately turned him out of the yard. Coxon and Stibbs – sober – and grumbling also very much I discharged also, the rest after that were willing to listen and having told them that if they behaved well this week their lost wages should be made up to them next week.

Throughout his career it was Isambard's technique of management to withhold pay on some pretext and then hold it as a hostage against 'good behaviour' for the future.

Later in this entry he wrote: 'I think we must pay our men a little more seeing the fine weather above ground and the fatigue and the wet below. The men on both shifts are anything but sober and this, combined with the wretched state of the ground, accounts for our slow progress.' The men did not, of course, get this pay rise, for while Isambard had full powers to sack men and withhold pay he had no power to give them more money.

In the evening he left the tunnel unsupervised when he took Gravatt to his celebratory dinner with his father and mother, sisters and brother-in-law. Marc asked Isambard if the tunnel was safe to be left, whereupon Isambard was obliged to tell a white lie to reassure his father and gain entrance to his dinner. Marc Brunel wrote in his diary: 'Isambard's birthday. He being of age. He came with Gravatt to dinner. Both very agreeable guests as they had left things very comfortable or they should not have come. It is a satisfaction to me to know that things should have improved so suddenly under such ground.' Two days after this, Marc wrote: 'The tunnel is still in the same dangerous condition as it has been for some weeks.'

Broken glass, old boots and other debris were coming into

the frames and the river was obviously very close overhead. The watermen on the river told Marc that he was tunnelling into an underwater quarry where gravel had been dredged out. If so, the shield would break through and the tunnel would be flooded. Marc decided to examine the ballast hole in the river-bed and made a party of the occasion. On 25 April a diving bell was hired from West India Docks. It was, literally, an open-mouthed bell. Lit by candles, it was lowered on a chain into the river and fed with air from a pump on the support barge. Ingress of river water was prevented simply by the air pressure within the bell but those sitting on seats around the wall of the bell could step or fall into the water.

Isambard took his mother, her friend Mrs Baldwin and his brother-in-law Ben Hawes down in the bell and discovered the hole just as predicted. An iron tube was then pushed through the soft mud to the frames and with this as a speaking tube a light-hearted conversation was held between those in the bell and those on the frames.

Although Marc had protested against the admission of the public to the tunnel and although he knew it could collapse at any moment, on 15 May he allowed Richard Beamish to escort his 'dear friend' Lady Raffles and her large entourage right up to the frames. Marc and Isambard were on tenterhooks the entire time as the visitors satisfied their curiosity and the river cascaded down over the staves and hissed through gaps in the poling boards. Somewhat wilting, these flowers of the Establishment were returned safely to street level. Three days later, as the tide was rising, increasing the weight of water over the frames, the tunnel collapsed.

The diving bell was hired again. During one of his subaqueous expeditions Isambard was accompanied by an assistant called Pinckney who, seeing one corner of the frames, tried to step on to it from the diving bell, slipped and would have been lost in the mud had not Isambard instantly put one leg into the water. Pinckney grabbed hold and Isambard dragged him back into the bell. By 11 June the breach had been sealed with 19,500 cubic yards of bagged clay. The pumps were started and on 25 June 150 ft of the tunnel was clear of water.

Isambard was first to explore. Taking with him in a punt a few miners, those who had been the last to leave the frames on 18 May, he set off into the flooded archway, the men holding candles to relieve the Stygian darkness. Eventually the punt bumped softly on to the bank of silt which had been washed into the workings. Isambard got out of the boat, crawled on to the far from firm bank of earth and got through to the frames. By the light of one candle he could see that they were leaning over and buried to their staves in mud but otherwise intact. He crawled back over the slime and his men took him back to the shaft.

He relished the drama of his gruesome and hazardous journey. Isambard was always supremely confident at work of his indestructibility. He loved the excitement, the danger, the attention, the sense of creation that would lead to fame.

Although the tunnel was in a dangerous condition, very important persons still asked to be shown around. Isambard did not welcome such visitors into his world and would turn upon them Brunellian scorn. He probably felt a certain resentment towards them: they were coming simply out of curiosity to where he and his men daily risked their lives. When Charles Bonaparte and his party insisted on punting along to the buried frames Isambard took them, pushing against the roof to move the boat over the water. Well down the tunnel he gave way to a mischievous urge to give them greater excitement than they bargained for. He stood in the boat and began to rock it from side to side saying, 'Now then, gentlemen, if by accident there should be a rush of water, I shall turn the punt over to prevent you being jammed against the roof and we shall be carried out and up the shaft.' Charles Bonaparte, rather stout and very scared, had just replied, 'But I cannot swim,' when Isambard, rocking the boat too violently, fell overboard. He *could* swim, however, popped up like a seal and was hauled back into the punt.

Isambard and William Gravatt carried on the entire supervision of sealing the breach in the river bed, pumping out the water, digging out the frames, righting them, repairing them and, on 1 October, setting the shield once more in motion. Late on 7 October 1827 Isambard was walking in the dark from his office to the shaft, when he fell into the water-tank, which was sunk in the ground and stored water for the boilers of the pumping engines. It was normally covered with an iron lid but this had been left open.

He was badly hurt, his leg swelled up, but he would not go home nor even remove his boots to inspect the damage. He wrote in his diary afterwards that he was scared to take them off in case he could not get them on again should some emergency arise. But he had had a very bad fall and as the hours passed he felt ever more sick and shaken. At 2 a.m. on 8 October he finally surrendered. Gravatt was allowed to remove Isambard's boots and to send him home by cab. He reported the event to Beamish, also off-duty through illness:

> Your humble servant, with his usual good luck, is laid up with a contusion (confusion it ought to be) in the left knee, having made use of that leg and opposite arm to stop his further descent into the river water tank which some kind old woman left open and which, with extended jaws, swallowed his right leg and lower trunk. I trust our not seeing you is due to nothing more serious than a dish of turtle soup. You must excuse a short and badly written note inasmuch as reclining on a sofa, however luxurious for a Roman alderman, is not equally convenient for a pen-man.

He was away from work until the 24th when he made another friendly report to Beamish ending with the words: 'I think I shall give the men a bit of beer and beef in the West Arch on Saturday but I don't know yet.'

In fact a banquet was held in the West Arch of the tunnel for the Directors and their friends on 10 November. Marc generously stayed away so that Isambard could preside and have the credit he deserved as Resident Engineer. The archway was draped suitably in crimson and the band of the Coldstream Guards played – deafeningly, it must be assumed, in that echoing arch – while 120 workmen were regaled with beer and beef in the East Arch. These latter, forgiving past pay cuts, came out of their arch and presented Isambard with a pick and shovel as a token of their respect; that speaks volumes for young Isambard's character. He led by example and, by working harder than anyone else, he drew his men to him and made them give of their best. He drove the shield – and the men – on with great determination against seemingly impossible odds, but in this he relied very much on the skill and courage of his miners, men such as Collins and Ball.

On 2 January 1828 some of the rocks which had been thrown down into the river-bed breach came through into the frames. Isambard did not stop mining to throw down more clay on to the river-bed but decided, according to Richard Beamish's memoir, to tunnel on quickly, believing that he would get past the weak point and have the brick arch built to support the river-bed before the mud collapsed. This would appear to be an early example of Brunellian self-deception. With water pouring through the frames he kept the men at work, day after day. On 11 January Marc escorted a party of dignitaries to the frames and noted in his diary that he found everything satisfactory. The next day disaster struck.

Isambard was on the shield, at 6 a.m., on Saturday 12 January 1828, supervising the tunnelling, with miners Collins and Ball on duty with him. Richard Beamish was above ground in the site office, handing out vouchers for beer and gin to the wet, cold workmen coming off shift. Suddenly the door burst open and in rushed the watchman yelling that the tunnel was full. Beamish grabbed a lantern and dashed outside, to the east or workmen's stairs, but he found them packed with men struggling upwards so he went to the west staircase, the visitors' stairs, smashed down the locked door and hurried down the steps.

As he ran down he saw, by lamplight, the unconscious body of Brunel. Had Beamish been a few seconds later the wave would have received, taking Isambard with it into the depths and there would have been an end, but Fate had use for Brunel yet. Beamish grabbed Isambard's clothing and hauled him to safety. Isambard the Indestructible.

Pandemonium reigned as men poured out of the shaft and stood around shouting. Below, the roar of the Thames could be heard clearly. The flooding later turned out to have caused six deaths. Despite the shock, Isambard refused to go home but at once wrote a report to the Directors and then insisted on going on board a barge with the intention of directing the lowering of the diving bell to examine the damage. When they came to lower the bell they found the chain faulty and asked Isambard if they could use a rope. Isambard was so ill that he could barely summon the strength to whisper, 'Don't go down.' With that he was taken home, feeling, he said, 'never so queer, as if I was going to break into pieces'. The men on the barge lowered the empty bell by the rope; the rope broke.

After a few days in bed Isambard had recovered to the extent that his doctor allowed him to go to Brighton to convalesce. There he indulged his love of theatre and acting, attending plays and fancy-dress balls – for he also had a keen eye for a pretty girl. On 4 February 1828 he wrote in his diary: 'Pleasant company. Very comfortable. Strolled on the pier smoking my meerschaum before breakfast – breakfast at noon. Rode about visiting works (sea-wall being built).

Dined at 7.' But on 8 February he recorded: 'Violent haemorrhage after riding horse.' On the 11th he was 'still bleeding' and on the 15th, 'Still ill and retrieved by Beamish in a hired chariot which brought on more bleeding.'

4

Ambition versus Love

On 16 October 1827, during the period of enforced idleness caused by his fall into the rain-water tank, Isambard began a secret journal in which he bravely admitted to himself his gravest failings and most private thoughts. It reveals a mirror image of the public man. Where he was in public a masterful officer, in periods of quiet reflection he was insecure, fearful of the future and impatient for fame.

It was 22 April 1828 before he was sufficiently recovered from his narrow escape from drowning to commit his feelings about that time to his secret journal:

> Here I am in bed at Bridge House. I have now been laid up useless since 12 January. I shan't forget that day in a hurry. Very near finished my journey then. When the danger is over it is amusing rather than otherwise. While hope remained it was an excitement which has always been luxury to me. When knocked down I certainly gave myself up, for I never expected we should get out. The roar of the water in a confined space was *very grand*, cannon can be nothing to it. Apart from the loss of those six poor fellows the whole affair was well worth the risk and I would willingly pay my share of the expenses.

His private confessions were rigorous and he was understandably concerned about secrecy. So nervous was he on this score that, even though the journal had a strong lock and was kept in a locked strong box, he 'could hardly believe that it is really private'. In the journal he tried to be honest with himself when often his instinct was to deceive himself. By acknowledging his faults he hoped to moderate them, and he must be given credit for that, but he never lost them entirely and much nocturnal repentance on minor matters did not survive the following day.

'Pleasure' and 'sensations' were very important to him – as they are to everyone – but the way Isambard uses the words gives the impression that they were especially important to him. One reason for writing the journal was that he thought, 'The pleasure I shall derive hereafter, in reading and comparing the remarks made at different times, will, I promise myself, be very great,' and then, as if this was altogether too indulgent, he added, 'I think also much utility and some good lessons may also be got.' He had always been taught to look for 'utility' in what he did and had been steered away from mere pleasure. He had to keep his pleasures secret, locked away.

He bought the book which was to be his journal three months before he began to write in it. He took himself to task for this procrastination on the first page. 'Why have I not begun before?' he asks and replies sternly, 'I have postponed it! I am very prone to say "tomorrow" and yet I am not irresolute nor do I want firmness in greater matters. I must cure myself of this.' Having made this resolution not to put off till tomorrow what should be done today he writes:

Tomorrow I will begin

The next day and the day after he wrote ordinary entries concerning work on the tunnel but on the third day, 19 October 1827, he made a brutally honest examination of his conscience:

When thinking of this journal whole volumes crowd in on me – [about] my character [and] my *châteaux d'Espagne* yet now I am without an idea. As to my character. My self-conceit and love of glory or rather approbation vie with each other which shall govern me. The latter is so strong that, even of a dark night, riding home, when I pass some unknown person who perhaps does not even look at me I catch myself trying to look big on my little pony. . . . I often do the most silly, useless things to appear to advantage before, or attract the attention of, those I shall never see again or whom I care nothing about. My self-conceit renders me domineering, intolerant, nay, even quarrelsome with those who do not flatter.

His ambitions, what he sometimes called his 'castles in the air' or *châteaux d'Espagne*, were what he lived for, their fulfilment constituted his reasons for living and nothing was to be allowed to get in their way. Unfortunately for his plans he had been in love for seven years, since the age of fourteen, with a girl in Manchester whom he identified as 'Ellen Hume'. (This surname was probably a misspelling of Hulme, a name that crops up in the journal with regard to a friend who lived in Manchester.) Isambard had it in his head that he must marry this girl – he truly loved her – but he felt he was too young, too poor, to marry and that, more to the point, marriage to a girl without her own money and from an insufficiently elevated class of society would hold him back in his ambitions. So he wrestled with his feelings through the months and through the pages of his journal.

19 October 1827
Q. Shall I make a good husband? Am doubtful. My ambition or whatever it may be called (it is not the mere wish to be rich) is rather extensive but still – I am not afraid that I shall be unhappy if I do not reach the rank of Hero and Commander-in-Chief of His Majesty's Forces in the steam (or Gaz) boat department. This is a favourite 'Castle in the Air' of mine. Make the Gaz engine answer, fit out some vessels (of course a war), take some prizes, nay, some fortified town, get employed by Government contract and command a fine fleet and fight – fight – in fact take Algiers or something in that style. Build a splendid manufactory for Gaz engines, a yard for building the boats – and at last be rich, have a house built of which I have even made the drawings. *Be the first Engineer and example for all future ones.*

Isambard's ambitions were indeed extensive and very much ahead of their time since he envisaged the privatisation of the Royal Navy 160 years before the Royal Ordnance and the Naval Dockyards of Britain were sold to private enterprise.

His youthful enthusiasm left little space for caution and in his resolve 'not to be prevailed upon by others to do what I think imprudent' he was, I believe, concealing from himself a more basic fact: he was never going to listen to anyone's advice, because advice which did not coincide with his own prudent – naturally – inclinations was by definition imprudent.

On 4 November he was experiencing a panic over the slow progress of the tunnel and therefore of his career and at 3 a.m., in a break from supervision of the tunnel works, wrote:

I have today been to London Bridge. Am full of my skeme [later altered to 'scheme'] for a 300-ft arch, mutual joints. Sketching centering for arch. My father's negotiations with his friends may yet turn out something.

What will become of me? To go to France is to lose my connection and damage my prospects here yet to stop here at my age I cannot expect to be employed.

A tunnel at Gravesend or Liverpool, eh?

Mr Pitt was only 22 Prime Minister and for *the first time in his life!*

I may be said to have almost built this tunnel having been active Resident Engineer. What Castles!

My Gaz engine—a tunnel—tunnels.

What a field—yet I may miss it.

He spent 21 November 1827 at a London factory supervising the manufacture of a 'screwing gauge' for the 'screw jacks' that would push the tunnelling frames forward. In the journal Brunel describes his pleasant homecoming that evening. The 'sensations' which are stirred within him give rise to luxurious thoughts of bachelorhood. These feelings sweep away, momentarily, previous doubts as to the future and instead he weighs the pros and cons of marriage and recollections of past girlfriends, for even 'EH', his great love, is now behind him.

The entry is a fascinating insight into Isambard's spontaneous feelings, a good example of his unselfconscious selfishness, his one-sided attitude towards women at a time when a woman and all her worldly goods were a man's chattels. There is no denigration implied in stating this. Isambard was a conventional, honest, hard-working young man of his time, but his times were not those of the virtuous, reform-minded Victorian; indeed, Isambard cannot really be described as a 'Victorian' at all, since his formative years were in the unreformed, unvirtuous 1820s – and his roots lay in the eighteenth century. He wrote:

Having smelt the cold, frosty, night air, I entered my parlour. A nice, blazing fire, my table before it, papers, books, neatly arranged thereon. The whole inspired such a feeling of comfort that I could not resist sitting down and imparting my sensations to this book as to a friend.

As long as health continues, one's prospects tolerable and present efforts, whatever they may be, tolerably successful then indeed a bachelor's life is luxurious. Fond as I am of society 'selfish comfort' is delightful. I have always found it so. My *châteaux d'Espagne* have mostly been founded on this feeling. What independence! For one whose ambition is to distinguish himself in the eyes of the public such a freedom is almost indispensable – but on the other hand, in sickness, how delightful to have a companion whose sympathy one is sure of possessing. Her dependence on you gives her power to support you by consolation and however delightful may be the freedom and independence, still we find that certain restraints are necessary for the enjoyment of pleasure.

I have always wished and intended to be married but have been very doubtful on the subject of children. It is a question whether they are the source of most pleasure or pain.

I have had, as I suppose most young men have had, numerous *attachments*, if they deserve the name. Each in its turn has appeared to me *the true one*. EH is the oldest and most constant, now however gone by. During her reign, nearly 7 years, several inferior ones caught my attention, I need only remind myself of Mme D.C., O.S. and numerous others. With E. Hume it was mutual. The sofa scenes must now appear to her, as to me, rather ridiculous. She was a nice girl and had she improved as a girl of her age ought . . . [The rest of the page, about thirty lines, has been cut out, thus losing the overleaf as well. The journal continues:] have served me right if I had been spilled in the mud – certainly a devilish pretty girl, an excellent musician and a very sweet voice – but I'm afraid those eyes don't speak of a very *placid temper*.

Women were there for Isambard's benefit, there was no question of a sharing partnership.

The difficult progress of the Thames Tunnel project made its future very uncertain and Isambard's prospects with it. On 7 May 1828, feeling frustrated and insecure, he wrote:

Here are these Directors damning the tunnel as fast as they well can. If they go on at this rate we must certainly stop and then – by Jove – where the money is to come from I know not. What money we may get from the Battersea concern [the sawmill] will produce at most £300 a year, most likely not £200! The Gaz may never realise . . . where will be all my fine castles? Bubbles!

The young Rennies – whatever their real merit [Isambard evidently did not think very highly of them] – will have built London Bridge, the finest bridge in Europe, and will have such connection with Government as to defy competition . . . while I shall have been engaged on the tunnel which failed, a pretty recommendation.

It's a gloomy perspective yet bad as it is I cannot bring myself to be downhearted . . . after all, let the worst happen – unemployed, *untalked-of*, pennyless (that's damned awkward) I think I may depend on a home at Benjamin's. My poor father would hardly survive the [failure of the] tunnel. My mother would follow him – here my invention fails. A war now and I would go and get my throat cut and that would be foolish enough. I suppose a sort of middle path will be the most likely one – a mediocre success – an engineer sometimes employed and sometimes not – £200/£300 a year and that uncertain.

A dozen or so lines further on he actually contemplates giving up his pretensions to greatness and thinks instead of taking a sinecure and living comfortably in happy mediocrity: 'Why should I not get some situation? Surely I have friends enough for that? Get a snug little berth and then a snug little wife with an interesting little somewhat to assist in the housekeeping? What an interesting situation.' But the thought horrifies him as the implications become clear: 'No luxuries! None of your enjoyments of which I am tolerably fond. Oh horrible! And all this because the Directors can't swallow when the food is put into their mouths.'

In this period of doldrums Isambard experimented with the Gaz engine, did small jobs for his father and led a quiet social life, including meeting a highly eligible young woman whom he allowed to slip through his fingers. It was the sudden realisation of this loss which stirred him to confide again to his journal, on 7 June, his first entry for a month. He had rediscovered his love for Ellen Hume just as he met this new woman and his feelings for Ellen got in the way of a very profitable marriage. Isambard describes the new young lady's attributes as a modern man might describe the virtues of a car he had been thinking of buying:

> June 8 1828. 1 a.m. Who would have thought I should ever have lost anything from over-modesty? It appears that I might really have had A. B . . . w, a fine girl, plenty of accomplishments and £25,000, no joke. . . . It would never have done to have married then – quite absurd, so young and when it came to the point I should have found too late what I now find – that I have returned to my first love. Ellen is still, it seems, my real love. I have written her a long letter today. Her answer shall decide. If she wavers I *ought* to break it off for I cannot hope to be in a condition to marry her and to continue in this state of suspense is wronging her.

Isambard, I assume, gave her a blunt appraisal of his prospects and his lack of money and asked her if she would be willing to marry on those terms. In his journal he continued: 'After all, I shall most likely remain a bachelor . . . for me my profession is my only true wife.' This is a brave, sad, line which he immediately follows with: 'Oh! That I may find her faithful.' His mind then turns to the miserable events surrounding the tunnel: 'How time and events creep on. Next Wednesday in the public meeting [the shareholders on whether or not to continue digging the tunnel]. Shall we get the money? "To be or not to be?" We must try and get the Government to begin borings at Gravesend.'

This is an astonishing line, given Isambard's detestation of government departments and government interference in the affairs of individuals and must be a measure of his desperation for money. At this his mind snaps back to Ellen and he wrestles to and fro, between true love and expediency. 'Oh! Ellen, Ellen, if you have kept up your musick and can even play only tolerably we might be very happy yet – and starve – it won't do – however, we'll see . . . If I had married A. B . . . w I should certainly have been independent, though I should hardly have liked depending on my wife, she'd have made a good one though – but it would have spoiled my future prospects. I'm afraid to settle too early. Oh for a lighthouse. . . .' So he continues agonising over his dormant or failed schemes and his possibilities. He ends with: 'Damn it, Ellen, how you keep creeping up on me, how I am thinking of you, well, until I have your answer . . . it is no use to think of you.'

He was longing for a positive reply from Ellen yet his feelings were ambivalent – wanting her to marry him but at the same time wary of the prospect, in case it should get in the way of his ambition.

He began a correspondence (now missing) with Ellen which lasted until May 1829. He was 'half afraid of my old attachment binding me yet I have not the heart to break it off' but he managed to steel himself to the task and on 1 June he wrote: 'I have had a long correspondence with Ellen which I think I have managed very well. I may now consider myself independent.' So his ambition had got the upper hand and he had managed to extricate himself from love. But he did it gently and he and Ellen Hume remained on good terms.

As he 'ran down' his love for Ellen he understandably became emotional and his friendship with Benjamin Hawes developed. It was deep and lifelong even though in later years Hawes became a very important cog in the governmental bureaucracy Isambard so much detested. On the eve of his twenty-third birthday, just before he finally broke off his 'engagement' with Ellen, he wrote affectionately to Hawes. It was not a normal letter, not to be posted on the morrow, but a testament, for Ben to read after Isambard was dead:

> I had always intended that this book should perish with me . . . but having [decided] to make my will I found how poor I was and how unable I was to leave you anything which could give you an idea of my attachment to you. The greatest proof I could imagine was to leave you this, my private journal and if you could form an idea of my secretiveness, of my horror

of telling anybody that which I wish to be secret, you would be able to value this mark of my love.

I conceal things from myself and it was to get rid of this load of secrets I had to keep, that I imagined this staunch friend. Yet I always have my fears. I keep the key [of the journal] always about me, the book itself in my strong box with a secure lock but when from home I am always afraid. My dear Benjamin, ever since I have known you I have esteemed you and now my attachment is as strong and perfect as I think possible on earth. My passions are not warm but they are staunch and true and unchangeable.

II

Great Western Railway

5

The Bristol Connection

In June 1828 Isambard was pronounced fit enough to go away on sick-leave, not, however, to the stimulating ambience of Brighton but to a relative's house in Plymouth and later to Clifton, Bristol. Chance rules our lives and it was Isambard's good fortune to be in Clifton at that time. In 1753 an alderman called William Vick had left £1000 to be invested until £10,000 had been accumulated. Then the money was to be used to bridge the Avon gorge. By 1829 a sum of £8000 had been reached and a committee formed to raise the balance and hold a competition to find the best design. Isambard was thrilled with such a dramatic location, and with the chance to show what he could do. He at once entered the competition.

Isambard gave the Clifton Bridge Committee a choice of four sites at which a suspension bridge could be built across the sheer-sided gorge, with spans varying between 870 and 916 ft, the longest suspension spans proposed up to that time. While the bold conception was Isambard's, much of the detailed design was Marc's. His diary records, day after day, 'Working on Isambard's bridge'.

Isambard by now had made a home for himself with his sister Sophia and his brother-in-law, Ben Hawes, at Barge House, Lambeth. Obviously this was more congenial to him than remaining with his parents. He was in his early twenties and doubtless felt more his own man with his knees out from under his father's table.

Back in Bristol Thomas Telford was called in to judge the various entries and rejected them all, Isambard's on the grounds that the spans were too long. No suspension bridge could be more than 600 ft long, he said, which just happened to be the exact length of his Menai Strait Bridge. Telford was then asked to present his own proposals and produced a freakish design in which a suspension bridge was supported by ornate Gothic towers which rose from the bed of the gorge, 200 ft below the proposed roadway. Isambard was incensed and wrote one of his beautifully polite/sarcastic letters to the Bridge Committee:

> As the distance between the opposite rocks was considerably less than what has always been considered as within the limits to which suspension bridges might be carried, the idea of going to the bottom of the valley for the purpose of raising at great expense, two intermediate supporters, hardly occurred to me . . . what a reflection such timidity will cast on the state of the Arts today.

The Bridge Committee went into a huddle and Isambard travelled to the North of England, most uncomfortably, by stage-coach, looking for work. In making his way, joltingly and slowly, about the country he must often have wondered if there was not a better way for busy entrepreneurs to travel. Railways were certainly on his mind. Early in 1829 he applied for the post of Engineer to the Newcastle & Carlisle Railway and in May was informed that the contest was between himself and Francis Giles. Giles had tried to oust Marc Brunel as Engineer of the Thames Tunnel and was one whom Isambard would certainly have considered 'mediocre'. It is easy to imagine the sharp disappointment he would have felt when Giles was appointed – especially when he was told he would be called if Giles proved to be unsatisfactory. But at least his endeavours up to that time, his work in the Thames Tunnel, his draft designs for the Clifton Bridge and his experimental work on the carbonic gas engine, had not gone unnoticed for on 10 June 1830, at the early age of twenty-four, he was elected a Fellow of the Royal Society.

One small but successful job he did carry out under his own name, late in 1830, was a drainage scheme between the marshes and the sea at the village of Tollesbury in Essex. The fee for that job would have been as welcome as water in a desert. He had always to take a chance on whatever project he tendered for, spending borrowed money while he ate, worked and travelled. The cost of hiring a horse and carriage for a twenty-mile journey was 15 shillings in 1830 and the fare from London to Sunderland by stage-coach was £7 9s 6d, when the weekly wage for a workman might be 10 shillings. His parents and brother-in-law must have done much to support him as he sought to find his niche.

On 16 March 1831 the Clifton Bridge Committee announced that Isambard's plans had been adopted. He had reduced his span to 630 ft to conform to the prejudices instilled in the Committee by Telford. To reduce the bridge span, Isambard introduced a stone abutment rising out of the rocks on the western, or Leigh Woods, side of the gorge. For this unnecessary work the Committee were to pay £14,000 and there it stands today, a memorial to Telford's jealousy, supporting forever the memorial to a bolder engineer.

Isambard was very excited about the Committee's acceptance of his plans, especially when they gave him a free hand to produce the grandest possible effect. The suspension chains were to be supported by 240-ft-high towers bestriding the road like some colossal Ancient Egyptian monument. The towers themselves were to be clad in cast-iron reliefs, to illustrate the processes by which the iron was formed into the bridge and to show how the bridge was raised. There was possibly a touch of Ozymandias about Brunel's conception, almost as if he intended to crush his rivals with the weight of his genius: 'Look on my works, ye mighty, and despair!'

While he – and his father – were working on the plans for the bridge, Isambard completed plans for an astronomical observatory in London for James South. It had a fully revolving dome bisected by the telescope slot which was covered by shutters. South had approved the plans, the building was erected under Isambard's supervision and on 20 May 1831 he was the guest of honour at the opening of South's new toy. 'I lionised it till six,' Isambard wrote in his diary.

His triumph was short-lived. Isambard had for the first, but by no means the last, time, exceeded his estimate of costs. South was furious, refused to pay and caused an anonymous article to appear in the *Athenaeum* which described the work as 'an absurd project which had no other object than . . . to produce effect on the part of the architect'. South had agreed the plans and had enjoyed the glory of owning such a splendid building so his criticism was especially cruel. Isambard was furious and wanted to sue South for libel but Charles Babbage and Edward Blore persuaded him against it.

In June Isambard returned to Clifton where the ground was being cleared to begin work on the bridge. He basked again in adulation at the opening ceremony on the 21st, listening to flattering speeches and drinking champagne toasts while the navvies quaffed beer. After the ostentatious opening, however, the Committee discovered that they had insufficient money to build the bridge, and before more cash could be raised Bristol went up in flames, literally.

The reason lay in the widespread simmering discontent that high prices and low wages had caused, particularly among the labouring classes, but the precipitating cause of public disorder was the strong emotion aroused by the proposed Reform Bill by which tens of thousands of men hoped to gain the right to vote and thus elect Members of Parliament more likely to represent the views of Everyman. Those Tories who opposed this democratic measure were very unpopular men.

Isambard was in Clifton on Saturday 29 October when the Recorder of Bristol, Sir Charles Wetherell, vehemently opposed to Reform, arrived in the city for the Assizes. He was accompanied by a detachment of Dragoons under Lt-Col Brereton and was met by a stone-throwing mob. Brereton took no action and Sir Charles was forced to take refuge in the Mansion House, the Mayor's official residence in Queen's Square. When the crowd refused to disperse, Brereton not only refused to charge but actually fraternised with the mob and withdrew, whereupon the mob stormed the building and tore it apart while Sir Charles and the Mayor made their escape across the roofs.

At noon on the 30th, Col Brereton marched his men out of Bristol and the mob took over. Isambard and his friend Nicholas Roch were sworn in as special constables and as the gaol was opened and fired, and the toll houses, Bishop's Palace and Mansion House also put to the torch, the two friends did what they could at the Mansion House and Palace to salvage valuables and to discourage looters.

Although Isambard was small of stature he arrested a looter and forcibly marched the man away to a magistrate, the first part of his journey to Botany Bay if not the gallows. On the way Isambard's prisoner was rescued by a man acting as a constable but whom Isambard had seen looting earlier. He retrieved his prisoner by warning the man of what he had seen, but shortly afterwards the same man wrested the prisoner away again, and this time for good.

Isambard reported the incident to the magistrate but was unable to make any identification due to the darkness and the very frightening situation which had existed at the time. When Charles Pinney, the Mayor of Bristol, was tried for neglect of duty, Isambard gave evidence and of course was still unable to identify any of the rioters or looters. This has since been put forward as proof of Isambard's humane feelings and that he held 'liberal and radical views'. Had he been a radical he would have been setting fire to Bristol with the rioters, not desperately trying to place a rioter in custody, with the gallows as a likely punishment.

In the context of the times, Isambard was certainly a liberal and once, in a moment of great stress, he did indeed threaten to join the radicals. In his diary for February 1832 he described a family called Frampton as, 'terrible, anti-reform, anti-catholic, anti-free-trade people'. The Framptons were obviously true-blue Tories and clearly Isambard disagreed with their outlook. But Isambard rebelled against any law which restricted the freedom of the individual – except, of course, laws against theft, murder and the like. He believed in every man's right to follow his own best interest without interference from government, he believed that the free play of the market would solve all problems for the best. That is what 'liberal' meant in his time, but it is not what we today understand by the term.

On 14 November 1831 he set out on a 268-mile stage-coach journey to Monkwearmouth, where local businessmen wanted to build a dock on the north bank of the Wear estuary. He hoped to persuade them to appoint him as their engineer. Though he described them as 'shrewd, clever, fellows – but a rum set', they were in fact not so shrewd because the site they had chosen was inconvenient for naviga-tion, and when finally built the docks were little used. The business-men were, however, shrewd enough to recognise a hungry young man when they saw one and to give him the job – but no expenses.

Isambard trekked home circuitously, visiting and admiring Durham Cathedral and looking very scornfully at the Scotswood Suspension Bridge which took the Stockton & Darlington Railway over the River Tees. The floor of the bridge deflected 12 in. under the weight of a couple of coal trucks and creaked dismally as it returned. He studied the S&DR, the buildings of Darlington, the people of Hartlepool whom he considered to be 'a remarkably fine race of men', he looked at canal and harbour locks, and at York and Beverley Minsters, and then made his way across to Manchester to visit the Hulmes and their daughter, Ellen.

It was while he was in Manchester, on 5 December 1831, that he took his first train ride and in his diary drew free-hand circles and lines whilst the train was in motion. He wrote: 'I record this specimen of the shaking on the Manchester Railway. The time is not far off when we shall be able to take our coffee and write whilst going noiselessly and smoothly at 45 mph. Let me try.' From that it seems plain that his railway, wherever it was, would be for the middle and upper classes. He refers to 'we' meaning, I suppose, people like himself, for the labouring classes did not write or 'take coffee'. He came back to London from Manchester via Chester and Birmingham, the whole trip having cost him – or a friend – £18.

The plans he made for Monkwearmouth were so ambitious that Parliament threw them out. The time and money he had expended on designs for a naval dry dock and repair yard at Woolwich were also wasted when the Admiralty lost interest in the project. There was nothing he could do but keep on trying and in the meantime seek solace in the company of his friends.

Isambard could be a witty actor in home-produced plays and, as we have seen, was an energetic person outdoors, used to rowing boats on the Thames as a means of transporting bits of Gaz engine and also for pleasure, with William Hawes. They would take the 4 a.m. stage-coach out to Kingston and then row to William's home in Lambeth. In February 1832 Ben Hawes introduced Isambard to the Horsley family who lived at 1 High Row in rural Kensington. William Horsley was an organist and composer, his wife Elizabeth was the daughter of an organist-composer and all but one of their five children were either musicians or artists. The house was the meeting place for the musical establishment of Europe: Brahms, Mendelssohn, Chopin, Joachim, Paganini and Bellini were welcome visitors there. John Horsley became a Royal Academician and the youngest child, Sophy, would have made an international career as a professional pianist had it not been for the opposition of her eldest sister, Mary.

Mary was said to have been very beautiful but otherwise possessed of none of the abilities of her siblings. She had, it has been said, 'nothing to be proud of but her face'. Perhaps it was her lack of accomplishment that led her to adopt the proud, haughty and some-what overbearing attitude for which she was well known and which caused her to block her sister's career. Mary and Isambard gradually grew closer and it must have been love that drew them since neither had any money and she could play no instrument – both attributes which Isambard had once considered of vital importance in a young woman.

In August 1832 the Reform Act was passed and middle-class families such as the Brunels and the Hawes got the vote for the first time, although their erstwhile allies – the working people – gained nothing. Ben Hawes offered himself as MP for Lambeth and Isambard supported him at public meetings. Isambard was feeling very 'blue devilish' at the time; the small engineering jobs he was getting were insufficiently exciting or challenging for him and in spite of the beautiful Mary Horsley he became depressed.

Ben Hawes was returned as MP for Lambeth in December. Isambard wrote in his diary: 'So many irons in the fire and none of them hot . . . Woolwich Docks, Monkwearmouth, the Gaz engine, Clifton Bridge.' All were in abeyance and he had received no payment for the outlay he had made for them. There was one new project: 'Bristol Docks. I am still waiting in the expectation of something being done but have heard nothing decisive since my report.'

The suspense of waiting, week after week, would have been a miserable burden for him, made worse when on 30 January 1833 he had to admit defeat on the Gaz engine. He wrote: 'All the time and expense, both enormous, devoted to this thing for nearly ten years are therefore wasted . . . it must therefore die and with it all my fine hopes – crash – gone – well, well, it can't be helped.'

He had reached rock-bottom. The situation might well have crushed the morale of anyone else but he kept his courage and continued to look for work. After the limited increase of voting rights granted by the Reform Act of 1832, confidence returned to the country, money once more became available for investment and the Committee for Bristol Docks, of which Isambard's friend Nicholas Roch was a member, took up once more the problem of improving the navigation. They agreed to adopt Isambard's suggestions for improving the 'Floating Harbour' and in February 1833 Isambard began supervision.

Bristol, eight miles or so from the sea, up the tortuous, tidal River Avon, had been England's second largest port since the Middle Ages, and ships' masts formed a forest of spars through the centre of the town as they lay moored against the river quays. In 1804 the Avon was diverted via the 'New Cut', around the south side of the city, and the old course of the river, through the city centre, became the 'Floating Harbour', between the Neetham Dam at the upper end and the lock gates of the Cumberland Basin which gave access to the river. The hope was that the bed of the new enclosed harbour called the 'Float' could be kept deep by the scouring action of water passing through with the operation of the locks; unfortunately, however, they silted up, so that ocean-going ships tended to run aground within the harbour. Bristol's commerce depended on the river but, owing to the inefficiency of the Corporation, the Avon was being choked with mud. By 1833 the city was beginning to lose its importance to the far better placed, newly developed, port of Liverpool.

In 1830 and 1831 Isambard had drawn up a list of improving works to be carried out on the Floating Harbour, including a steam-powered 'drag boat' which could winch itself backwards and forwards across the Float while a scraper below the hull dragged the mud to a culvert which could be opened and the mud washed out into the river. The riots in Bristol and the unsettled state of the country generally sapped confidence and prevented these ideas being adopted but in 1833 the drag-boat system was installed in the Cumberland Basin and worked well – although it merely transferred mud to shoals in the river.

It has been said that his work for the docks and on the designs for the Clifton Bridge earned him a reputation as an engineer with the people that mattered in Bristol – the merchants, manufacturers and bankers – which was shortly to stand him in good stead. But these people did not fall over themselves to employ him in the great railway adventure which began in the autumn of 1832. He had earned no special reputation for what was undoubtedly some very good work. What his work did bring him was the valuable friendship and respect of the Quay Warden, Captain Christopher Claxton, RN, a very capable, half-pay naval officer, and of Thomas Guppy, an exceedingly wealthy, artistic, well-educated owner of a sugar refinery who was also an engineer, having served a five-year apprenticeship at Maudslay's.

On 7 May 1832 two local surveyors, William Brunton and Henry Price had proposed a direct – but somewhat hilly – line of railway from Bristol to London, going via Bath, Bradford-on-Avon, Trowbridge, Devizes, Hungerford, Newbury and Reading. The great men of Bristol liked the idea but for some unknown reason took a dislike to Brunton and Price. They closed ranks against them so that they did not obtain the subscriptions they needed to go ahead with their scheme. The idea, though, continued alive and well.

In the autumn of 1832, four Bristol merchants, George Jones, John Harford, Thomas Guppy and William Tothill, met in a little office in Temple Backs and formed themselves into a committee for the purpose of making the Bristol Railway. They canvassed Bristol Corporation, the Society of Merchant Venturers, Bristol Dock Company, Bristol Chamber of Commerce and the Bristol & Gloucestershire Railway Company and on 21 January 1833 they held their first full meeting. Prospects appeared good and in February the money was raised to pay for a survey. They decided to put the job of surveying the route out to competitive tender and, further, to give the job of Engineer of the railway to the man who submitted the lowest building estimate. Brunton and Price were obvious contenders, as was William Townsend, a local man who had surveyed and supervised the construction of the Bristol & Gloucestershire Railway, a 10-mile-long coal tramway from Coalpit Heath to the Floating Harbour. Isambard's friend, Nicholas Roch, who, with three others, formed the sub-committee which was to find engineers or surveyors willing to make the survey, put forward Isambard's name.

Isambard knew of these preparations and on 21 February he recorded in his diary 'BR', for Bristol Railway:

> BR. Rode over to Cumberland Basin – dragging going on well. Came back in search of Mr Roch. He came to Mr Osborne's and informed me in *his* presence that a sub-committee was appointed for the purpose of receiving offers from me in conjunction with Townsend and also from Brunton and Price as to what terms and in what time we would make a survey and on what terms we would afterwards undertake to lay out a line for Parliamentary plans.

Isambard and Roch then went to find and inform Townsend. Naturally, Isambard was not pleased to be yoked to Townsend. He realised that the Bristol to London railway was exactly what he had been looking for – the greatest single railway undertaking in Britain to date. Great glory would accrue to its engineer and he certainly did not want to share that with a 'mediocre success' like Townsend.

'How will this end?' Isambard asked in his diary that night. 'We are undertaking a survey by which I shall be considerably a loser but succeeding in being appointed Engineer.' He had no doubt that he would get the job yet he adopted an antagonistic attitude – curiously undiplomatic – towards the wishes of his would-be employers. The Bristol Railway was big enough for him and he wanted the job badly – but even so he would take it only on his own terms. Isambard was contemptuous of the idea of allowing the man with the lowest price to build a major railway line and spoke his mind boldly, without fear of the consequences – knowing that Roch preferred the idea of a competitive tender. 'You are simply giving a premium to the man who will make the most flattering promises,' he told Roch. 'The route I will survey will not be the cheapest – but it will be the best.'

The following evening, 25 February, Isambard invited Townsend to join him at dinner with Robert Osborne, the Committee's solicitor. Osborne left the room and Townsend asked Isambard to explain 'frankly' what the relationship between them would be. Isambard tactfully showed him his subordinate place and recorded in his diary: 'I have no wish to be otherwise than a gentleman, perfectly on an equality, yet as our standing would distinguish us, he having generally acted as Surveyor, I as Engineer, that there would be no fear of our interests clashing and therefore we would pull together.' Townsend was agreeably humble before Isambard's genius and the latter noted that Townsend 'did not aspire to stand on an equality with Mr Brunel, that he was not known in London and thus although he felt himself quite capable of undertaking such a work *yet he should not pretend to put his opinions in opposition to mine but he would yield to me.*'

Isambard also learned from Townsend that Brunton had no friends on the sub-committee; 'if so,' wrote Brunel, 'we may secure the ground to ourselves. Townsend's gratifying humility did not soften Isambard's attitude and he ended his entry with a bad-tempered: 'How the devil am I to get on with him tied to my neck.'

Isambard stated uncompromisingly his case in writing to the sub-committee. That letter was to be his only representation to his prospective employers. He handed it over to Roch on 4 March and departed at once for London where, in his capacity as Resident Engineer, he was to attend the annual meeting of the Thames Tunnel Company.

On the 6th, immediately after this meeting, Isambard boarded the night mail-coach from London and, riding 'outside' for the sake of economy, arrived in Bristol next morning, tired, stiff and chilled to the bone, whereupon he made his way to Osborne's office. The Bristol Railway Committee met that morning to consider the applications from would-be surveyors. Of all the applicants only Isambard saw the line for what it would be – a strategic trunk route. Indeed, not even the Committee saw it like that and, whatever reputation he might have had thanks to his work for the Floating Harbour, his talk of 'not the cheapest but the best' did not go down well.

The argument went on all morning as Isambard waited in Osborne's office to hear his fate. At 2 p.m. a messenger brought a note from Roch – Isambard had been appointed as Engineer of the Bristol Railway and was required to attend at the Council House for the appointment to be formally confirmed by the Chairman, John Cave. At dinner that evening, Roch told Isambard that he had got the job by a majority of one vote with Cave voting against him. But the narrow margin mattered not at all: Isambard had the job. A glorious prospect had opened before him and on 9 March 1833 he and Townsend set out on the survey.

Isambard boasted later, to a Select Committee of the House of Lords, that he 'was the first, and for sometime the only employee of the Bristol Railway'. He forgot that Townsend, officially his equal, had been appointed on the same day as himself. Isambard had for so long worked in his father's shadow that he was not going to share the glory of the Bristol Railway with anyone.

The two men set out to survey the country from Bristol to Bath along a route suggested by Townsend; using his tramway to climb steeply on to the heights north-west of Bristol before turning south-east through Wick to descend upon Bath over Lansdown Hill! This was merely a circular tour of some of the steepest hills in the West Country and says nothing at all for Townsend's conception of what a main line railway should be. Isambard took him back to Bristol through the Avon valley, the shortest – and virtually level – route. Isambard not only determined upon using that line but also decided on placing the terminus of the railway at Temple Meads. Townsend soon accepted his inability even to keep up with Isambard's energetic horse-riding, much less conceive a trunk main line, and was glad to remain in the Bristol area working under Brunel's instructions.

Isambard was then unleashed. At last he had the enormous project all to himself and set out to show what he could do. He was gambling on his future, drawing on his credit with the West of England Bank, living an itinerant, horseback life, to lay the foundations of what he prophesied would be 'the finest work in England' and so achieve the one great honour he desired – to be a household name, to stand out as England's greatest engineer.

There were two possible routes from Bristol to London. Both went via the Avon valley to Bathampton, where one went via Bradford-on-Avon, Devizes, Marlborough, Hungerford, Newbury and Reading while the other had to climb the escarpment east of

Bathampton and pass through Chippenham before setting out over 60 miles of exceedingly remote grassland to reach Reading. From there the line would run through the Thames valley to make one of several entries into London.

This vast area had to be surveyed on horseback, the preferred line decided upon, approximate levels taken and landowners won over to the idea of the railway passing through their property – and all in about ten weeks. Brunel's diary shows the frantic energy with which he pursued his aims:

Thurs. 18 April. Got a hack and rode out to Woodley Hill according to a letter from Hughes [a surveyor he had engaged; after some searching he found him – on the wrong track]. Directed him . . . to push on to the Thames across Earley Court and Upper Earley . . . I then rode on to Bagshot Heath (at least 10 miles) and returned by a line going at the back of Easthampstead Park.

Isambard must have ridden 40 miles that day. He would have had to ride fast to cover the ground in daylight and indeed he records that his horse fell on the way home.

On Sunday 21 April he went to church at St Lawrence in Reading and then rode to Wantage via Blewbury, 26 miles along the main road but Isambard would have been scouting to and fro, spying out the land, and would therefore have covered more than that distance. It was late when he arrived at the Bear in Wantage market place but at six next morning he was in the saddle, heading back for Reading, surveying as he went. At Streatley he turned right at the Bull and rode up the 1 in 4 hill to the open downland where he 'determined the outer line winding round the undulating ground'.

Back at his Reading hotel he had a quick meal and then rode out to Theale to search in vain for Hughes. Next day the weather was warm and sunny. Isambard rode out to Theale again, and after much searching found Hughes, reclining in the buttercups by the canal side, 'a beautiful place to be in this hot weather', conceded Isambard to his diary, although one supposes that he was not so easy on the skiving Hughes.

On 30 July Isambard explained his proposals at the first public meeting of the Bristol Railway. He announced that the line would be 116 miles long and would cost, complete with stations and locomotives, £2½m. Although that was a huge sum for the times, it was nearly a triple underestimate on Isambard's part. On 22 August the Bristol Committee went to London to meet the recently formed London Committee. Isambard described them as, 'rather an old women's set, a regular jobbing committee. Must hope for somebody to give them a little life and sense.' The man to do just that arrived on 27 August as the London Committee's Secretary: Charles Saunders. Isambard and Saunders liked each other instantly and Saunders was to be his staunchest supporter. On 27 August Isambard was confirmed by the London Committee as Engineer of the line and that evening he wrote in his diary that magic combination of letters, GWR – Great Western Railway. It was the use of his father's 'Great' that worked the magic; the conventional title would have been 'Grand Western Railway'. How weak that sounds.

With an entire railway to be designed he needed a drawing office and raised a loan to rent a London office at 53 Parliament Street. Here he installed a staff of draughtsmen and a chief clerk, one Joseph Bennett, who was to serve him for twenty-six years. Hired hacks and stage-coach services were no longer sufficient for his transport so he designed and had built a four-horse britschka which presumably required a coachman and which would have cost a great deal in livery charges each night. It had a bed, a drawing board, and cupboards for all his drawing and surveying equipment plus his box of fifty cigars which he chain-smoked. The navvies were to nickname it the 'Flying Hearse' and in that they were closer to the truth than they realised. Isambard drove himself as mercilessly as any slave.

His assistant surveyors could not enter on any land until Isambard had been to see the owner and, very often, placated his outraged Tory feelings. Isambard used the word 'Tory' privately to describe anyone short-sighted enough to oppose his wonderful railway. However, he left his sarcastic wit outside when he interviewed landowners and with grace and tact managed to charm almost all the dukes, lords and gentlemen – like a latter-day John the Baptist, announcing the advent of the Great Western Railway and calling on all and sundry to join it.

He had not only to persuade them not to oppose him in Parliament, he also had to ask them to buy shares in the Company. He detested this part of his job, 'sad, harassing work' he called it, but it had to be done. If he was to see his great dream realised he had to persuade several thousand strangers to take up shares in the £2½ m. company. Parliament would not even look at his Bill until he had the right number of shareholders. Isambard wrote all the letters arising from the survey, checked all the accounts before they were paid and scrutinised all important legal documents – in spite of there being a company solicitor. Although he had several assistants to whom he issued instructions, he double-checked to make sure they had been carried out correctly.

Finally everything was done. A mere nine months after his first riding out of Bristol with Townsend, complete and specific plans for the Great Western Railway were deposited in the Parliamentary Bills Office, together with proof that the necessary number of shares had been taken up. When the Bill came before Parliament early in 1834 it was for a railway which varied somewhat from that which came to be built. It was to come out of London from Vauxhall, near Waterloo, go through Brompton and Hammersmith to South Acton and then, after passing through a tunnel, join the line as built at Ealing. There would have been a mile-long tunnel under Sonning Hill. This was longer than was required by engineering criteria but was extended to hide the trains from the MP for Berkshire, Robert Palmer, whose house stood near-by and who was implacably opposed to the line. The Avon would have been bridged four times instead of twice, as it in fact is.

Opposition to the Bill was fierce. Farmers around London were frightened of produce coming from far away to give them competition, the stage-coach and canal companies were against it, but most formidable of all was the unlikely alliance between the London & Southampton Railway and Eton College. The former wanted to make a line to Bath from Basingstoke, while the latter was afraid that the GWR would put the brothels of London within easy reach of the aristocratic schoolboys – thus demonstrating a singular lack of faith in their pupils' strength of character.

On 16 April 1834 the Bill went to its Committee stage. Isambard was the main witness for the Bill and was subjected to cross-examination by Serjeant Merewether who attacked him as if he was a criminal. Isambard remained unruffled throughout. Merewether asked him how many landowners on the route had assented or dissented to the line and Isambard not only told him which man belonged to which camp but also gave the precise mileage of railway through each county. He could also give the depth and length of all his cuttings and embankments and produced figures to show that deeper or longer or higher earthworks existed elsewhere. Merewether would interrupt Isambard's flow with a silly question, such as: 'How far is a chain?' Isambard would politely inform him and then pick up at exactly the point he left off.

Sometimes a member of the Select Committee would interrupt with a naïve question: 'Have you selected, in your judgement, the best line of communication?'

'Of course the line I have selected I consider the best,' replied Isambard tartly.

Some of the questions were downright stupid. 'You have spoken of two lines, one to the north of the Marlborough Downs, the other to the south. If you were a conjuror and could conjure the whole population on the north of the Downs to the south, which line then would you recommend?'

'I really cannot say,' replied Isambard impatiently. 'I should prefer the south line. It is a pity people live on a part of the land so high but choosing to live there they must take the consequences.'

Isambard chose the northern of the two routes because it passed over a lower summit than the Marlborough route, and because the northern line was strategically more important. The Marlborough route would have been a parochial line, winding through hills and in and out of several river valleys to connect various small towns with London and Bristol. The northern route was a major trunk line connecting the two most important centres of commerce in England with, as nearly as possible, a level way. It was perfectly feasible to send out major branch lines northwards and westwards into the far west of England and west Wales – for Ireland. It is significant that the English lords who owned land in Ireland and the Irish nationalist politician, Daniel O'Connell, all supported the GWR.

The Committee passed the Bill, which went for its second reading. But opposition to the Vauxhall terminus from the inhabitants of Brompton was so strong that the Company abandoned it – leaving the line without any terminus. Opposition counsel called the GWR 'neither Great, nor Western, nor even a Railway' and the Bill was thrown out by the Lords on 25 July 1834. The GWR company came back in 1835 with fresh proposals. The terminus of the line was proposed as Euston, with the GWR joining the London & Birmingham at a junction in the vicinity of the present-day Queen's Park station. Because the mile-long tunnel under Sonning Hill had not removed Robert Palmer's objection to the line its length was reduced to 625 yds to make the work cheaper.

Isambard was grilled by Merewether for eleven out of the forty days that the revised Bill was before Committee and answered the questions – some sensible, others intended to be disconcerting and a few merely fatuous – with the same cool skill he had shown the year before. He was centre-stage throughout that time, with members of both Houses coming to watch his performance at some time or other. He was making his reputation and there can be no doubt that he enjoyed the limelight. When it was all over and he was asked how he had remained so cool and collected in the face of Merewether's onslaught, Isambard replied with that recognisably Brunellian mixture of innocent arrogance and boyish truthfulness: 'Because he could not possibly know as much about engineering as I.'

6

Ambition Uppermost

King William IV gave his Royal Assent to the Great Western Railway Bill on 31 August 1835 and the way was clear for Isambard to realise his dream of creating the finest railway in the country. He wanted high speed and smooth riding – something no other engineer had, up to that time, set out specifically to achieve. He did not envisage his railway as a common mover but as a luxury transportation system. His passengers were going to 'take their coffee whilst travelling at 45 mph'. He set out to achieve perfection for those who could afford to pay for it.

He was well aware of the serpentine motion of the narrow, short wheel-base, four-wheel carriages on the Stephensonian 'coal-cart' gauge of 4 ft $8\frac{1}{2}$ in. and of their up-and-down motion as they trundled over short rails laid across stone blocks. The rails were laid correctly at the start but the blocks subsided randomly under the weight of trains and could not easily be re-aligned. Isambard had seen how not to do it and believed he had discovered the correct method. What was needed was a track which was capable of maintaining its perfect level both longitudinally and across the rails. His rails would be screwed to continuous wooden bearers held down tightly against hard-packed sand by being attached to heavy, wooden piles driven 15 ft into the ground.

The lost Bill of 1834 included a clause restricting the gauge to the Stephensonian standard but between losing that Bill and coming to Parliament again in 1835 Isambard decided he wanted a gauge of between 6 ft 10 in. and 7 ft, and he asked Lord Shaftesbury, in charge of drafting Bills, to omit the gauge clause. He was at once challenged by a member of Shaftesbury's staff, a Mr Palk, who asked Isambard what he would do about the inevitable problem of break of gauge. Isambard said he did not think this was important, even though the GWR was seeking to run over L&BR standard-gauge metals into Euston. Thus Isambard was well aware, from the very beginning, of the objection to having two gauges in one small country.

The opposition to the 1835 Bill were so busy listening to Dr Dionysius Lardner's learned discourses on excessive oxygen consumption in tunnels on steep inclines, which would leave no air for the passengers to breathe, and so busy attacking imaginary lines on Isambard's plans that they did not notice the lack of a gauge clause. Had they done so they could probably have prevented the passing of the Bill. Sheerly by chance, therefore, Isambard was left free to use any gauge he chose and on 15 September 1835 he wrote to his Directors proposing a broad gauge. His reasons were based on much mathematical calculation, at which he excelled and with which, as usual, he dazzled himself and the people who would have to pay for his theorising. He wrote:

> The resistance from friction is diminished as the proportion of the diameter of the wheel to the axle is increased . . . we have therefore the means of materially diminishing this resistance . . . by simply widening the rails, so that the body of the carriage might be kept entirely within the wheels, the centre of gravity might be considerably lowered and at the same time the diameter of the wheels be unlimited. I should propose 6 ft 10 in. or 7 ft as the width between the rails . . . I am not prepared at present to recommend any particular size of wheel . . . but my great object would be in every possible way to render each part capable of improvement in what appears to be an obstacle to any great progress in such a very important point as the wheels – upon which the resistance, which governs the cost of transport and which governs the speed obtained – so materially depend.

The Stephensonian system was indeed sadly lacking. The shortcomings of the Liverpool & Manchester Railway had led Isambard to look for a better way of doing things but his desire to make spectacular scientific advances – largely for the good of his public reputation – led him into an over-reaction to the problems. He could have done all that was necessary and still used the standard gauge. I do not think that this is a verdict from hindsight. Judged by the light of his own times he might be said to have acted rashly. From the very first the practical difficulty of the incompatibility of gauges had been pointed out to him, not merely by parliamentary officials but by Robert Stephenson of whom Isambard had once written, 'he is *decidedly* the *only* man in the profession whom I feel disposed to meet as my equal or superior.'

The GWR Board adopted Isambard's generalised proposal for a wide gauge on 29 October 1835 but the actual width of 7 ft was not announced formally until the half-yearly meeting at Bristol in August 1836. Meanwhile, several inventors laid their schemes for track-laying before the GWR Directors who passed them on to Isambard for evaluation. One of his replies to the Board, dated 9 January 1836, sums up the way Isambard was always willing to look at other men's ideas and to copy and improve upon whatever he thought was worth while. The reply was also a masterpiece of Brunellian manipulation, keeping the Directors under his control:

> The scheme is only one of numerous others which will doubtless follow. During all this competition the Company is placed in a peculiarly advantageous position . . . we do not have to make a decision for a twelvemonth . . . we can study all systems and take the best from each . . . I should wish to keep myself perfectly uncommitted that I might impartially advise you when the time comes.

Having thus established his impartiality he dampened their enthusiasm for outside assistance by a cunningly oblique reference to cost: 'If any of the suggestions be adopted I should be the first to recommend that this Company pay *liberal compensation* to the inventor, proportionate to the use we might make of his invention.'

Having secured his position he then reassured the Board of the conventional nature of his own system:

> I have no new plan of my own . . . on the contrary, the result of the best considerations . . . induces me at present to give preference to a slight modification of the oldest system of railway building used in England . . . namely rails of simple form laid on longitudinal beams of wood . . . I beg to repeat . . . that in this system there is nothing new . . . each part is old and has at some time or other been subject to experiment.

Isambard was being devious here, for while there was nothing new about longitudinal sleepers, the use of piles and the spacing of the rails – neither mentioned in this particular letter – were revolutionary. He was obviously playing down the gauge question since he knew it was controversial and problematic.

In the meantime Isambard had been trying to persuade Robert Stephenson to co-operate in allowing the broad gauge into Euston. Knowing Stephenson's practical objections to his elegant theory, Isambard adopted his most charming and conciliatory tone in his letter of 15 October 1835: 'My Dear Stephenson, I am requested by my Directors to see you upon the subject of the best means of carrying our rails along your line from the point of junction, Kensal, to the depot, Euston.' Isambard followed this with a very peculiar sentence: 'Our rails being placed at a greater width than yours – I believe – are, I think this may be done without difficulty.' Surely he knew very well what was the gauge of the L&BR? In his efforts to be charming he seems to have carried delicate reticence beyond the bounds of common sense.

Isambard continued to purr gently and discreetly into Stephenson's ear: 'I think this may be done without difficulty. You may, *perhaps*, differ with me in this opinion. Have you any objection to talking the thing over with me to tell me the difficulties you foresee, if any? I will endeavour to meet them or be prepared to yield to them.'

Neither copious draughts of Brunellian oil nor Isambard's genuine friendship and respect had any effect on Robert Stephenson and the L&BR. The company simply did not want the GWR at Euston. On 16 November Stephenson sent a heavy hint of this to Isambard in the form of some sketches of Euston's proposed layout: the L&BR had made no provision whatsoever for the GWR. In December the GWR Directors abandoned Euston as a terminus and decided on their own line to a terminus on 'a certain space of ground adjoining the basin of the Paddington canal in the Parish of Paddington' and set out to obtain a fresh Act of Parliament for the construction of this line – the Paddington Extension Railway.

On 26 December 1835, aged nearly thirty, Isambard took stock of his situation. Certainly he was in cheerfully uninhibited spirits, like a little boy counting up his toys, childishly proud, greedy and condescending, viewing even his friends, men who were his intellectual equals, as objects to assist his own advancement. He wrote:

When I last wrote in this book I was just emerging from obscurity . . . the railway is now in progress. I am their Engineer to the finest work in England – a handsome salary – £2000 a year – on excellent terms with my Directors and all going smoothly, but what a fight we have had . . . it is like looking back on a fearful pass – but we have succeeded and it's not this alone but everything I have been engaged in has been successful.

Clifton Bridge – my first child, my darling, is actually going on – recommenced week last Monday – Glorious!

Sunderland Docks, too, is going well.

Bristol Docks. All Bristol is alive and turned bold and speculative with this railway – we are to widen the entrances and Lord knows what.

Merthyr & Cardiff Railway. This I owe to the GWR. I care not about it.

Cheltenham Railway. Of course I owe this to the Great Western – and I may say so myself. Do not feel much interested in this. None of the parties are my friends. I hold it only because they cannot do without me. It's an awkward line and the estimate's too low. However it's all in the way of business and it's a proud thing to monopolise all the West as I do.

Bristol & Exeter Railway. This survey was done in the grand style – it's a good line too – and I feel an interest as connected to Bristol to which I really owe much. I think I shall carry this Bill – I shall become quite an oracle in the Committees of the House. Gravatt served me well in this B&E survey.

Newbury branch. A little go, almost beneath my notice. It will do as a branch.

Suspension bridge across the Thames (Hungerford foot-bridge) I have *condescended* to be engineer of this but I shan't give myself much trouble about it. If done it will add to my stock of irons.

I forgot also the Bristol and Gloster Railway.

Isambard then totted up the amounts of capital each project represented and found the total to be £5,320,000 – 'a pretty considerable capital to pass through my hands and this at the age of 29 – faith, not so young as I always fancy tho' I can hardly believe it when I think of it'.

Although he was Engineer to so many large undertakings he did not consider that he had done more than lay the foundations of his fame and fortune. He ended his survey:

I am just leaving 53 Parliament Street where I may say I have made my fortune – or rather the foundation of it – and have taken Lord Devon's house, 18 Duke Street. A fine house. I go sometimes with my four horses – I have a cab and a horse – I have a secretary – in fact I am now a *somebody*. Everything has prospered . . . I don't like it, it can't last, bad weather must surely come. Let me see the storm in time to gather in my sails.

Isambard believed that possessions made him a 'somebody'. The more he owned, therefore, the larger the 'somebody' he became and without possessions he was a 'nobody'. Status was everything to him. This catalogue had been devoted to himself. Only one line, the last, mentions his future wife, a status symbol not yet in his possession – indeed, he had not then even proposed to her yet he confidently wrote: 'Mrs B. This time 12 month I shall be a married man. How will that be? Will it make me happier?' He was still writing about himself.

In April 1836, rather against his will because he did not like the parties involved, he accepted the post of Engineer to the Oxford, Worcester & Wolverhampton Railway. 'Here's another £1,500,000 of capital,' he wrote in his diary, 'really my business is something extra-ordinary.' In May he landed the job of Engineer to the South Devon Railway from Exeter to Plymouth and with yet another iron in the fire he evidently considered himself sufficiently well supplied against disaster to ask Mary Horsley to marry him. She accepted him on 14 May 1836.

Did he love her? One supposes so, although not in the same way as he had loved Ellen Hulme. Mary, it is generally agreed, had neither the talents nor the money which Isambard had once thought essential in a wife. She was narrow-minded, strong-willed, bigoted, snobbish and bossy, yet submissive to Isambard. However, without talents she constituted no threat to his ego, for Isambard admitted no equals except Robert Stephenson. She was publicly acknowledged to be very beautiful, which would be a feather in his cap, she came from the right class in society so she would not be a bar to his progress.

She would, without doubt, be an adornment to his career – for a man had to be seen to be wealthy before he could be accepted into society. He would lavish upon her fine clothes and expensive jewellery – she would be his creation as much as the Great Western Railway. She would gain an exceedingly charming husband whose fame and fortune were all before him. In a luxuriously appointed home, decorated to Isambard's impeccable taste, she would be delighted to become a society hostess, hold fashionable court and maintain an oasis of culture to which Isambard would return, from time to time, as his work allowed. A cynical view, perhaps, but then it can be argued that Isambard had given up true love for his ambition – his first love was now his work, that is to say his ambition.

Isambard was working under tremendous pressure, whether

designing his SS *Great Western* or surveying his several railways. He could never say where he would be more than a week ahead so when he could clear a date he and Mary were married by special licence in Kensington Parish Church on 5 July 1836. She was twenty-two. Marc Brunel, then sixty-seven, took a day off from the Thames Tunnel and came with Sophia. He was so deeply bound up with the tunnel that his diary page for that day was full of work sketches. On the sole remaining line he recorded, 'Isambard married today.'

At the wedding breakfast back at High Row, the crowd packed the house and spilled out into the summer garden. Some of Isambard's assistants were there, including William Gravatt who appalled Mary's rather giggly younger sisters by his lack of small-talk and his awkward manners. Gravatt loathed the fuss and the idle chatter and felt ill at ease. The younger Horsley girls quickly detected this and, in trying to set him at his ease with extra attention, terrified him so that he half-emptied Mr Horsley's snuffbox. They later described him as 'partaking of the Wild Beast'.

Isambard's idea of a honeymoon was a fourteen-day tour by stage-coach. They went to North Wales, explored the romantic, gloomy passes of Beddgelert and then trekked all the way to Devon before trudging home to Kensington. Exceedingly lengthy letters from Mary's mother and sisters pursued them, full of family chatter, references to Gravatt's lack of style and requests to know what Isambard had done with the wedding presents, in particular with a pair of silver salt cellars which could not be found anywhere. Doubtless Isambard saw much of engineering and indeed of artistic interest but it must have been hard work for Mary, completely unused to jolting about in a long-distance coach and in any case an indifferent traveller, not willing to put up with any hardship. Still, she was riding on the cushions of young romance, which probably made it all bearable.

Mary returned home to 18 Duke Street and at once set about creating her world. She was as intent on grandeur as Isambard and could stand on her dignity better than most. She was obsessed with her social status and was very much aware of the need to be seen in all the 'right' places, wearing the 'right' clothes and with the 'right' people. She and Isambard began to accumulate servants, only four to begin with, including a liveried footman who always accompanied her when she ventured forth to promenade in St James's Park opposite their house. When she was presented to Queen Victoria she was so absurdly overdressed that her niece, Maria Hawes, wrote in her diary: 'The Queen never took her eyes off Aunt Mary, but followed her to the end of the room and I had no chance of being noticed, coming behind her immense crinoline.'

Mary's concern for always doing the 'right thing' led her to forbid utterly her second son, Henry, to marry the girl he loved, Isobel Froude, daughter of the scientist William Froude and a very close friend of the family. The reason for Mary's objection was that William Froude's brother, Hurrell, had, under the influence of Dr John Henry Newman, become a Roman Catholic – considered at that time not only very unfashionable but even an unpatriotic thing to do. So strong was her objection and so intimidated was Henry by it that, even after his mother's death, he still could not marry 'Issy' and remained a bachelor to his death.

Mary Brunel's sister Fanny became an accomplished amateur pianist and was encouraged by the violinist Joachim to play professionally. Fanny wanted to do this but Mary's influence in the family was so strong that she was able to prevent it by pointing out that Fanny would be engaging in trade. The irony of this was lost upon Mary's invincible arrogance – her elegant home was situated on the floors above Isambard's offices at 18 Duke Street. She herself was living 'over the shop'.

7

Fishponds and Flattery

In 1836 a small railway with a big name, the Birmingham, Bristol & Thames Junction Railway (BBTJ) had obtained its Act to build a north/south railway from the L&BR at Willesden to the Thames at Chelsea Basin. The route cut across the proposed line of the Paddington Extension Railway (PER) at Wormwood Scrubs (the present-day Old Oak Common) on the level and one wonders if this was an attack on the GWR inspired by the L&BR. The BBTJ Directors were hostile and were to give Isambard a great deal of unnecessary annoyance.

Isambard toyed with the idea of using the atmospheric system of traction over the PER, for in his sketchbook No 22 he drew a plan of a large air pump under the heading London Extension Railway. The Bill for the PER came before the House in 1837 and even without the complications of atmospheric traction it was subjected to severely hostile delaying tactics. On 16 July 1837 Isambard wrote in high dudgeon to Thomas Osler, a Bristol Director:

> My Dear Sir, A new delay has occurred in the progress of our Bill, a new crotchet has come into some Lord's head and a new clause is sent to the Commons for approval. This utter, wanton disregard for the interests of parties waiting is really disgusting. The tyranny exercised is as great as it could be under the most despotic government and the only answer one gets to the strongest appeals is ridicule and insult. If I had not been a *Radical* before, I should become one now. Yours very truly, I.K. Brunel.

While he was designing or supervising the construction of several railways, the SS *Great Western*, the Monkwearmouth dockyard in

Sunderland, and fending off requests for assistance – the Great Northern wanted his help in Parliament in 1836 – he had also to recruit and train the engineering assistants who enabled him to take on so much work. Michael Lane was Resident Engineer at Monkwearmouth, George Frere was Resident Engineer for the Bristol end of the GWR and John Hammond was in charge of the London end with Robert Archibald his assistant.

The best-loved assistant was the one who could read his mind and do what the great man would have wanted had he been there, the one who remembered that friendship would never be allowed to stand in the way of the work – since the work was intended to advance Brunel. George Frere was such a man and Isambard's letters to him occasionally show a relaxed and friendly attitude. Isambard dished out orders in minute detail and expected those orders to be minutely observed. He allowed no independent action. The rare few who were his equals in engineering science and mental ability – Gooch and Gravatt, for instance – were uneasy subordinates and he watched them carefully for signs of independence so as to keep them firmly in their place – as servants.

Isambard's manner was very strict at the start and the first trial any applicant had to pass was the letter he received which laid down the conditions under which the aspiring engineer would be employed. Only the most determined would have replied to the letter Isambard addressed to the young W.G. Owen (who became Chief Engineer of the GWR in 1868) on 16 January 1836:

In consequence of Mr Bennett's [Brunel's clerk at Duke Street] strong recommendation I authorised him to write to you on the subject of your being employed upon the Great Western Railway . . . but as I have not the means of judging your capability I must explain to you the terms upon which you, or any other gentleman, must enter the service of the Great Western Railway. The sub-assistants must be considered as working entirely for promotion, their salaries and their continued employment depend entirely upon the degree of industry and ability I find they possess. Their salaries commence at £150 p.a. and may be increased progressively up to £250 and perhaps in some cases to £350 p.a. They must reside on such part of the line as required, consider their whole time, to any extent required, at the service of the Company and will be liable to instant dismissal should they appear to me to be inefficient from any cause whatsoever and, more particularly, to consider themselves as on trial only. If these conditions appear to you encouraging you will come to Town immediately and call at my office, 18 Duke Street, Westminster.

Isambard took more trouble with his young men than the letter to Owen suggests. He directed them to jobs, gave them their chances, watched their progress, encouraged them and tongue-lashed them should the occasion arise. He had to have well-trained men and he undertook their training and discipline along with the rest of his creation. In practice a man had to be inefficient over a long period before he was sacked. The only quick way to dismissal was to behave in a manner unbecoming of a Great Western Railway officer and gentleman. Lethargy was given at least one chance to repent. During the early part of 1836, in spite of all his pressing problems, Isambard appears to have cared sufficiently about a young sub-assistant called Harrison, working under Hammond at the Hanwell Viaduct, to write him the following letter:

My Dear Sir, I am sorry to be under the necessity of informing you that I do not consider you to discharge efficiently the duties of assistant engineer and consequently, as I informed you yesterday, your appointment is rescinded from this day. A great want of industry is that of which I principally complain and thus it is entirely within your power to redeem this situation. I shall have no objection to you continuing on trial at the Bristol end of the line and I sincerely trust that you will see the necessity of making greater exertions . . . and that at the expiration of a month I may be able – with justice to the Company – to reinstate you in as fine an opportunity of advancing yourself in your profession as a young man could possibly have.

Unfortunately for young Harrison, just after Isambard had sealed this letter with hot wax he received from an instrument maker the bill for a circumferentor which had been supplied to Harrison. Isambard had ordered Harrison to buy the circumferentor, a surveyor's instrument now superseded by a theodolite, on the principle that no aspiring surveyor should be without one, but young Harrison thought that Isambard must have wanted it for the Company – so he sent the bill to his employer. There was no doubt in Isambard's mind that this was an act of insolence. He broke the seal on the letter and added this:

PS: You have acted with reference to this in a manner which I do not choose to pass over. It indicates a temper of mind which excludes all hope of your profiting from the new trial I had proposed. You will please consider yourself dismissed from the Company's service on receipt of this letter.

The railway was to cut a swathe through fields and houses. Some landowners welcomed the rails, others were reluctant and some hostile. Handling these people was a delicate and time-consuming problem for Isambard but one which he handled with great skill and charm. Where a landowner was enthusiastic for the railway Isambard would give him the job of smoothing down those less enlightened.

One such early railway enthusiast was called Wilkins, who owned most of the village of Twerton, near Bath. Wilkins, to quote Brunel writing to his Directors, 'has allowed us the most perfect accommodation in allowing us to pull down such houses as were in our way *before the line was finally determined and before the terms of purchase were agreed'*. The railway line was planned to go down the main street, requiring the demolition of practically the whole village which then had to be re-built beside the line. Isambard realised the intense feelings that might be generated by such an upheaval and advised the Directors to allow Wilkins, 'rather than strangers', to carry out the work. Wilkins was a really practical businessman. He took the contract and was paid to demolish and rebuild the village while at the same time receiving compensation for the loss of his houses.

On the Bristol & Exeter line Isambard found no such enthusiastic helpers. He and his assistant, Ward, had to spend great efforts with Stanford, the newly installed owner of Nynehead Court, near Wellington, and also with the pugnacious Revd Proctor Thomas of Wellington itself. The railway ran through their lands and neither wanted it. A Brunellian embankment was scheduled to fill in the clergyman's fishpond and he was far from forgiving. Ward went to see him, an exciting visit apparently, because Ward reported to Isambard suggesting he should come and try his charm on the man, 'you should see the size of his fists'.

Isambard's sense of humour failed him and he replied tartly on 9 January 1836:

> The idea of my going 180 miles to see a man's fists is rather absurd . . . I hardly have the conscience to put the Company to such expense for any Proctor Thomas in history. However, be very civil to him and as he is coming to London request him to have the goodness to drop me a note when he is in Town to say where he is or to favour me with a call.

Some landowners, seeing the railway coming, suddenly thought of improvements which they could make to their lands which would be made impossible by the railway. Naturally they demanded huge sums of money as compensation for their 'loss'. The B&ER embankment just north of Wellington would cut across a corner of Stanford's land, and block the way for an as yet unbuilt ornamental drive which he said he was going to make across the park from the parish road to his house, Nynehead Court. Isambard wrote to him on 11 January 1836 promising that if Stanford allowed the railway through, he would provide a sumptuous bridge in the embankment through which the private road could pass. He wrote:

> It shall be a stone bridge of the same style and architecture as the existing canal bridge [Grand Western Canal] but superior in every respect as regards proportions, materials and workmanship. It will be substantial and well built and if required I will include a lodge house in the abutments or wing walls.

Stanford relented and the handsome bridge, complete with lodge for the gate-keeper within the wing wall, was built together with ornamental stone walls on each side of the intended road between the railway and canal bridges which were about 100 yds apart. But the rest of the mile-long drive was not constructed because Stanford went bankrupt soon afterwards.

With this settled, the course of the line could not be altered for the benefit of the Revd Proctor Thomas's fishpond. Isambard briefed Ward, by letter, on how to break the news to him: 'I cannot remove our line owing to my promise to Mr Stanford but I will make him a dozen fishponds for about the same money that my visiting him would cost the Company.' Isambard suggested that flattery would go down well: 'Remember that he is a man who wishes to act very fairly – and these sort of men like to be told so.'

Even noble lords were not above a certain dishonesty. The GWR embankment in the vicinity of Taplow was to pass over Lord Orkney's land and his lordship, through his Land Agent, tried to get a bridge built through the bank, large enough for a coach and horses, under the pretext of providing for a water-course that did not exist.

Although Isambard was building the GWR and the B&ER for the sake of his public reputation, he also saw it as a great public work. It was, after all, funded by the cash of hundreds of middle-class people – clergyman, spinster, army officer and gentleman appear as occupations in the lists of shareholders as well as merchant, industrialist and banker. In a letter to Sir J.W. Gordon, who owned part of Wormwood Scrubs, which the GWR had to cross to reach

Paddington station, Isambard said: 'I need hardly remind you that although the application is made on behalf of a Company, it may be fairly considered to be made on public grounds, since a proper entrance into London for the whole of the west of England traffic depends on it.'

The Great Western was, in Isambard's mind, a proper, gentlemanly investment, not a matter for speculation. He loathed all speculators. There were, in his eyes, a self-serving interest and an enlightened self-interest. The former was vulgarly commercial and therefore ungentlemanly, the latter sought to earn a living while giving something in return. When the self-seekers got in his way they roused his ire. In January 1836, Exeter City Corporation was 'out to make a killing' on the land which the B&ER required for their terminal at Exeter. The approach to the city was along the Exe valley, the terminus could be in one spot only – and that land was owned by the Corporation which was demanding an exorbitant price.

Isambard gave stage management directions to his assistant, Ward, telling him how to deal with the greedy aldermen:

> Exeter Corporation is behaving in that unfair and illiberal manner which has disgusted us on the GWR. They forget the immense advantages they will have by our coming there and can think only to exact from us as much as they can. *Treat them with a high hand.* Let them know we are sure to get our Bill and that we are angry at the idea that Exeter – for whose sole benefit this line is made – should dare to offer us the slightest impediment.

Isambard had estimated the cost of the GWR at £2½ m. and his constant worry was to keep costs down, for it was soon obvious that the estimate was too low. Among much else soaking up hard-to-come-by cash was the purchase of property and it was of the utmost importance that the vendor should have no idea that he was selling to the GWR. Isambard directed all estate agents working for the GWR and ordered them to use great discretion. To a Mr Hawkes of Reading he wrote on 20 August 1836:

> I have received your letter of 19th and I do not feel inclined to increase my offer for the properties in Crane Street and Friar Street. I consider £1800 quite sufficient and I shall hope to hear that you have concluded the purchase. It seems to me rather injudicious to have disclosed the Great Western Railway Company as the purchaser, it was understood between us that this should not be disclosed – as the knowledge of it was not likely to have procured the property at a reasonable price.

On 8 March 1836, he was riding about the village of Saltford – a difficult place for Brunel. The route came from Bath, down the Avon valley on a long curve, almost dead level, and was obliged to go through the village which stood on a hilly spur projecting into the valley. A cutting would have destroyed the house of a Major James, who, believing the GWR to be a money-bag of unplumbable depth, had put a very high price on his property. Isambard hated to feel that someone had the upper hand and rather than buy the house and make a cutting he planned a tunnel which would have to dive deep under the house to avoid harming its foundations. Isambard found this up-and-down kink in his otherwise superbly level track irksome and was looking for a way of dispensing with the tunnel and of maintaining the level.

Scouting quietly through the houses, Isambard saw that if he went through the adjoining property he could not only shorten the tunnel but also keep his level and ease the sharpness of the curve through the village. One wonders why he had not noticed it back in 1833. Anyhow, without being recognised, he was able to negotiate with the owner who was quite happy to sell the house and an acre of land for £700. This was an opportunity too good to miss and Isambard shook hands on the deal without first having the Directors' permission to make the expenditure. He then handed over to his local estate agent, Goodridge, to make the formal arrangements.

Isambard wrote the draft contracts for every job and re-examined all the closely written pages of legal language forming the final contract documents. He frequently noticed errors in drafting and referred back to the Company's solicitor: 'There is an error on page 26. It says "and the whole work will be completed in 20 months". As it stands this might be taken to mean only the whole of the bridge. Please insert the words "and the whole of the works included in this contract . . .".' He would employ himself on far smaller details, without doubt to the detriment of his supervision of the main work. To one of his clerks, Leane, he wrote: 'You have paid Mr Herschel Babbage this last quarter's salary. Mr Babbage left us at the end of last quarter. You must consider this as a mistake on your part.' Indeed, Isambard had even formulated the accountancy system.

Isambard's one dislike was handling money, because, sometimes, when he had paid cash from his own pocket to buy items for the Company's use, he would lose the receipts and could not ask to be reimbursed. On 10 March 1836 he wrote to Saunders:

I have no wish to avoid trouble in anything but I do not want to increase my responsibility in money matters. Not only is it a source of great anxiety but I find myself a loser of a pretty constant percentage through small bills which are omitted from the accounts or are paid without regular vouchers and which in consequence I do not like to charge for. I shall feel obliged if you can make arrangements which will prevent money passing through my hands more than is necessary.

Isambard's phenomenal energy in directing the construction of his SS *Great Western,* the GWR, and other railways, naturally leads to the idea that he was tremendously strong physically, so it is worth remembering that, even as a boy, he was not blessed with robust good health. In a letter to Saunders written in 1836, Isambard excused his delay in answering: 'I have been unwell, *my old complaint.*' Whatever it was, it seems to have been well known and recurrent, and the tendency to illness which he seems to have had would have been exacerbated by the pace at which he lived his life.

The construction of the line, embankments, cuttings, bridges and stations was let out to contractors, although the Company did employ their own men when the need arose. The line was divided into contracts lettered by area – 'L' for London, 'R' for Reading, 'S' for Swindon, 'C' for Cirencester and 'B' for Bristol. Box Tunnel contracts were numbered under the heading 'Box Tunnel'. The contractor arrived at his price for a job by simple arithmetic – he estimated the cubic yards of earth to be moved or piled, the number of bricks required, and the number of horses. There seems to have been no allowance, or inadequate allowance, made for additional costs owing to bad weather or unforeseen difficulties, and as a result a contractor frequently got into financial trouble.

Usually, Isambard gave the contract to the man offering the lowest price, provided he could find a bond of £2000–5000 cash for each contract he signed. The bond was the Company's security for the performance of the work 'in a good, substantial and workmanlike manner'. The contractor was also bound to maintain his work for a year after completion. When those conditions were met the bond would be returned – at least in theory.

Isambard employed far too many low-calibre contractors and as a result spent far too much time supervising their efforts to the detriment of his proper work and indeed to his health. But it was the breath of life to him to be 'in charge' and to be seen rushing hither and yon, ordering the works. Isambard was particularly difficult when authorising payment to contractors. Calculations of the work done were made by his Resident Engineers and once these figures were approved by Isambard they were sacrosanct – even if they were wrong – and the errors were usually in favour of the Company. The matter could go to arbitration but as Isambard was, by the terms of the contract, the Arbitrator, the contractor received little or no satisfaction. Isambard's position was most curious since he fomented the disputes in the first place, and was also a shareholder in the GWR, while his infallibility complex ill-qualified him to be impartial.

Had Isambard employed the strongest contractors, Brassey or Betts for instance, he would have been spared a great deal of labour. These men had the capital and the expertise to build a railway quickly and to the agreed price. Isambard would not have been overwhelmed by mundane, supervisory duties and could have performed his job as Engineer to the greater satisfaction of the Company. Indeed, the Directors were soon to beg him to take some assistance in day-to-day management.

Isambard would not employ such men because in his mind a Betts or a Brassey in charge of day-to-day construction would detract from his status as Engineer in sole command. Thus he wasted time coaxing 'lame-duck' contractors like William Ranger and when he was forced to replace Ranger by a really capable contractor like Hugh McIntosh he ill-treated him and hindered his work. The same fear of losing his status was evident, many years later, in his behaviour towards John Scott Russell, the designer and builder of Isambard's SS *Great Eastern*.

The Scottish firm of Hugh and David McIntosh was Isambard's most reliable contractor. They were solvent, they owned their own horses and plant and they had well-trained, Scottish, engineers as their foremen. Hugh was elderly and blind but with David his son and several other close relations as his 'eyes' he had carried out many large works including the Menai lighthouse, the Dutton Viaduct for George Stephenson, the Belper contract on Vignole's North Midland Railway, and miles of heavy earthworks for Locke on the London & Southampton Railway. Isambard merely took advantage of the firm of McIntosh, he worked them extra hard, withheld payment – because the firm had the strength of credit to continue without pay – and generally behaved in the 'dictatorial, illiberal manner' he so much detested in others.

He made his life unimaginably and quite unnecessarily hectic by trying to supervise everything himself. No one but he knew how to do anything. He was in charge and thought that by issuing a constant stream of sharp little letters, peremptory orders, demands and exhortations to hurry, he could steam-roller over everyone and even be in several places at once. The organisation of the undertaking, in 1833–41, without benefit of any communications more sophisticated than a goose-quill pen, was bound to have been difficult, but Isambard's single-handed management style made matters worse. He took all decisions on himself and, as a result, his orders were sometimes confused, planning errors were made, there were mistakes in drawings and omissions on the legal side, all of which lost time and incurred extra costs.

8

'For the love of fame'

In a letter to Isambard on 24 January 1836, one of his engineering assistants, Robert Archibald, wrote:

> The embankment [near Acton] has gone down very unequally. At Church's culvert it has gone down 3 ft, at various other places from 15 to 22 in. and in other places it has gone down like deep potholes which I have filled with clay but at the place where the two tips meet it has not gone down above 3 or 4 in. so that nearly all that has been allowed for sinking has to be dug away for a distance of 10 chains [220 yds]. This I have been unable to do on account of the frost being *2 ft* into the ground. Likewise, we have had a considerable difficulty in spreading the ballast properly on account of its being caked into hard lumps by the frost. This was so intense that in many instances I have seen the ballast hard frozen in the waggons from the time it was filled at the pit to when it was tipped and it was only with the greatest difficulty we could get it out of the waggon at all.

When we say 'Brunel built the Great Western' it would be well to remember those who helped him at the job.

In December 1836, Isambard ordered Hugh and David McIntosh to take possession of the garden of the Feathers public house on Ealing Green so as to progress with the track bed. Unfortunately, although the price had been agreed, Isambard had – typically – omitted to pay the landlord of the pub for the land, so there was an altercation. Three months later Isambard had still not authorised the payment. On 28 February 1837, James Leishman, McIntosh's foreman, wrote to his employer: 'It is now nearly 3 months since you had notice to go on with this work and as yet I have not been able to get into the garden; in consequence I have not been able to do anything beyond Ealing Green and waggons and horses for that work have been standing, doing nothing.' And, of course, Isambard would write to complain about 'lack of progress'!

Four days later Leishman wrote a similar note and then drew attention to a fresh problem: 'It is impossible to build the bridge in Hanwell Church Lane without removing Mr Hoffenden's garden wall as the wing walls of the bridge stop up a road that they [Isambard] have made no provision for.' Leishman called Robert Archibald to examine the site, the latter agreed that Leishman was right and a note was sent, that day, to Isambard, making him aware of the problem. Isambard had a certain way with what seemed to him to be criticism – he ignored it for as long as he could. On 14 June no guidance had come from Brunel, and Hugh McIntosh wrote asking again what was to be done. It was 23 June before Leishman heard, at third hand, that Isambard intended to erect a temporary bridge.

The high embankment approaching the Hanwell viaduct from the east was Contract 9L, let to Hugh McIntosh, and that leading away from the west end of the viaduct was 3L, let to David McIntosh. Enormous difficulty was experienced in raising the banks owing to the soft and waterlogged nature of the ground; the banks sank and the soil slipped. McIntosh had hundreds of men at work, digging spoil from cuttings through Ealing and with horses and carts taking it to the tipping end of the embankment. Part of the railway in Ealing cuttings, through the property of a Mr Woods, had to be hidden in a 'covered way' by means of a brick arch which would be covered in soil and this, too, was part of Hugh McIntosh's contract.

Work progressed slowly. Deep drains had to be dug along the foot of the bank to the River Brent, more men, horses and equipment were required and on 16 May 1837 Isambard, the GWR Directors and Hugh McIntosh agreed to complete the work one month earlier in return for a bonus of £2500. 'I shall be glad to hear from you that you have already commenced active proceedings for carrying into effect the arrangement,' Isambard wrote to McIntosh in mid-May.

McIntosh wrote back at once asking when a large bank of clay, lying across the path of the embankment close to the viaduct and under the responsibility of the Company, would be removed. On 22 June he wrote again, with old-world politeness: 'Knowing your anxiety to get 9L as forward as possible I took the liberty of asking when the heap of clay near the Brent viaduct might be removed to the south side of the embankment as well as the north? I see no harm that could ensue, it would hasten the work and would enable the waggons to team earth over the wooden bridge very soon.'

Isambard was actually on his travels when this letter was brought to him so he replied with untypical vagueness on 24 June:

> With respect to the removal of the clay heap near the viaduct. I do not understand exactly where the place is that you propose to put it – on the south of the embankment and east of the bridge which would do or in the south-west corner of the Company's property close to the Brent. My principal desire being not to disfigure that piece of land more than I can help.

He did not want piles of clay spoiling the view of his magnificent viaduct.

He did not take decisive action until 2 July when he visited the site and then having caused the delay wrote to McIntosh urging him to hurry:

> I have been to Hanwell this morning. A temporary bridge must be formed from the present tip-head to the old clay heap and the embankment pushed on in two branches . . . I have to request that every possible exertion be used and the works continued day and night to expedite the draining of the ground . . . make it 10 or 12 ft wide and carry it well down into the clay and extend it across the fields to the ponds on the north side . . . if the draining of the ground should not effect a complete stoppage in the moving of the ground . . . I shall build 4 arches at that spot and the temporary bridge should be so arranged to allow these being built as far as possible.

But it was easy to write orders for huge drains to be dug and large temporary bridges to be built – without getting in the way of permanent arches which might or might not be raised. Others had to do the physical work, men and money had to be found. Robert Archibald reported to Isambard on 5 July that 'the Hanwell embankment has a great number of cracks on the top and the ground is giving way at "X" . . . we have not yet come to clay in the drain, we are down 8–9 feet – there are 112 men on this work.' All this extra work was, of course, funded by the contractor. The new arches cost McIntosh £9037 16s 10d whereas the same length of embankment would have cost him £6212 16s 6d. The legal wrangling over who should pay these extra costs were then given to Isambard for arbitration, to be added to an existing list of disagreements over payments which was already far too long.

On 6 July Isambard ordered four arches to be raised to replace this section of troublesome embankment. On 5 August Isambard completed the drawings for the arches and ordered David McIntosh to prepare foundations for them. There is no doubt that Isambard's obsession with being seen to be in charge of every aspect of the work led to expensive delays and muddled thinking as this note from David McIntosh to his father shows: 'The Covered Way is ordered to be gone on with forthwith but at the same time I have orders to see Mr Woods and arrange to do away with it.'

David McIntosh and Isambard, I believe, took an instant dislike to each other. They were both the products of a lengthy schooling from an early age – at a time when many children received scant education, if any at all. McIntosh, I think, resented Isambard's hectoring manner while Isambard detested McIntosh's demonstrated independence. From a note from John Hammond, Isambard's Resident Engineer in the London Division to his assistant, Robert Archibald, I wonder if, even amongst Brunel's 'loyal' employees, there was not a certain amusement at their master's pretensions. The note, dated 14 July 1837, said: 'My Dear Sir, By all that's good you must get on faster. You must crowd in men everywhere by working night and day. I begin to feel queer about our completion. . . . For the love of fame and our great master's name – push on the work.' The work – navvies, foremen, horses, Isambard and all – floundered on through the mud of an unseasonally wet July and August.

The contractors Grissell & Peto undertook to build the 300-yds-long Hanwell Viaduct. There were eight arches each of 70-ft span, springing from stone caps on top of the 65-ft-tall brick piers which were of a curious tapered proportion, designed to look 'Egyptian'. Isambard was fond of this device and had intended to use the same shape for the suspension towers of the Clifton bridge. As with the Clifton bridge, upon whose designs Marc lavished weeks of work, the Hanwell Viaduct also received Marc's close professional attention. On 14 March 1834 and for several weeks afterwards there is, in his diary, a daily entry, 'working on Isambard's Brent Viaduct'. With the cessation of these 'Brent Viaduct' entries, there are no further references to Marc doing any work for Isambard, although, during 1835, he went with Isambard to visit the Hanwell site. Marc, then aged sixty-six, notes, ruefully I think, that Isambard kept him outside until long after dark.

Isambard visited the viaduct regularly and was critical of this or that. After an inspection on 26 February 1836 he returned home to Duke Street, fuming, and wrote the following to Grissell & Peto:

> I have just returned from Hanwell where I observed that by far the largest proportion of bricks upon the ground and actually in use were of a quality quite inadmissible. I examined those bricks on Monday last and gave particular orders to your Foreman, Lawrence, respecting them. Those orders I find he has neglected to obey and has in one instance, privately [*sic*] or by trick, directly evaded them. I must request that he be immediately dismissed. I find upon the works such causes for complaint that I feel called upon to take some decisive steps to protect the interests of the Company. At the same time I am most desirous of avoiding coercive measures and still have hopes that you will be induced to proceed with the work in a more satisfactory manner. I shall be obliged by your calling on me tomorrow morning at 10 o'clock.

Isambard was an ingenious and resourceful designer of many durable bridges – indeed only two of all his bridges failed. One was his exceptionally 'flat' brick arch over the River Parrett where the out-thrust from the arch was too great for the marshy ground in which the abutments were founded. The other was his cast-iron beam-bridge over Uxbridge Road. Isambard had covered the iron beams with timber, and when in 1847 this was set alight by a piece of burning coal from an engine the resulting heat cracked the cast-iron. Isambard did not like beams of cast-iron as the metal was treacherous, liable to break under a heavy blow or to be seriously weakened by cavities within, invisible from outside. He did, however, after load-testing, use cast-iron beams at Uxbridge Road, over a couple of streams near Wantage and to carry the rails over the Wilts & Berks canal at Swindon station.

To carry roads across the double track, broad-gauge railway, Isambard produced a standard, 30-ft-span, arch. The soffit of each arch, which could be built in brick or stone, has a uniquely Brunellian, broad gauge, profile, a flattened horseshoe shape. Between Bath and Bristol a 'Brunellian Tudor' arch was provided. All these types are still in use today, from Southall to Penzance. Isambard took great pains to ensure that his bridges did not suffer from undue settlement and issued strict instructions as to how the bricklayers were to lay the bricks and how his assistants were to check for subsidence. He wrote to Hammond, on 3 September 1836:

> I am not quite sure that I have given you the same strict injunction as providing against the sinking of a bridge arch that I have given to Frere. While I think of it, therefore, I write to you. In the first place I expect to have a very accurate measurement taken of the sinking of all arches from the smallest bridge to the largest. This must be done by drawing a straight line across the arch just as soon as you can after the mortar is dry. This may be done with a straight edge and after that by whipcord stretched to its utmost. Then, from time to time, and particularly after the centering is struck, this straight line must be examined and its deviation noted down. Until the results are accurately obtained we must provide for the probable settling. Over all arches, therefore, the courses of brickwork of the spandrel walls and the string-courses and coping stones must be set up out of their straight line – whether this be a straight or a curved one – by about 1/20th in. per ft span and in this manner. Sketch supplied.

The bridging of the Thames at Maidenhead presented Isambard with a difficult problem. The river was almost 100 yds wide with a central island. His first plan was for a triple-arch viaduct, but later he evolved the beautiful design which is still in use today. Over the 53 miles from Paddington to Didcot he had planned a road rising towards the west at 1 in 1320. The Thames then carried sailing barges whose tall masts had to be accommodated – even though once the railway was complete the barges would rapidly go out of business. Isambard did not want to create a 'hump' in his superb railway just to give headroom to the masts of sailing barges and, squeezed between the masts and the level of the track, he evolved the famous 'flat' arches so much admired today.

The railway approaches the river on a tall embankment which gives way to four, conventional, semicircular arches, one of which spans the tow-path. The latter was not part of Isambard's original plan but, typically, he constantly altered his design, not only before but sometimes during the construction period. As built, the tow-path arch had a 21-ft span and the rest 28-ft. Then from the tow-path the great elliptical arch leaps over 128 ft of water to land on the central island and then leaps again, 128 ft, to meet four more land arches. The maximum rise of the river arches, from the point of springing to the crown is only 24 ft 6 in., most of the rise occurring in the first quarter of the span. Thus he rapidly gained height over the water without forcing the track-bed upwards to clear the arch.

Isambard worked out the general aspect of the bridge in his sketch-books, trying half a dozen styles from the florid and fussy to the superbly clean lines which were his final choice. The mathematical details he worked out on a few sheets of 10 × 8 in. cartridge paper, the famous profile of the elliptical arches surrounded by a mass of arithmetic, tiny figures written neatly in pencil.

Isambard had to balance hundreds of tons of brickwork in the Maidenhead bridge. The weight of bricks in the haunches had to be sufficient to support the long 'jib' of the arch while the weight in the centre had to be sufficient to compress the bricks in the haunches. If the haunches outweighed the crown, the centre of the arch would be forced upwards while the compression forces had to balance so that they ran within the ring of bricks all around the arch from springing to springing and down to earth through the massive, brick piers.

He would have had an easy life if arithmetic had been all that he had to worry about, but from the outset his design was attacked in order to lower the value of GWR shares, to discredit him and bring about his downfall and thus an end to the broad gauge. Before even the piers of the bridge were started he received a strong complaint from the Thames Commissioners, who repeated a rumour as if it was incontrovertible fact: that work on the bridge was blocking the tow-path and the river. Isambard's charm was decidedly ruffled. The Commissioners had obviously not visited the site. On 29 August 1836, he replied with an unusually angry letter:

Sir, I have taken all due steps to ensure the security of the navigation during the construction of the bridge – and at considerable expense – and in a much more complete manner than I believe you yourselves would have provided had you been executing the work. I have designed the largest arch of any bridge above Southwark for the express purpose of including the whole of the present navigation channel and the wide towing path under the same arch. I have done that which I suspect I will be severely criticised for, namely, made a 2-arch bridge for the purpose of throwing the only pier required on an existing island. I believe this will be the only instance upon the entire river of a bridge being built without in the slightest degree altering, still less, injuring the navigation. After doing all this – far more than we could have been compelled to do – unasked – it is rather vexatious to be interfered with in the manner we have been.

Having frozen the opposition with icy words of rebuff he seems to be asking for an apology: 'I hope you will put it all right and restore the good feeling you seem disposed to cultivate. I have explained what I intend and cannot be responsible for the statements others may choose to make. The bridge has been designed peculiarly with regard to the navigation and without consideration of expense on the part of the railway.' He finishes with a straightforward threat in strong language. 'If the Commissioners are discontented and troublesome, there is still time for me to save £10,000 and still build a bridge as they can find no fault with – but it would by no means be as convenient as the one at present intended.'

The work of constructing the bridge began early in 1836, by contractor Thomas Bedborough. He may or may not have been an efficient engineer but he was certainly short of money and was soon in trouble. Bedborough had to excavate the foundations for the great brick piers on each bank and on the mid-stream shoal and to protect the holes with coffer-dams. Hammond, the Resident Engineer, kept a close eye on matters and reported daily to Isambard on the impecunious goings-on. On 5 December 1836 Isambard visited the site and the next day wrote as follows to Bedborough:

> Sir, The progress in the dams of the Maidenhead bridge is not merely slow but most unsatisfactory to me. There does not appear any probability that in their present state they can be sufficiently water-tight, particularly the western coffer-dam. For the safety of the construction of the foundations I shall be obliged to call on you to drive another row of piles or take such steps as necessary to make the coffer-dam fit for its purpose as required by the contract. I must remind you that the defect arises in great measure from you not having taken out the gravel before driving the piles as you were advised to do by Mr Hammond.

Isambard tried to help him by relieving him of the approach embankments so that he could concentrate his resources on the bridge, but it was no use. Bedborough ran out of funds and was dismissed on 17 March 1837. The contracts for the embankments went to a Mr Oldham, while that for the bridge went to a Mr Chadwick.

9

'If I ever go mad'

Early in 1836, among his multifarious duties, Isambard found contractors, Paxton & Orton, who were willing to sink exploratory shafts into Box Hill along the line of the tunnel the Great Western Railway would need there. He instructed them to start work. He also interviewed several prospective site engineers, and, in May, offered the job to William Glennie. In his letter accepting the post, Glennie spoke enthusiastically about becoming Resident Engineer of the tunnel. This was too presumptuous and Isambard wrote to correct him on 18 June:

> You have entirely misunderstood me. . . . I think I explained that this position of Resident Engineer was attainable by you – not promised by me . . . all I can offer you is the post of Assistant Engineer . . . I must guard against holding out the expectation to you . . . on the contrary, what I now offer must not be a certain or permanent position. My responsibility is too great to allow of my retaining . . . anyone who may appear to me to be inefficient . . . it is an understood thing that all under me are subject to immediate dismissal at my pleasure. . . . I am anxious that you should not entertain any expectations. . . . it is for you to decide if you are likely to proceed satisfactorily and whether the chance is sufficient inducement. . . . I wait for your answer to determine the destination of an offer from an Engineer who, like yourself, is desirous to be a Civil Engineer.

I feel that that final sentence, very cleverly, hints at kindly feelings towards Glennie on Isambard's part. Glennie took his chance, was appointed, and went at once to Box Hill.

Paxton & Orton dug the six permanent and two temporary shafts from the bottom of which, and from the cuttings at each side of the hill, the tunnel would be dug. These shafts were about 25 ft in diameter and varied in depth from about 85 ft to 260 ft through limestone or dense blue clay. The work was difficult and Isambard asked his father for some of his miners from the Thames Tunnel to assist. During the winter of 1836 an additional problem was created by the flooding of the shafts. Expensive steam-pumps were brought in, which drained the contractor's purse more than the shafts.

On 12 April 1837 Isambard advised his Directors to make 'a liberal act' and give Paxton & Orton financial help so as to expedite the work and quash the rumours which were damaging confidence in the Company. Ever since 1834 the tunnel had been described as 'monstrous, extraordinary, most dangerous and impractical' and now that the contractor was in difficulties, the gloomy prophecies were raked up once more. But the Directors were not disposed to be liberal, the contractor retired, the shafts filled with water and GWR share prices slumped. The work was taken over by two local quarry owners, Lewis of Bath and Brewer of Box. They were experienced in quarrying the Bath stone for building work but were ill equipped for sinking the shafts. The steam-pumps they installed were small and unreliable, forcing Isambard to spend considerable time travelling to Box to show them how to do the job and to coax them to use better machinery.

Lewis and Brewer completed the shafts in the autumn of 1837 and took the contract to dig 880 yds of tunnel from the Corsham end through the Bath stone they knew so well, but Isambard had great difficulty finding anyone willing to dig the remainder through some very difficult strata. The tunnel, described as 3193 yds long in 1841 and now stated to be 3212 yds, was the longest then undertaken in Britain. In February 1838 George Burge of Herne Bay, an important man of his time, agreed to take on the job and to complete it in thirty months.

Throughout 1837 Isambard was constantly on the move, visiting locomotive builders in the North of England, rail-rolling mills in South Wales, the SS *Great Western* in Bristol, as well as patrolling the GWR from end to end – all this in his horse-drawn britschka. On 18 July, a young locomotive engineer called Daniel Gooch wrote to Isambard offering his services as Works Manager for a 'locomotive manufactory at or near Bristol'. Isambard knew the engineering ability of the Gooch family and recommended the GWR Directors to hire Daniel Gooch at once. Given a free hand, he met Gooch in Manchester on 9 August and immediately appointed him as Locomotive Superintendent. On Monday, 14 August, ten days before his twenty-first birthday, Gooch began work in the GWR's engineless depot at West Drayton.

Isambard considered Gooch as no more than a Resident Engineer and awarded him a salary of £300 per annum against his own £2000. Gooch was at least Isambard's equal, not only intellectually but also in his energy and commitment to the job. He was far in advance of Isambard as a locomotive engineer. They complemented each other: the one a civil engineering genius, the other a brilliant locomotive engineer. Isambard was short of stature, passionate, wordy, somewhat theatrical, cultured, charming and artistic; Gooch was tall, gaunt, somewhat puritanical, of few words, without drawing-room charm, a practical man who, unlike Isambard, never stepped outside his subject. Furthermore, Gooch had no overwhelming desire for public acclaim – plain old-fashioned wealth would do for him.

At the end of August the GWR Directors announced that in November 1837 the line would open to a station they called Maidenhead, at the $22\frac{1}{2}$ mile post, just east of the Thames. They must surely have consulted Isambard before issuing this notice – how he allowed it to be made is a mystery. Either it is an example of Brunellian self-deception or else he was so distracted by his various problems that he agreed without giving the matter any thought. No track had been laid, the Hanwell embankments were sinking and the Thames Junction contractors were blocking the line with earth as they tried to dig a tunnel under the Grand Union Canal. Supplies of timber for the track either did not arrive or arrived in embarrassingly large quantities, the tanks for immersing the wood in the preserving fluid – the kyanising process – leaked, bridges on the Paddington Extension and even Paddington station were very far from complete – and there were neither locomotives nor carriages!

Gooch soon felt the dictatorial nature of Isambard's rule. Early in November 1837 the Great Western's first locomotives – Mather Dixon's *Premier* and Charles Tayleur's *Vulcan* – arrived at West Drayton on a canal barge after a sea voyage from Liverpool. Lifting tackle was supplied by John Hammond. Isambard had expressed some reservations about the gear but he had not forbidden its use and, with some additional chains and ropes and with the use of an elm tree for an 'anchor', Gooch unloaded the engines without waiting to be supervised by Isambard or by Hammond. This display of independence annoyed Isambard and he gave Gooch a strong rebuke. But Gooch was no ordinary employee and demanded to know 'whether you look to Mr Hammond or me as the responsible party for the unloading? For if I am responsible it is hardly fair that I should take his opinion.'

On the 28th, Robert Stephenson's *North Star* arrived in a Thames barge at Maidenhead. Isambard supervised the erection of a sheerlegs complete with safety rope to steady it. While he was directing operations the safety rope was cast off prematurely, the sheer-legs collapsed, killing a workman and only narrowly missing Isambard's head. Over forty years later Gooch wrote in his *Memoirs* that his sense of satisfaction would have been much greater but for the death of the man. The sense of injustice still rankled: 'One feature of Brunel's character, and it was one that gave him a great deal of extra and unnecessary work, was that he fancied that no one could do anything but himself.'

While he demanded total obedience from his 'inferiors' Isambard was always conciliatory towards any 'equal' opposition. He always tried to be helpful towards any party that had the power to delay him, this being the cheapest and quickest way of getting what he wanted. But none of his blandishments had any effect at all on the peculiarly aggressive Birmingham, Bristol & Thames Junction Railway.

In February 1837 he suggested that the spoil from Great Western cuttings through Wormwood Scrubs could go towards making embankments for the Thames Junction – the GWR contractor could make the Thames Junction's embankments or the Thames Junction's contractor could make the GWR cuttings and cart the 'fill' to his embankments. He intended to create good will and wrote to the Thames Junction's man, Hoskins: 'Any accommodation that can be mutually afforded we shall be as ready to give as, I trust, you will be.' The letter ended with a typically Brunellian flourish, 'Money arrangements', he wrote, 'are questions merely of amount which cannot amount to a difference of opinion.' Isambard had a gentleman's lack of concern for anything as sordid as money, but it was not a businesslike attitude and the other firm took him for a fool.

Hoskins pursued an ungentlemanly course while taking advantage of all Isambard's friendly proposals. On 13 August Isambard was in Bristol for the launch of the SS *Great Western* and on his return he was at once embroiled with Hoskins. The Thames Junction Company had taken over and fenced off land belonging to the Great Western without the formality of paying for it. Isambard wrote plaintively to Hoskins: 'I do not understand the reasoning by which, because we did not reply to your letter, your company has the right to take possession of land without even settling a price.'

Hoskins then suggested that 'it would be more convenient for all concerned' if his contractor was to haul earth from GWR cuttings to Thames Junction embankments in GWR wagons. Isambard declined the suggestion with graceful hints about the trustworthiness of Hoskins's minions: 'Our proceedings have always followed our desire to be neighbourly . . . and therefore you must not suppose that I wish to act otherwise now – but I see many practical difficulties . . . in running wagons off our line into other hands.'

Isambard's SS *Great Western* sailed into the East India Dock, London, to take on her engines on 23 August. Isambard then had to visit the dockyard regularly while trying to pull his railway together, a task which included the removal of the faltering contractor William Ranger from works at the Bristol end of the line. Ranger had taken contract 8L, Sonning cutting, 1, 2 and 3B – that is the Avon Bridge at Bristol, three tunnels on the eastern approach to Bristol and the Twerton Tunnel west of Bath. Ranger does not seem to have had the driving personality necessary to organise such large works and, owing in part to the several bonds of £5000 he had had to hand to the Company, he was short of money.

Isambard did not want to sack him completely, as contractors were not easy to find, but he wanted him to concentrate his resources on Sonning cutting. It was a tricky legal situation because Ranger did not want to go. Meanwhile, Brunel was in touch with Hugh McIntosh as a suitable replacement for Ranger. Hugh McIntosh was willing to take over William Ranger's large contracts but his son David was not enthusiastic. David McIntosh, seven years older than Brunel, was an experienced and capable engineer and certainly not over-awed by him. The family firm already had plenty of work and he was concerned that they should not over-burden their resources – especially in view of Isambard's reluctance to pay for work already performed on McIntosh's Contract 9L.

David McIntosh was right to be suspicious of the forceful little Isambard, with his air of Brunellian infallibility. When Brunel had interviewed Hugh McIntosh his attitude had been more that of a master to a servant than one businessman asking another for help. Isambard reported to his Directors: 'I have great hopes of Mr McIntosh – but for a relative. . . . I gave him my estimate of about £75,000 and told him he was wasting my time if he could not come somewhere near that. He has requested time for *his person* to go over the ground. The delay will suit my personal convenience and I recommend the Directors give him this time.' It would appear that Isambard's choice of phrase was disdainful. Hugh McIntosh's 'person' was, in fact, his son, David, and it appears that he was guilty of not falling in at once with Isambard's wishes. Without doubt Isambard could not bear a 'servant' to maintain an equality or independence before him.

Hugh and David McIntosh finally agreed to take on Ranger's three Bristol/Bath contracts. Hugh McIntosh did not live long after this but he lived long enough to regret the agreement. Once he had them signed up, Isambard began to squeeze them, refusing to pay, refusing to recognise the true amount of work performed. Gates which had cost McIntosh £5 each were marked down, by Isambard, to £3 10s. McIntosh was asked to do extra work – which diverted men and resources from existing contracts – and Isambard then complained when those contracts fell behind schedule.

Stone for the façades of the Twerton Tunnel, which Brunel agreed to supply, did not arrive owing to another contractor's slow progress. When the stone did arrive, to be erected according to contract as coursed rubble, Isambard forced the masons to cut it so smoothly and to lay it with such precision that the finished quality came close to ashlar work. This extra work took extra time, costing McIntosh several thousand pounds which Isambard refused to pay. When McIntosh's navvies uncovered a Roman mosaic floor in contract 3B near Newton, west of Twerton Tunnel, Isambard ordered the digging to cease while the same men erected a fence around the site until the pavement was lifted for preservation. All very laudable, but Isambard had no right to use McIntosh's men, and their wages, for such work.

Not surprisingly McIntosh was unable to meet his contractual deadlines for completion of work, whereupon Isambard called upon him to pay a financial penalty as agreed in the contract. McIntosh refused and after some argument Isambard conceded that, as McIntosh had worked very hard, and as the delays were 'nobody's fault' (that is, they were Isambard's fault), McIntosh would not have to pay the 'fine' at once but it would be suspended to ensure his future good behaviour. This was a similar technique to that used by Isambard over the miners' pay in the Thames Tunnel.

Simultaneously Brunel was withholding payments to Hugh McIntosh for work performed on contract 9L, on the pretext that David McIntosh had submitted no account for 3L. When Hugh tried to get his money he was fobbed off. On 4 January 1838, David McIntosh wrote to his father: 'My Dear Father, Today with Mr Brunel again after being put off and put off. The account for 9L without ballasting is £12,000 in round numbers. He disputes some figures – the wages are too high compared to others, another set of accounts he wants time to consider and so on till he makes a deduction of £6000 . . . he kept me in the City from 1 till 4.'

Isambard had estimated £2½ m. as the cost of building the whole line complete with rolling stock. In January 1838 that figure had long been spent and the railway was not even open to Maidenhead. On 23 February he, Charles Saunders and a Director, G.H. Gibbs, spent all night going over the estimates to see how much more money was required. Gibbs recorded in his diary: 'From his [Isambard's] manner and expressions I fear that we shall require at least £666,666 more, making in all four millions [*sic*]. I wish this may be enough.' So worrying was the lack of funds that Saunders recommended that at the forthcoming meeting of shareholders the report on finances should be made so that 'without in the least deceiving the public, [it] would not give them at once the real state of the case'. No wonder Isambard was attempting to make McIntosh subsidise the GWR.

Isambard was too steeped in matters of class to see the incongruity of ill-treating a first-class contractor who was building miles of line for him, while bending over backwards to be conciliatory to the odious Hoskins. To Isambard, McIntosh was no more than a superior servant but Hoskins was an equal, however obnoxious. On 4 September 1837, Isambard had returned from accompanying his Directors to Bristol and Box and found the Thames Junction Company in an obstructive mood once more. The GWR contractor had wanted to pipe water away from the Wormwood Scrubs cutting and the natural outlet was down the southbound slope of the Thames Junction's unfinished embankment. This was the kind of co-operation Isambard had envisaged when he had extended his co-operation to the smaller company but in spite of all, the Thames Junction Railway would not allow GWR water pipes on their land. Isambard wrote in terms of sorrowful rebuke to Hoskins:

> The Directors have naturally been much annoyed on hearing that when the most trifling accommodation is required by us it is wantonly resisted by persons in the employment of the Thames Junction Railway, while they, on the contrary, take advantage of our forebearance when they come through land belonging to us before any agreement is made . . . we have lent your men tools and plant, and when we wanted it we ought to have received a reciprocal accommodation.

Instead of engaging Hoskins in such constructive discussions as what kind of track-work would be used on the flat, 90-degree crossing of the two lines, Isambard became embroiled in an exchange of acrimonious letters. Hoskins's reply to Isambard's letter of 5 September is not known but it infuriated Brunel and prompted one of his most peculiar letters, dated 21 September:

> Your quotation of the fable reminds me of the practice imputed to a certain old gentleman – who had better remain nameless – who could quote the Bible to suit his purposes. Anything may be perverted. I should say that the character of the Wolf and the Lamb were used not merely symbolically of the stronger and the weaker parties in the bustle of this world but also of two parties, one of whom has the means of harassing the other. We are the Lamb, very willing to be left alone, wishing to annoy nobody. You brought an Act, we could have prevented you easily, we did not, but only required non-interference from you. We could have hindered you, if not stopped you [getting the Act of Parliament] – we did not, but on the contrary have in a quite inoffensive style, suffered some annoyance and never by a single act annoyed or hindered you. I defy you to name one. It is then like the Wolf that you have shown your teeth – snarled at us – would find one little thing after another as grounds of complaint. All we say is leave us alone and I think you will find us to continue as lambs. I fancy I can see the Wolf screwing up his lips and giving a slight snarl. On this point, perhaps, on our turning over the leaf, we may come to some other fable.

All this imagery got Isambard nowhere. On 12 October he had to write again, beginning with the friendly 'My Dear Sir, Are you aware that your workmen are actually tipping their earth from the excavation for the canal bridge directly into our line, forming a large bank in the middle of our railway? Will you have the goodness to have it removed?' Hoskins did not have the goodness and two weeks later the earth bank was still blocking the Great Western track-bed.

Isambard kept a confident and at times arrogant face to the world but on 3 December 1837, at 6 a.m., after a whole night of letter writing, he relaxed completely and in a long letter opened his heart to his friend, Charles Saunders:

> My Dear Saunders,
>
> A hint or two from the other end is useful to remind me of what, however, I am fully sensible of – your exceeding kindness in relieving me of everything you can and still more strongly shown in your silence and absence of complaint.
>
> In my endeavours to introduce a few – really but a few – improvements in the principal parts of the work I have involved myself in a mass of novelties. I can compare it to nothing but the sudden adoption of a language, familiar enough to its creator but understood by nobody about him. Every word has to be translated. One alteration has involved another and no one part can be copied from what others have done. I have thus cut myself off from the help usually received from assistants. *I am obliged to do all myself.*

He was being very unfair to his dedicated assistants such as Frere and Hammond who worked so hard to carry out his wishes. Without Gooch and his men the locomotives, whose shortcomings were almost entirely the fault of Isambard's defective theories on locomotive design, would not have turned a wheel. Isambard went on to make the unique admission that the problems were of his own making:

> As regards the Company I have never regretted one instant the course I have taken. The conviction which daily grows stronger, that eventually they will profit immensely from these changes is my only relief from my own annoyance . . . I want you to know that if I appear to be taking things coolly it is because I feel them so acutely that I am obliged to harden myself a little to be able to bear them and also because I do believe that I am doing my best to lead the Company through the temporary difficulties I have got them into.
>
> If I ever go mad, I shall have the ghost of the opening of the railway walking before me, or rather standing in front of me, holding out its hand and when it steps forward, a little swarm of devils in the shape of leaky pickle tanks, half-finished stations, sinking embankments, broken screws, missing guard-plates, unfinished drawings and sketches, will quietly, and quite as a matter of course, lift up my ghost and put him off a little further than before.
>
> What a note I have written you – well I don't think it is altogether

wasted – I hope you will feel the same. Yours sincerely, I.K. Brunel. PS: Mary asks how Florence is.

While he kept his fears and loneliness to himself, except in very private moments with friends, his great ambitions drove him on relentlessly.

10

Transatlantic Visionary

There is a much-quoted anecdote which illustrates both Brunel's impatience with faint-hearted colleagues and his own unbounded vision. At a meeting of GWR Directors in October 1835, when one of them complained that the railway line was too long to be built, Isambard immediately retorted, 'Why not make it longer? Build a steamship to go to New York and call it the *Great Western*.' Some of those present may have thought that this was a typically brusque Brunel rejoinder to an unwelcome remark, but the interest of his friend Thomas Guppy, the engineer-businessman, was aroused. After the meeting he and Isambard went off to discuss the idea and the Great Western Steamship Company was the result.

While Isambard created every detail of the civil engineering of the Great Western Railway and jealously guarded his highly paid position as Chief Engineer, he worked without salary on the SS *Great Western* and actually suggested that a building committee be established to work with him in the design and construction of the ship. The committee consisted of Isambard and his close friends Thomas Guppy, the highly capable old sea-dog, Captain Christopher Claxton, and the Bristol shipyard-owner William Patterson. The ex-Chief Surveyor to the Royal Navy, Sir Robert Seppings, the Chief Shipwright at Woolwich Royal Naval Dockyard and other Admiralty engineers gave advice and allowed the committee access to naval drawings of hulls.

The SS *Great Western* was very much the result of a co-operative effort between several skilled men each making his special contribution, and no one man can take the whole credit. However, Isambard initiated the idea, not only of regular transatlantic steam navigation but of linking the ship to the railway. He was the director and central figure.

Oddly, Marc Brunel, whose designs for marine engines and boilers were so progressive, was not one of those who helped. Perhaps Isambard did not want his father to take part in *his* project, perhaps the Great Western Steamship Company did not want to pay royalties for the use of Marc Brunel's patents, but certainly Marc, like Dr Dionysius Lardner, believed that transatlantic steam navigation was impossible: they thought that the larger the hull to carry the coal, the more coal would be required to drive the hull through the water, a vicious circle from which there would be no escape.

Isambard realised that the carrying capacity of a hull increases in *cubic* yards while the surface of the hull opposed to the water increases only by *square* yards; a hull could be built large enough to carry all the coal required and then extended to accommodate a sufficient payload of passengers and cargo. He also saw that the increased length would make for better speed and a smoother passage while the larger the ship was the smaller the power plant would be in proportion to the carrying capacity.

Isambard has been credited with discovering these facts but he himself wrote, in 1835, that they were 'well known' among some shipbuilders. Among the enlightened few was John Scott Russell – two years younger than Brunel – the Scottish naval architect, scientist and shipbuilder, who, in 1835, had defined in mathematical terms the old, rule-of-thumb principle of the wave-line hull. Claxton, Guppy and Patterson went to shipyards in Liverpool and Glasgow to study methods of steamship construction and in the report they wrote for Isambard they pointed out the advantage of a large ship over a small one. Isambard took an existing idea, and showed how it could be developed.

Dr Lardner, typically, refused to leave the Pit of Fallacy and at meetings of the British Association for the Advancement of Science in Dublin and Liverpool in 1835 asserted that transatlantic steam navigation was about as likely as 'a trip to the Moon'. He repeated this – using more cautious language – in Bristol, at a lecture to the British Association on the evening of 27 August 1836, the day that the foundation stone for the abutments of the Clifton Bridge had been laid.

To expedite construction work on the Clifton Bridge, Captain Claxton and Isambard supervised the erection across the gorge of a $1\frac{1}{2}$-in.-diameter iron bar, 1000 ft long, with the intention of suspending from it, on pulley wheels, a 'travelling basket' strong enough to carry building materials or men. Claxton's letter to the *Bristol Gazette* gives us the diameter and tells us that the bar was made up of sections welded together on the western or Leigh Woods side, and that on 23 August 1836 it was hauled across the 630-ft chasm to the Clifton side by a 10-in. hawser on a capstan. The bar was landed on the Clifton side and the men were giving three cheers when the hawser broke and the bar sprang into the air, falling 200 ft to the river where it stuck in the mud. It was bent in the middle but was raised and fixed in position by next day, in time for the ceremony of laying the foundation stone for the bridge abutments on the 27th.

Modesty and humility were not conspicuous features of Brunel's character. On the contrary, he had a high opinion of his own merits and regarded it as his due to be given public recognition of his achievements. This trait was very evident on the occasion of the laying of the foundation stone of the abutments of the Clifton Suspension Bridge by the Marquis of Northampton, President of the British Association. Preceded by a band the Marquis headed a procession of eminent scientists, engineers, civic dignitaries and townsfolk. Brunel, however, held aloof from the throng and asserted his pre-eminence, as designer of the bridge, by walking alone immediately behind the Marquis's carriage and ahead of the rest of the procession.

Events subsequent to the foundation stone-laying ceremony are open to doubt. According to the *Bristol Mirror* nothing further was done till the afternoon of 23 August when a few spectators left at the site saw the travelling basket being prepared to cross the gorge from the Leigh Woods side. A man was seen to enter the basket which then ran down the sloping bar to the centre where it stopped on the central 'kink'. The hauling rope had not been wound in as the basket ran down the bar so the rope looped downwards towards the river as the steamer *Killarney* was coming past. The rope became entangled in the mast and the bar and basket were on the point of being swept away when somebody cut the rope, leaving the basket 'swinging to and fro with fearful rapidity. We hear that it was only with the utmost effort that the gentleman could keep himself in it. When it ceased to swing the gentleman was drawn to the rock.'

Isambard was said to have been 'much vexed' that anyone should have crossed without his permission – or, more likely, to have had his thunder stolen. After a new rope had been attached, Isambard entered the basket, apparently alone. The basket then rolled down to the centre where it stuck fast on the kinked bar. The *Bristol Mirror* reported: 'Mr Brunel endeavoured by swinging it to and fro to release the car but being unable to do so, this intrepid gentleman mounted the car, climbed the ropes and released the car when swinging over this tremendous chasm.' How he did this when his whole weight was on the pulley is not shown. He was then hauled back to the rock.

None of the other Bristol newspapers reported this dramatic event, indeed even the *Bristol Mirror* only had the story as hearsay since the report used the words, 'we hear that . . .'. It is also worth mentioning that on the 23rd the same paper had to print an apology to one William Palmer whose trial for theft the newspaper had published. The report stated that he had been found guilty and sentenced to 14 years' transportation when in fact he had been found innocent and set free.

The *Bristol Advocate* deliberately ignored the ceremony and made no mention of the events reported above, but instead published a long complaint against Captain Claxton for neglect of his Quay Warden's duties due to his activities about the West Country and abroad on behalf on Isambard Brunel.

The *Bristol Gazette* stated that immediately after the foundation stone had been laid, a large block of stone was placed in the travelling basket which was then hauled across without difficulty. It was specifically stated – contrary to the *Mirror* and to Rolt – that no person crossed the gorge on 27 August.

A new bar was placed in position during September and on the 27th it was considered safe for use. Isambard went across in the basket at 6 p.m., accompanied, not by an 'un-named youth' as Rolt has stated but by Master Claxton – whom I suppose to have been Captain Claxton's son. Isambard made two more trips accompanied first by a Mr Coulson and then by a Mr Tate and all three journeys were accomplished 'with the greatest of ease' according to the *Bristol Gazette*, *Bristol Advocate* and *Bristol Mirror*.

To find a builder for the SS *Great Western*'s engine, a competitive tender was advertised but Isambard knew the best firm for the job and made sure that Maudslay Son & Field got the contract. This was nothing to do with favouritism. He wanted the men with the widest experience and the greatest expertise to do the work – the best, not the cheapest. Maudslay's had already designed and built several 'side lever' marine engines and got the contract to supply a pair, working as a 'V twin' to the SS *Great Western* according to Isambard's specification as to horsepower.

Each cylinder was 70 in. diameter by 84 in. stroke taking steam at 5 lb psi and driving directly on the paddle-shaft. Isambard introduced one highly significant innovation: a cam-operated valve-gear. By this means live steam entering the cylinder was cut off after only a fraction of the piston's power stroke, the piston continuing to be driven by the expansive nature of the steam imprisoned in the cylinder – thus saving a great deal of the expensive vapour. This was the first time anyone had used a variable cut-off device but Isambard did not patent his invention because he had philosophical objections to the system of patents.

The SS *Great Western* was, by a very large margin, the longest ship in the world at that time. Its wooden hull was 212 ft long and 35 ft 4 in. broad, exclusive of paddle-boxes. It was massively constructed in traditional oak, but trussed with wood and iron to a much greater extent than was usual. The keel ribs were tied through with iron bolts from bow to stern to withstand the fiercest Atlantic storms and the keel was copper-bottomed to resist the ship-worm *teredo navalis* and other marine nuisances.

The ship was launched at Bristol on 22 July 1837, her headlong progress across the river being checked by heavy chains. The rigging was erected and on 18 August she set sail for London accompanied by a steam-tug in case of need. She out-sailed the powered boat and arrived off Gravesend on the 22nd. Her steam engines were then installed and during March 1838 she steamed trials in the Thames, making 11 knots with perfect steadiness.

On 31 March the SS *Great Western* set out for Bristol under Lt Hosken, RN, as Master with Isambard and his naval assistant, Captain Christopher Claxton on board. They were abreast of Canvey Island when the wind was suddenly full of the smell of burning and shortly afterwards a fierce fire with thick smoke broke out around the base of the funnel. Stokers running up from the smoke-filled engine room saw land close-by and dived overboard to swim to safety while Hosken put the helm over and ran the ship on to some sandbanks.

The Chief Engineer, George Payne, turned on the water-feed to the boiler but could not reach the steam-cock which would activate the fire-hoses. As the flames licked around the top of the boiler there was every likelihood that the safety-valves would seize due to the heat and remain shut as pressure within the boiler increased. A disastrous explosion would have taken place but for the foresight of Claxton who had brought on board a hand-operated fire-pump. He organised a party of men to pump and went down into the engine room with the hose.

The fire had begun because the boiler lagging, made of felt, had been taken right up to the base of the funnel where there was the greatest concentration of heat; it was towards this area that Claxton directed his hose. Later, he and Payne were able to start the steam-pump and the fire began to be brought under control, but the floor of the room became inches deep in water. At this point Isambard attempted to come down from the deck to the engine room. Unfortunately the ladder was made of wood, its rungs were badly charred and the second or third rung broke.

The odds were heavily against his survival. There was a 20-ft drop to the floor which was covered in several inches of water. The room was full of smoke, neither Claxton nor Payne saw him fall and he should have been killed at once by a blow to his head or by being stunned and drowned, but by another of those quirks of fate, Claxton happened to be standing at the bottom of the ladder and thus broke his fall.

Claxton was knocked to one side and Isambard fell, face first into the water, unconscious. Claxton was stunned and could not see what had hit him, but then, gathering his wits, he saw a body half-submerged in the water. He grabbed the head out of the water, yelled for a rope and had the person hoisted out before returning to fighting the fire. Only when the fire was out and he went on deck did he discover whose life he had saved.

Isambard was taken ashore to Canvey Island where he was put to bed, seriously hurt. Even then he would not let go of his responsibilities and within hours of the incident he was writing directives to Claxton. When the SS *Great Western* arrived in Bristol on 2 April, there, waiting for Claxton, was the familiar letter from Isambard full of instructions and questions. He spent about three weeks in bed after this, the second heavy battering and near-drowning his small body had experienced, conducting the supervision of his works by letter from his sick-bed.

The SS *Great Western* was moored at Broad Pill 7 miles down the

Avon close to the Bristol Channel. After taking on coal and a few passengers – fifty people had cancelled their bookings when they heard of the fire – she steamed away, bound for New York, on 8 April 1838, the day before Isambard's thirty-second birthday. She was not the only steamship to be making the crossing. The Liverpool-based British & American Steam Navigation Company wanted the honour of being first across and as their ship *British Queen* was still being built they hired the 703-ton, Irish cross-channel ferry *Sirius* to make the transatlantic run on their behalf. This little ship, registered in Cork, with an Irish captain and crew, and twenty-two passengers, sailed from London to Queenstown (Cobh), where more coal was taken on, and then set course for America on 4 April 1838.

Isambard's ship was the faster vessel and was designed for the transatlantic run. The four-day start of *Sirius* was swallowed up by the SS *Great Western* and as the gallant little ship went aground on sandbanks at the entrance to New York Bay – the Captain had wanted to save time by not stopping to pick up the Pilot – so Isambard's ship came steaming past and docked in New York, on the East River, at 3 p.m. on 23 April. Isambard's dream of steam-powered, ocean-going liners had come true.

11

Patience in Adversity

Isambard started work again, before he was fully recovered, about the end of the month. George Gibbs noted in his diary for 1 May: 'Went today to Maidenhead . . . found two engines out for the first time with steam up. Brunel and his wife and Saunders were there. . . . I was more pleased than ever with the Maidenhead Bridge, of which the centres are now struck – standing free – and I liked the arrangements for the Depot [Maidenhead station] but I felt some doubts both here and at Hanwell as to the opening in May.'

George Gibbs, an enthusiastic Brunellian, had not noticed the slight damage to the brickwork of the eastern arch of the bridge. While Isambard was ill in bed on Canvey Island, the contractor, Chadwick, had, without asking permission, eased the timber centering away from the arches. He was premature in this; the cement in the eastern arch was not perfectly set and the lowest three courses of bricks extending about 12 ft on each side of the crown of the arch, extending under the arch for three courses, had sagged down about half an inch.

The damage was superficial and the western arch remained perfectly stable but Isambard's critics had a wonderful stick with which to beat him and they were delighted to use it. Soon, the slight sagging of a few dozen bricks became 'crevices you can put your arm into'. The GWR Directors called in Nicholas Wood and John Hawkshaw, a mining engineer who had worked in Liverpool and Venezuela, and who was then Engineer to the Manchester & Leeds Railway, to report on Isambard's masterpiece. Wood said that the damage was caused by the premature easing away of the centerings but Hawkshaw said that the design was faulty and that the arch lacked weight in the crown. He recommended that stone be substituted for brick at that part. Chadwick knew well enough what was wrong and when Isambard ordered him to make good the entire damage at his own expense he did so.

On 8 October 1838, Isambard ordered the centerings below the Maidenhead Bridge to be eased away from the bricks. Most intriguingly he directed that all the scaffolding was to be left in place so that, from the tow-path, it looked as if it was still supporting the arches. The most constant rumour about the bridge was that its 'flat' arches would fall as soon as the scaffolding support was removed. Isambard's removal of the supports while deliberately retaining the illusion that it was still in use must have been intended as a secret joke to give himself something to smile about in the dark days which he knew lay ahead.

One Saturday night in November 1839, after many days of heavy rain had put the Thames in a state of raging flood, a tremendous gale sprang up. Thinking that the centering would fall and with it the bridge, Lord Orkney sent a man to the home of one of Hammond's assistants, Bell, to say that the Maidenhead Bridge was endangered. Bell knew that no amount of wind could blow down the bridge, coolly sent the messenger on to Hammond, and then went back to sleep.

Brunel was incensed by Bell's lack of care and in a letter to Saunders wrote: 'Bell left it to chance whether Hammond might be in and whether a train might take a tumble into the river, in fact, taking no more trouble . . . than to forward this cock-and-bull story to Hammond who was 10 miles off when Bell was within a few hundred yards. I shall have my own quarrel to settle with Bell.'

Contrary to subsequent legend, the centerings withstood the gale and were still standing on 27 January 1840 because on that day Isambard wrote to Chadwick: 'You must immediately insert tie-bars into the spandrels of the western-most land-arch on the west side of Maidenhead Bridge and into the western arch of the east side and afterwards proceed with the others. You will oblige me by seeing to this having first settled the question of *removing the centres*.'

In June 1838 there were to be three important public events: Eton College festival of Montem on the 5th; the Derby on the 14th, in the presence of the soon-to-be-crowned Queen Victoria; and lastly her Coronation on the 28th. The traffic potential and the publicity advantage of introducing the railway to the public through these three famous events was too good to miss but it seemed an impossible task: engineering troubles were piling up. By 12 April 1838 just over 5 miles of double track had been laid and the embankment at Hanwell was still sinking. There were 17 miles of track-bed requiring pile-driving and track-laying, complete stations with offices, sidings, wagon turntables and water supplies were required. Paddington station was far from complete. There were locomotives to be given trial runs and all manner of details to be finalised.

Isambard was ill, in pain, and suffering from an unusual nervousness and he was not able to cope with the crisis satisfactorily. On some days he was absent altogether. Isambard's highly centralised style of management placed the whole works in jeopardy so, to lighten his load and to ensure against delays due to his absence, a few of his Directors were suggesting that he ought to accept assistance from a co-equal engineer. This last was Isambard's greatest worry.

On 11 May he wrote to Thomas Guppy:

> I am not particularly well in mind or body . . . I am still lame in the left foot and my back is weak. I don't write this letter without leaning back to rest and in consequence, I suppose, of the state of my stomach I am nervous, anxious and unhappy – in fact, *blue devilish*. An infinite number of things crowding in upon me, requiring attention and thought – all in arrears and I am quite incapable of getting through them. Everything seeming to go wrong – we talk of the 30th for opening and now everyone believes it – but me. I suppose I need a dose of salts.

On 19 May he wrote again to Guppy, in a fever of anxiety over the lack of news of the SS *Great Western* on her return voyage from New York. In the course of this he wrote:

> The GWR goes on well – I trust – but what with the circumstances of not having seen much of it and what with my nervousness I am very frightened. I can hardly say of what I am particularly anxious – Hammond and the others have my instructions *but still one's own eye is the only one after all*. [He then alluded to the suggestion that he ought to have a co-engineer:] I wish I could follow your advice . . . but the press is too immediate for any remedy now – it would require more thought of method to avail myself of the assistance of a person new to [the situation] than to struggle on as it is.

On 22 May the navvies had driven down piles and fixed the longitudinals to them over most of the 22½ miles from Paddington to Maidenhead, and on that day the Directors took a successful train ride over 11 miles from Hayes to the Maidenhead station. Later the same day, it was decided that the railway would have a private opening for the Directors and their friends on 31 May and that the public opening, for passenger traffic only, would take place on 4 June, Whit Monday. On 29 May George Gibbs wrote in his diary: 'At the railway office making sundry preparations for the opening. Went afterwards to Paddington and could hardly believe that we can be ready by tomorrow night.'

But they were. At 11 a.m. on 31 May 1838, 300 guests, including Isambard and Mary, and Marc and Sophia Brunel, foregathered at Paddington where two trains were waiting to convey them to Maidenhead station. The first, hauled by the pride of the Great Western, *North Star*, left at 11.30 a.m. and arrived 49 minutes later, an average speed of 28 mph. The guests were entertained to a cold luncheon in a tent where many toasts were drunk before they boarded their trains and returned to Paddington in somewhat livelier manner than they had come, one train making an average speed of $33\frac{1}{2}$ mph, start to stop. It seems likely that the engine driver had had a few pints while waiting for the exalted company to return, and Thomas Guppy must surely have been intoxicated when he walked along the roofs of the carriages as they see-sawed up and down at 50 mph over the hastily laid track.

The opening of the line to Maidenhead station, on 4 June 1838, only increased Brunel's troubles. The track had been carefully calculated, which is more than could be said for any other track at that time, and a great deal was expected from it, so the uncomfortable ride it gave was all the greater disappointment. Isambard believed he had designed a perfect track and had described his method in a letter to Nicholas Wood, on 12 February 1838:

> I take a timber 14–15 in. broad by 6 in. thick and, fastening [it] securely at intervals of 15 ft I beat the ground underneath it to almost any density . . . using hard blows on the timber, the sand below it is as dense as soft sandstone. Contact everywhere is perfect. Along the irregular surface of the timber is laid a plank which is planed true to the required level. Upon this are screwed the rails with a piece of felt under the joints . . . to prevent the ends squeezing into the wood. Plates [*sic*] are then tied across to maintain the gauge. The piles [driven into the ground] are for . . . holding down . . . and vary in length between 9 and 14 ft in cuttings

and [up to] 30 ft on embankments so as to reach the original ground. The piles are of beech, the timbers [are] American pine, the hardwood American elm, oak or ash and the whole is kyanised. The ballasting is brought up to the surface of the timbers. . . . It is greatly superior to anything I have seen in the ordinary mode.

This construction enabled Isambard to use a very strong but light-weight rail – his own invention. Railway rails were, at that time, usually made of cast iron – a material quite unsuitable as a load-bearing beam. Rolled, or 'wrought', iron was also used and while this did not snap like a casting, the running surface was liable to split open and become very uneven, a defect caused by uneven cooling as the heavy mass of iron passed through the rolling mill. Isambard designed a relatively light 'bridge' rail, an inverted 'U' section and at a stroke showed how to produce quickly – and therefore cheaply – miles of strong rail which, because it had not the mass, cooled evenly, and was free of latent faults. Typically, he did not patent the idea.

To reduce friction at the axle bearings and thus save fuel while increasing speed, he required large diameter wheels – in excess of the usual 3 ft. To have large wheels beneath a carriage would, in the conventional wisdom of the time, have raised it too high above the rails for safety so Isambard originally planned to sling the body low, between the wheels – and to do that without making the accommodation impossibly cramped he had to use a wider than usual distance between the rails. He could then, he reasoned, have carriage wheels of any diameter he chose and indeed envisaged wheels spinning round within sight of the windows.

The carriages, which were constructed by builders of horse-drawn road vehicles, at first ran badly due to a lack of knowledge of how to make railway vehicle springs and the lack of expertise in making properly balanced wheels. To avoid the unpleasant, serpentine motion of the little four-wheeled carriages of the Northern railways, he sensibly decided to use a six-wheeled chassis with relatively long wheelbase. This he could have done without recourse to the 7-ft gauge. To prevent the constant bumping over rail joints he decided on a continuous support beneath the rails with the whole held firmly to the hard-packed ground; neither did this require the broad gauge.

Isambard used 4-ft-diameter wheels for his first carriages but the only passenger carriage to have the body within the wheels was the 'Super 1st Class posting carriage'. The interiors of these were 'fitted up in a style not met with in any other railway conveyance in the Kingdom (except the Royal carriages)' but unfortunately their width at floor level was only 6 ft and the system was not repeated. Instead of slinging the body between the wheels – the whole point of the broad gauge – it was placed conventionally, over the wheels and was kept low by allowing the wheels to come up through the floor where they were accommodated under semicircular covers.

With this construction there was no need for the broad gauge. He could have had large-diameter wheels to reduce rolling resistance, long wheelbase, six-wheeled carriages for stability and used the standard gauge of the country. The only incontrovertible advantage of the broad gauge was 'economy of scale'. A GWR six-wheeled 1st class coach weighed 588 lb per passenger while an L&BR four-wheel 1st weighed 631 lb per passenger fully laden. It was easier to fill the smaller carriage than the larger one so the economy of scale advantage did not always operate.

There could be only one gauge for the major rail routes in one small island and, for better or worse, that gauge had been established in 1829 when George Stephenson's Stockton & Darlington Railway opened to anyone who wanted to run wagons on it. The average gauge of railways in the Newcastle area was 4 ft 8 in., thus Stephenson placed the rails at the best width to suit the majority of wagons of the district. Obviously this was not the best way to approach the matter of trunk railway construction. Stephenson himself admitted he would have preferred the gauge to be the round 5 ft, but after the S&DR came George Stephenson's Liverpool & Manchester, Robert Stephenson's London & Birmingham and Joseph Locke's Grand Junction, all to the 'standard' gauge. By 1835 it was too late to do anything to change matters. The die was cast.

Isambard did not see the case in that light at all. Although he did foresee that there would be a trunk railway network, he argued that the Great Western – having created a monopoly in its area – could run in splendid isolation from the rest. He desperately wanted to be right and no objection, however basic, would he recognise. He had settled on his own 'sacred cow', the 7 ft gauge, which was entirely unnecessary to the success of his venture, and thus created an unnecessary obstruction for national north/south rail traffic, while within the vast territory he had marked out as his own, he actually intended to stifle the inter-company competition he professed to find so important.

He was certainly a man of enormous energy and courage who pursued his vision with unanswerable, mathematical logic – unless mathematics did not support his case in which case he abandoned mathematics. His calculations served him brilliantly, particularly in his bridges, but when the future of his vision was threatened by some tiresomely mundane practicality – such as the incompatibility of gauges – he fled into a forest of figures and refused to come out. Sometimes he got completely lost in the wood.

In 1838 he was asked by the editor, Mr Oaks, of an encyclopedia published by the Society for the Diffusion of Useful Knowledge, to read and if necessary to correct the entry on railways. The author of this piece had written that railway wheels had flanges to guide them along the rail and to prevent them falling off. Isambard was having none of that. He wrote to Oaks:

> The flanges are a necessary precaution but they *ought never* to touch the rail and therefore they cannot be said to keep the wheels on the rails. They ought not to come into action except to meet an accidental, lateral force. A railway with considerable curves might be travelled over with carriages at any velocity and with wheels without flanges. The wheels are made conical, the smaller circumference at the outer edge. The pair of wheels are fixed to the axle and thus if anything throws the wheels in the slightest degree to one side the wheel is immediately rolling on a larger circumference than the other and the tendency to roll back is introduced. The carriage is kept always in the middle of the track. A beautiful arrangement.

Isambard's explanation omitted two essential points: a flangeless wheel needed precisely super-elevated curves, while the angle of the coned wheel would have to be not less than 30 degrees. His track, and indeed modern track, could not be maintained to the necessary perfection, and the steeply coned 'tread' of the locomotive's driving wheel would make insufficient adhesive contact with the rail. All wheel profiles would require frequent re-profiling to prevent derailments and, last but not least, without flanges it would be impossible to switch a train from one track to another. Isambard's enthusiasm for beautiful theories often blinded him to the mundane practicalities of the daily grind.

He maintained he despised 'dogma'; that nothing should be laid down as a hard-and-fast rule because everything was capable of improvement; that which was impossible now might become possible through experiment, hence a multiplicity of views was essential to progress. These were his individualistic, free-thinking views. So it is strange to read of Isambard's Lardneresque dogmatism concerning flanges or locomotive design.

He left the design of the locomotives to the various contractors after ordering them to adhere to the following conditions: 'A velocity of 30 mph is to be considered as standard and this is to be attained without requiring the piston to travel at a greater rate than 280 ft per minute . . . the weight of the engine not to exceed 10½ tons.' On 2 June 1836 he had written to Sharp, Roberts & Co., locomotive builders: 'I hope to attain 40 mph or more which would cause the piston to travel at 337 ft per minute which is the utmost that ought to be allowed.' Isambard's lapse into error is inexplicable. On the Liverpool & Manchester at that time they were running happily at 30 mph on 5 ft 6 in. wheels with a piston speed of 504 ft per minute and with engines weighing well over 10½ tons. His specifications obliged the locomotive builders to supply engines with very large wheels, undersized cylinders and, to keep within the totally unrealistic weight restriction, very small boilers.

His error must be attributed to his obsession with doing everything himself, qualified or not – 'he fancied that no one could do anything but himself,' Gooch had written. Yet where the SS *Great Western* was concerned Isambard had happily collaborated with a committee and as a result the ship – and its engines – was a complete success. By mid-1836 a certain orthodoxy of locomotive design had evolved. All Isambard need have done was to order some 'standard' machines from the well-known manufacturers, suitably scaled-up for the broad gauge – as the 'standard' Maudslay side-lever marine engines were scaled-up for the unprecedentedly large SS *Great Western*. Such locomotives would have had 6 ft 6 in. driving wheels and 15 × 18 in. cylinders, and would have weighed about 18 tons – no great weight for the massively strong track he had designed.

Isambard was unsuccessful as a designer of locomotives but he was very concerned about their looks because he saw the need to give his men something to show their pride in their work, the need for morale. In 1837 he specified a curved nameplate with raised, brass, serif letters to be placed over the central axle-box and on 5 March 1838 he included in a letter to the locomotive builder, T.E. Harrison, an exhortation to make his engines more pleasing to the eye:

We have a splendid engine of Stephenson's, it would be a beautiful ornament in the most elegant drawing room . . . and another of Quaker-like simplicity carried even to shabbyness . . . the difference in the care bestowed by the engineman, the favour in which it is held by others and even oneself, not to mention the public, is striking. A plain young lady, however amiable, is apt to be neglected.

The final sentence, it seems to me, gives a delightful insight into the good-natured side of Isambard, his warm-hearted temperament and love of beautiful things. What Isambard's livery would have been we do not know because Gooch, a real locomotive engineer, counter-manded the order. In February 1840 he wrote to R.W. Hawthorn & Co: 'I should like the other brass plates to be made as invisible as possible, having an objection to too much brass about an engine.'

By the end of the first week the railway had carried 10,360 passengers and on 28 June the first excursion train ran, when the scholars of Eton College were taken from Slough to London for the Coronation ceremonies of Queen Victoria. The Great Western Directors were particularly glad to do this because the Governors of the College had been implacably opposed to the railway and had forced the GWR to take extraordinary measures in order to have the merest semblance of a station at Slough. By 20 June the weight of traffic rolling over the track had beaten it into a 'roller-coaster' shape. At the centre of each 15-ft length it was pressed into the ground while at each end of the section it was held up to the original level by the massive piles.

Isambard acknowledged that his road was in a bad state owing, he said, to his use of sand and fine ballast below the longitudinals rather than coarse stones but on 20 June he was obliged to make an experiment whereby a half-mile of track was released from the piles and laid on coarse ballast while another half-mile was reballasted with coarse stones but left on the piles. All this cost extra money and the train service had to be reduced to allow the work to be carried out. Once again, ridiculous and untrue rumours sprang up concerning the safety of Maidenhead Bridge and the 'vast cost' of constructing a 7-ft gauge railway.

The Northern shareholders, some of them major industrialists who were excluded from becoming Directors of the GWR, used these several large sticks to beat Isambard, in the hope of thereby lowering the value of GWR stock which they could then buy to gain control of the Company and alter its gauge. The GWR Directors were unhappy and divided. Some, including Casson, Mills and Sims, were willing to admit the Northerners and thereby effectively dismiss Isambard. Others, such as the gentlemanly banker George Gibbs, loathed the Northerners. In his diary for 30 June 1838 he wrote: 'I abhor their selfish, illiberal and ungentlemanlike minds which lead them to measure everything that is done by the rule of pocket.' A very Brunellian sentiment.

Gibbs wanted to retain Isambard while forcing him to delegate the details of construction to an Assistant Engineer: 'We feel more than ever the necessity of pressing for more efficient assistance for Brunel, as a great deal of our work is getting far behind.' Isambard's faults and virtues were frequently discussed by the GWR Board after 21 June and by 13 July, as the difficulties continued, even Gibbs began to have doubts about him – he was trying to do too much. Gibbs wrote in his diary on 13 July 1838:

> . . . saw Casson and Saunders. The latter . . . showed me a letter from Brunel expressed in a cool and very proper manner but showing great feeling with regard to the loss of confidence which he believes he has seen on the part of the Directors and even of Saunders. Poor fellow, I pity him exceedingly and I know not how he will get through the storm that awaits him. With all his talent he has shown himself deficient, I confess, in general arrangement. There have been too many mistakes, too much doing and undoing. The draining I fear is imperfect and the carriages made under his direction have not worked well; but I cannot help asking myself whether it is fair to decide on a work of this kind within a few weeks of its opening; and is not the present outcry created in great measure by Brunel's enemies? I hear that at the meeting Brunel's dismissal is to be moved. Now the strong bias of my mind is that our only chance of comfort and safety is that our line should be carried out by Brunel with efficient assistance and on a more stringent system of control.

It was becoming clearer to the Directorate that Isambard was conducting an experiment with the shareholders' money, he was learning to shave on the chins of the shareholders. He needed to be controlled. Isambard was acutely aware that most Directors wanted him to be shackled to another Engineer while a few actually wanted him removed. The knowledge galvanised him; he lost his aches and pains, went into his 'Napoleonic' mode and on 12 July wrote to Guppy a fighting note full of defiance and military allusions:

> A splendid storm is brewing and although I have no umbrella or shelter and must weather it out I am curious to know beforehand whether it will be snow, hail, rain or all three with thunder and lightning to boot. An

active canvas is going on to do no more or less than condemn all my plans in the GWR and to dispense with the necessity of giving me any further trouble. I need hardly say that Liverpool is the gun whence all the shot comes . . . this is no joke but a serious attack. Our Directors certainly look on it as 'une affaire finie'. I am by no means disposed to treat it lightly, *a good attack always warms my blood and raises my spirits*.

Isambard's apparent enthusiasm for the 'fight' was almost certainly a disguise for the enormous apprehension he felt.

About 13 July, Isambard boldly suggested that two engineers should be called in to survey the line and report their opinions to the Board. On the 16th, the idea was accepted. Casson went even further and urged that Robert Stephenson be made co-Engineer with Isambard. Gibbs, Sims, Fenwick and Charles Russell knew this was tantamount to dismissing Isambard. They wanted to retain him while 'correcting with a firm hand everything that might be wrong and to pursue such a system . . . as on close examination may be found to be best'.

On the evening of the 16th Gibbs and Saunders went to see Brunel and put to him the results of the meeting. Isambard said he would resign rather than accept anyone – even his great friend Robert Stephenson – as his co-Engineer. It seems likely that Isambard suggested that the gentlemen Directors should take a ride on Stephenson's railway and see how *he* was managing because the following day Gibbs, Casson and Saunders went for a ride on the London & Birmingham Railway from Euston to Denbigh Hall, near Bletchley, 47 miles each way. They went down in a 1st class carriage and returned in an open 2nd class. To Gibbs's great relief they found a great deal wrong: 'The bumps and jolts at the joints are very frequent indeed . . . the road is under repair in many places . . . and they still have an immense expense to incur in replacing the temporary, transverse, wooden sleepers with stone blocks.'

Gibbs was grateful for this small mercy but it did not win the gauge argument. That raged on. On 20 July Robert Stephenson and the President of the Institute of Civil Engineers, James Walker, were asked to inspect and report on Isambard's track. They both refused. Exaggerated reports on the expense of Isambard's methods abounded, along with half-truths concerning bridges breaking and embankments sinking, the normal incidents of construction blamed on some peculiarity of Isambard's design. In spite of the extra-ordinary pressures which fell on him through his work and the whispering campaign of malicious rumours, he kept up a brave, confident public face as he was forced to draw on his reserves of nervous energy to meet the crisis. His determination, courage and indeed his patience in the face of so much public hostility were outstanding.

12

Isambard at Bay

The shareholders' meeting on 30 August 1838 was packed to hear the attack on the broad gauge and Isambard's defence of it. He set out to disarm the critics by agreeing with them. He admitted that his track had been a disappointment but pointed out that the worst lengths were those laid while he was an invalid on Canvey Island. While this was true, it carried the implication that Isambard's system could be correctly installed only under the personal supervision of one man – which must surely be a disadvantage. He admitted that the system of piles to hold the track down was an expensive mistake and that he now intended to abandon it. It must be said that all engineers then believed that, ideally, rails should be laid on a hard, solid surface.

Isambard claimed that he adopted the broad gauge owing to

the peculiarity of the circumstances of this railway . . . [which] consist in the unusually favourable gradients and curves which we have been able to obtain. With the capability of carrying the line upwards of 50 miles out of London on an almost dead level . . . and having . . . for the whole distance to Bristol, excellent gradients, it was thought that unusually high speed might be attained . . . the attainment of high speed appeared to involve the width of gauge. *I take it for granted* that in determining the gauge, due regard has been had to the curves and the gradients of the line, which ought to form a most essential, if not principal condition. To adopt a gauge of the same number of inches on the (flat and straight) Great Western and the (hilly and curvacious) Grand Junction Railway would amount practically to the use of a different gauge in similar railways. *The gauge which is well adapted to one is not well adapted to another* unless some mysterious cause exists which has never yet been explained for the empirical law which would fix the gauge under all circumstances.

That was a splendid example of Isambard's idiosyncratic style of special pleading – or 'blinding with science'. According to him the gauge was determined by the radius of the curves. That being the case, the serpentine railway he was at that time laying out between Sapperton and Stroud and, later, under the red cliffs of Dawlish and up the steep flanks of Dartmoor, ought to have been laid down to the 4 ft 8 in. gauge but they had to be laid to the – unsuitable – 7-ft gauge since otherwise there would have been a break of gauge within his own railway empire.

There is no doubt that the broad gauge railway used only a small amount of extra land. Isambard pointed out that GWR embankments required 6.5 per cent more space than those of the L&BR. The space between the walls of bridges carrying the L&BR was 30 ft – just like the Great Western – but L&BR tunnels were 24 ft wide against the GWR's standard 30 ft. Isambard said he wanted to give plenty of clearance, for comfort and for future enlargement of rolling stock. He pointed out how much more steadily the broad-based broad-gauge coach rode and reasserted his belief that larger wheels reduced friction and therefore allowed for higher speed. He was laying much emphasis on the 12-in. difference in wheel diameters between his railway and Stephenson's.

He concluded his speech with these words: 'These advantages were considered important by you . . . and certainly everything which has occurred in the working of the line confirms me in my conviction that we have secured a most valuable power to the Great Western Railway and that it would be folly to abandon it.'

However, the Liverpool Party wanted to standardise the gauge. They proposed that Brunel be shackled to a co-Engineer and that one of their number be given a seat on the Board. Had the Northerners known that they held a majority they would have pressed for a vote and that would have been the end for Brunel, but Gibbs managed to hide this fact from the dissenters and Isambard's own suggestion, that independent engineers be brought in to inspect the line and report on it, was adopted. The Liverpool Party's choice was the Stephensonite John Hawkshaw and to his examination was added that of Nicholas Wood who brought with him none other than the great sage himself – Dr Dionysius Lardner. Their reports were to be ready in time for the renewed debate at a meeting of shareholders on 10 October 1838.

After the meeting Isambard was taken ill and 'went at once into the country and attended to no business of any sort'. He had been working furiously in the expectation of perfection, so the disappointment of the reality was proportionately crippling. The Thames Tunnel had failed while he was Resident Engineer, none of his schemes between that and the GWR had come to much – with the exception of the eminently successful SS *Great Western* – and now he was about to lose oversight of a truly great work, his beloved Great Western. The threat of imminent separation from his masterwork cast him into a paralysing depression which was not overcome by the love at home of the beautiful Mary, or his infant son, Isambard.

He had returned to London by 10 September but did not resume duty before the 11th or 12th. On the 10th Gibbs 'spoke very seriously' to him about the need to do as he was told and at the 17 September Board meeting, Gibbs

> expressed strongly my opinion that if he [Isambard] were spoken to plainly but firmly he would heartily co-operate with us in reducing expenses and putting everything on the best footing but with this view it [is] necessary to cheer him. He is at present *almost brokenhearted* and in this state of mind he *cannot exert himself* but if we treat him judiciously he will do what is right and it will be our own fault . . . if we do not make him an *invaluable servant* for the future.

When Isambard met Saunders and a deputation of Directors at Paddington on the morning of 19 September he was feeling in a very contrite and subdued mood – if one reads between the lines of Gibbs's diary report, which states: 'We spoke to him [Isambard] *very plainly indeed* and he expressed himself *anxious to co-operate heartily* with us in carrying out our views which we then discussed with him.' They first asked him the very revealing question 'are you willing to bow to our wishes' and then told him what those wishes were. One significant item was that, in future, no construction was to be made without a proper plan of it first being shown to the Directors for their approval.

Isambard had previously set himself above the Directors and now he had had his wings clipped. It must have been an unpleasant experience for him, neither could he have enjoyed the sight of Dr

Lardner dashing about his railway on the *North Star*, carrying out ill-considered experiments with the sole object of having Isambard removed from his post as Chief Engineer. The wonder of it is that Isambard remained as polite as he did and furnished promptly all the information required by his inquisitor.

By the time of the October special meeting of shareholders, Nicholas Wood and Dr Lardner had not completed their investigations so the Directors refused to produce the Hawkshaw report alone, which was implacably hostile to Brunel and the broad gauge. The Liverpudlian contingent was 'a good deal staggered' by this and, as they lacked their main evidence, had only a weak defence against Isambard's persuasive – if somewhat peculiar – arguments. The meeting closed peacefully leaving the gauge question in abeyance. The showdown was yet to come.

The Hawkshaw report was written in hard, direct, economical language, quite unlike Isambard's elegant prose. Hawkshaw advised an immediate change to the standard gauge in order to save £30,000 over the whole line. That saving, he said, was the figure *after* due allowance had been made for scrapping locomotives and carriages. Of the gauge he wrote:

> ... the 4 ft 8½ in. gauge is generally adopted ... perhaps if railways were just commencing in this country an addition of a few inches, five or six at most (Robt Stephenson's opinion) might be made; but the advantage of making it now ... would in no manner compensate the evil that will arise from a variety of gauges in one country.

Isambard's track, which, now that the piles no longer supported it, was far better than anything Hawkshaw had built, was curtly dismissed. 'The mode of laying the rails is, I think, attempting to do in a difficult and expensive manner that which may be done at least as well in a simple and more economical manner.'

Hawkshaw's comments on the locomotives were ridiculous and one wonders if he had even seen one of Isambard's freaks. He stated that the engines were not only too heavy but too powerful! He compared them to a 'ship of 200 tons burthen when there was no probability of ever obtaining a cargo of half the weight'.

Gibbs was rightly outraged and wrote that it was a 'thoroughly ill-natured production from beginning to end, the greater part of which might have been written without coming near the line'. Isambard continued to burn the midnight oil as he attended to the railway, or attended the Directors at their Board meetings in London, Bristol or Cheltenham to report the progress of the work, or the lack of it. He had also to produce his answer to Hawkshaw's criticism and this he did on 11 December 1838:

> The question of the disadvantage of differing in point of gauge from other railways and consequent exclusion from communication with them, is . . . undoubtedly an inconvenience. The Great Western, however, broke ground in an entirely new district in which railways were unknown . . . it commands that district . . . and has sent forth branches which embrace nearly all that can belong to it and it will be the fault of the Company if it does not . . . secure . . . the whole trade of this portion of England, South Wales and the south of Ireland, not by a forced monopoly which could never long resist the wants of the public *but by such attention to those wants as shall render competition unnecessary and hopeless.*

There seems to be here, again, that strange, Brunellian mixture of God-like condescension and self-deception. Isambard proposed that the GWR – and, *ipso facto*, Isambard – would be able to build all the railways required by the people of the West Country and Wales – that the population would wait while all necessary lines were built and those that were not built would not be required. He was forced into making these patently absurd assertions by his defence of the indefensible. In the same report, in justifying the breaks of gauge his system would bring about, he wrote: 'Railway carriages and wagons must belong to the particular line on which they run and, except in such cases as the Grand Junction and London & Birmingham Railways which form, in fact, one line . . . it will never pay to trust them in the hands of others.' Thus he would have denied to the public the convenience of through-coach and through-wagon working between railways.

The Wood report was handed to the Directors on 12 December 1838. It was couched in inconclusive language. For example, Wood could see no harm in making a broad gauge railway between Bristol to London because this main trunk was 'complete in itself between two sides of the island' but then professed himself unable to judge how great a disadvantage the broad gauge would be when it threw off north- or south-facing branches into standard-gauge territory. He said that there were no advantages to be gained from the broad gauge to make up for the disadvantage of its isolation from the rest of the system and then said, 'there are counter-acting advantages incidental to an increased width of gauge'.

Wood was sure that the piles were worse than useless – 'their action seems to prevent the contact of the timbers with the ground' – but approved strongly of the longitudinal bearers under the rails, if they could be made stronger. Without Isambard's piles and with a much thicker beam of wood, he thought the track would be a large improvement on Stephenson's stone blocks or on cross-sleepers, which, he wrote, 'cannot be considered as a permanent description of road'. Isambard had already dispensed with the piles.

His report on the *North Star* declared that: 'It is not advisable to attempt an extreme rate of speed and that 35 mph, with the existing engine power, may be considered as the limit of practical speed for passenger trains'. This alarming statement was based on Lardner's researches which showed that *North Star*, the GWR's best engine, could haul 166 tons at 23.3 mph, but only 33 tons at 37 mph and 16 tons at 41 mph while the coke consumption rose from 1.25 to 2.76 lb per ton per mile from the lowest to the highest speed.

His report finished inconclusively:

Almost all the results . . . go to establish a conclusion that 7 ft is beyond that width that may be considered the best – but these investigations are far from conclusive in the present state of our knowledge as to what width is . . . the most advisable to adopt . . . therefore, until we have determined in the most satisfactory . . . manner the precise extent of the injury arising from the present width of gauge . . . it appears to me the present width should be retained.

The Wood report was read at a Board meeting on 14 December and caused consternation. The pro-Brunel faction saw small comfort in it while the anti-Brunel faction felt that it showed that they were right – especially as the Hawkshaw report was so adamantly against the broad gauge. On that same day a Dr Squires had written to the Board suggesting that Joseph Locke, Engineer of the London & Southampton Railway and staunch supporter of the standard gauge, be taken on as co-Engineer with Brunel. Even Gibbs and Saunders, exhausted by the incessant wrangling, were agreed that 'for the sake of peace . . . and if the leading principles of the railway could first be settled . . .' to bring in Locke would be a good idea. Only Charles Russell, later to be Chairman of the Great Western, was staunchly in favour of Brunel.

Isambard's future career was hanging in the balance. One of the Directors, George Unwin Sims, visited him at home in Duke Street on the 13th and told him that a co-Engineer would have to be appointed. After hours of argument, on the 14th, the Directors' meeting broke up. The Directors Gibbs, Russell and Casson with their Secretary, Charles Saunders, went to Duke Street to sort matters out with Isambard. He was worrying and wondering about the future, with Ben Hawes giving him moral support as usual. Isambard could not compromise, he never did. He was going to have it his way or not at all. He kept a calm face to cover his anxiety and set out to gamble his future on one last, great fight.

The deputation told him that the Bristol Committee were unanimously in favour of attaching to him a co-Engineer and to admitting one or two Liverpudlians to the Board of Directors, and that most of the London Committee agreed with this. They were dissatisfied with the performance of the railway and the rapidly rising cost of construction – it appeared that the line would cost double Isambard's original estimate. They were also very much alarmed at the poor showing of the much-vaunted broad-gauge engines.

Gibbs wrote in his diary that night, that Isambard spoke 'in a very modest way', but, in my view, Gibbs was mistaking a quietly spoken voice for 'modesty'. Isambard was not modest, he was always certain he was right. According to Gibbs's account, Isambard said that 'the evidence which is accumulating against me appears too great to be resisted without injury to the Company and therefore I am prepared to give way. . . . I have no objection to it being said that I have been defeated for I feel confident of the correctness of my views and I am sure I will have opportunities of proving it.'

He was quietly defiant and said that they could have his resignation whenever they wanted it but he would not work with any other Engineer. Isambard's confidence was worthy of an accomplished player of poker. His gamble paid off. The Directors were thrown into new fits of indecision and divided loyalties; they were given furiously to think and went their various ways to do just that.

By 18 December Isambard had drafted his reply to Wood's vacillating report and had handed it to the Directors at the Princess Street, London, office of the Company. Dr Lardner had attributed the poor performance of the broad-gauge *North Star* to its wide frontal area. This was ludicrous and Isambard told the Directors that he was 'perfectly convinced that a great fallacy pervades it as may be shown and proved by experiment'. He gave hope for proving Wood and Lardner wrong and rallied back to his side Gibbs and one of the Bristol Directors, C.B. Fripp. With Russell and Saunders he then had five Board Room allies to argue his case.

While the Directors argued amongst themselves, for and against the Brunellian concept, Isambard and Daniel Gooch set to work to find out what was wrong with the *North Star*. Gooch was aghast at this engine's poor showing. He was convinced it was potentially the most efficient engine on the line and feared that the embattled Directors would blame him for its shortcomings. They were bound to lash out at someone – and indeed they did. On 28 December Gibbs wrote of the 'total unfitness of Gooch for his situation'.

Gooch and Brunel took the *North Star* for a run and at once achieved better performances than Dr Lardner's, simply by better driving and firing techniques. After the first run Gooch examined the blast pipe – that which discharges exhaust steam from the cylinders up the chimney – and discovered that not only was it $2\frac{5}{8}$ in. diameter – instead of the designed $3\frac{1}{4}$ in. – but that it was not discharging centrally up the chimney. The narrow pipe restricted the discharge and thus allowed a 'back pressure' to build up in the cylinders, while the eccentric siting of the pipe in the chimney did not produce a sufficiently strong blast on the fire to make it burn properly.

Gooch and Isambard worked throughout December and even on Christmas Day to rectify the faults and on 29 December they invited George Gibbs to come with them, on the footplate, from Paddington to Maidenhead. With a load of 43 tons they averaged 38 mph start to stop with a coke consumption of .95 lb per ton/mile. They were all delighted and excited. The news was given to the Board but otherwise it was kept a secret, intending, as Gooch wrote, 'to spring it as a mine against our opponents'.

13

Isambard Triumphant

In December 1838 and January 1839, problems with the locomotives reached crisis proportions. Isambard's impossible specifications to the builders, throwing away the very advantages for which he had built the 7-ft gauge, combining with the bad workmanship of the constructors and the lack of any standardised parts, led to poor performance, regular breakdowns and long periods under repair. Gooch was taking the blame and on 2 January he was summoned before the Directors who demanded that he explain himself.

Gooch did not directly criticise Brunel but he had to state the case correctly in his own defence. It was obvious to him that much of the problem stemmed from Isambard's lack of experience with locomotives – there had been a great deal of reasoned thought but no practical experience at all. Even without naming names, his meaning was obvious and he was required to make a full, written, report on each engine. He knew he was going to infuriate Isambard but he had no choice; his own job, as well as the future success of the Great Western, was at stake. In the meantime Isambard faced his own 'trial' before the Directors and assembled shareholders, to whom copies of the Hawkshaw and Hood Reports had been circulated, in the London Tavern, on 9 January 1839.

The debate was long and acrimonious. All the railways south of Watford had a Liverpool Party of North Country individuals and industrialists and usually these were resented as 'outsiders' – never more so than among the aristocratic and land-owning gentlemen of London and the West Country; Northern 'brass' was welcome but not Northern 'interference' in what was basically a West Country enterprise. The *Bristol Journal* wrote of the debate as a struggle between 'Mr Brunel' and the 'Men of the North', while the London *Sun* saw 'Mr Brunel' as standing for scientific progress against the conservative stagnation of the standard-gaugers. 'Mr Brunel' sat quietly in the body of the hall and awaited events.

The meeting opened with the Directors rejecting Hawkshaw's advice to scrap the broad gauge: 'The objection that the wide gauge might prevent a junction with other lines seems both to Mr Wood and the Directors to have but little weight as applied to the Great Western Railway.' This was followed by a statement of Company policy in the light of – or in spite of – the reports: 'The Directors, upon a deliberate reconsideration of all the circumstances . . . divesting the question of all personal partialities or obstinate adherence to a system, unanimously acquiesce in the abandonment of the piles, in having heavier timbers and rails [and] retaining the width of gauge . . . as the most conducive to the general interests of the Company.'

The resolution was then moved that the Directors' report be 'approved and adopted'. At once the 'Men of the North' moved the amendment that 'the reports of Messrs Wood and Hawkshaw contain sufficient evidence that the plans of construction pursued by Mr Brunel are injudicious, expensive and ineffectual for their professed objects and therefore ought not to be proceeded with'. And with that, battle commenced.

Around the walls of the hall, Dr Lardner had displayed charts of the data he had obtained during his tests on *North Star* and very technical they looked, too. A Mr Heyworth rose to attack the *North Star* using data provided by Dr Lardner. He insisted that high speed was impossible on the broad gauge and gave figures for trains running at 80 mph to prove it. Charles Babbage then stood up and showed that the good Doctor's 'facts' were worthless because they had been obtained with inaccurate instruments whereupon the assembled throng began to shout for Isambard, eagerly awaiting the quiet sarcasms by which, they were sure, he would put down the opposition.

Isambard told the excited throng: 'I had not intended to speak, but Mr Heyworth must be labouring under some misapprehension. I cannot believe that he has any account of engines running at 80 mph, thereby promising more "impossibilities".' This raised general laughter. Mr Heyworth was annoyed and replied that he was not referring to actual speed but to a calculation made by Dr Lardner as to degrees of resistance in the atmosphere based on five experiments. 'They are a scale founded on experiments,' he concluded, huffily.

'And so are all scales,' replied Isambard, urbanely, 'so were Dr Lardner's – but they might be mistaken.' This was greeted with cheers and laughter. He went on to say that the poor showing of the *North Star* under Dr Lardner had nothing to do with atmospheric resistance and everything to do with internal streamlining. He explained what he and Gooch had discovered and then read out the latest performance figures, pointing out that they were far superior to anything that Hawkshaw could show on his Manchester & Bury Railway.

Isambard had shown Dr Lardner to be a quack, Hawkshaw's railway to be inferior and, seizing the psychological moment, gave the audience some Brunellian facts. The GWR was nearer to a perfectly level railway than any in Britain, it had the most powerful engines and the most commodious carriages, it would be complete in itself from Bristol to London and would soon cover a vast area within which it would reign supreme. This was going to be a West Country and Welsh railway – who needed the Liverpudlians? Though it loftily ignored the thorny topic of incompatible gauges and such mundane considerations as the difficulty of finding money, men, materials and time to create a whole network of broad gauge trunk lines, nevertheless the vision splendid proclaimed by Brunel must have dazzled many of his listeners for he carried the day.

A Poll was demanded and the result was:

For the Amendment, those present		176
For the Amendment, proxy votes		5969
	Total	6145
Against the Amendment, those present		1984
Against the Amendment, proxy votes		5908
	Total	7892

The original motion was then put again and was carried unanimously. For better or worse, the Great Western was committed to the broad gauge – and to Isambard Kingdom Brunel.

Isambard had been able to defend the indefensible thanks to the incompetence of the supporters of the standard gauge. He won the debate because of the absurdities of Dr Lardner, whose exposure was largely the result of Daniel Gooch's work on the *North Star*. Isambard's arguments, which were based either on very shaky logic or irrelevances, had been delivered in confident, elegant terms and presented a vision of the future which the unimaginative, standard-gaugers could not match. Through his oratory, mixing technicality with charm, Isambard had swept along a large number of people in a tide of enthusiasm – and some local patriotism.

Though the result of the poll appeared to be a vote of confidence in Isambard, to his chagrin he had immediately to face what seemed to him to be a mutiny. Gooch's report on the locomotives was with the Directors by 10 January 1839. As Gooch put it, later, in his *Memoirs*: 'I could only tell what I believed to be the facts . . . and such facts would be displeasing to Brunel.' They were. Although Gooch mentioned no names and stuck to a factual statement and explanation of the condition of each engine it became obvious to the Directors that Isambard was to blame for the poor performance of the engines although some of the problems did stem from bad workmanship at the factory.

Brunel took great offence at Gooch's 'disloyalty' and wrote him 'a rather angry letter' which has not, unfortunately, survived the years. However, when he had calmed down and had time to reflect, Isambard wrote again to Gooch and in his *Memoirs* Gooch states that 'his good sense told him that I was correct and his kind heart did me justice'. Gooch's report to the Board resulted not only in his being instructed to prepare designs for new locomotives – Isambard could have coped with that – but Gooch was told to report direct to the Board and thereby became a Chief in all but name. Isambard's writ no longer ran in the Locomotive Department, a novel situation for him and an extremely distasteful one. He was the Creator of the railway, he was its 'first employee', and he wanted to remain in sole command – after all, he disliked accepting the over-riding authority of the Directors.

On 28 January, less than three weeks after being instructed to prepare new designs, Gooch had compiled, with the assistance of his Chief Draughtsman T.R. Crampton, meticulous plans and specifications for a new breed of locomotive based on Stephenson's *North Star*. They were not only well proportioned, free steaming and power-ful – they were the first in the world to be standardised in their com-ponents. Contractors were provided with detailed drawings, written instructions and templates to this end. The Locomotive Department, and later Swindon Works, became, in everyone's eyes but Isambard's, a separate entity under Gooch.

Isambard ought to have welcomed this – the railway was expanding and he could not have coped adequately with that part of the work taken on by Gooch – but his obsessive desire to be *seen* to be in charge of absolutely everything gave him no peace. As Gooch's 'empire' began to grow and become independent of his own, Isambard saw it detracting from his greatness. For years he bombarded Gooch with complaints and instructions, fussing like an old hen over a chick.

On 11 January 1840 he wrote to him:

> My Dear Sir, The *Dog Star* driving wheel is gone. It is barely capable of moving and quite unfit to use with a train and the *North Star* is going. Have you ordered any new ones or what do you propose to do? You must provide for them IMMEDIATELY. We are today as badly off for engines as we have ever been. The new tender alarms me very much. It is too weak and twisting. At first I supposed it was bad workmanship but on examining it I observed a radical defect in the construction. The whole weight is upon the inside frame except at the two ends. . . . This must be remedied immediately. . . . I was not aware of their construction or I should certainly have objected to it. *You should try and let me know where better to assist you.*

Isambard cast doubt on Gooch's management in the first few lines, cast doubt on his engineering ability next and finally tried to patronise him with offers of assistance. One day Isambard was on an engine which was priming – throwing sooty water from the chimney over the passengers. This could be caused by the interior of the boiler being dirty and as soon as he arrived in his office he wrote a fussy little note to Gooch: 'I insist on boilers being washed-out periodically. Do not fail to attend to this.' Or this thoughtless note on 2 June 1840: 'I cannot let you rest on the subject of the engines for Chippenham. [He meant the engines based at Chippenham which assisted trains up Dauntsey incline.] Every day is of the utmost importance . . . could we borrow one from the [London &] Southampton?' Isambard must have been somewhat distracted to suggest borrowing a standard-gauge engine which would have required conversion to the 7-ft gauge and back again. He ended with: 'P.S. What engine brought up the goods train and set fire to the luggage van? We must ascertain the cause and put a stop to the evil at once.'

Gooch, the Locomotive Engineer and Superintendent of the Department, was not even allowed to draft the 'Rules and Regulations to be observed by GWR enginemen and firemen'. Isambard wrote these and presented them to Gooch on 29 October 1840 together with a personal rulebook for Gooch himself: 'Certain rules for your guidance in the appointment of enginemen and firemen and in the meantime if you require to employ anyone let me know before appointing them.' In that same letter he turned to the subject of speeding: 'J. Hill brought up the *Cyclops* in 27 minutes from Slough [40 mph average start to stop] following the short train into Paddington within three minutes. This work must be put a stop to *effectually*. The Directors have determined to fine him ten shillings.'

But then the other side of Isambard came out. He was delighted by Driver Hill's *élan* but was concerned that the men should not become reckless. He had not given them any effective brakes neither had he prepared any signalling worthy of the name. He interviewed Driver Hill, explained his concern about safety and then refunded the ten shillings docked from his pay by the Directors.

Isambard's Bristol & Exeter and Great Western Railways, in 1842, were the fastest in the world, with speeds of 50 mph a commonplace. This was due mainly to the excellence of Daniel Gooch's standardised 'Star'- and 'Firefly'-class engines but also to the splendid track and track-bed engineered by Isambard. When Isambard travelled in a Great Western train he did not – as modern advertising suggests – 'let the train take the strain' and relax from his labours for an hour or so, but became a 'carriage-riding Inspector' and rode in each carriage, changing from one to the next along the outside footboards while the train was in motion. If he found any defect he would have the carriage removed for attention. The railway was, without doubt, the fastest but unfortunately the riding of the carriages at high speed left much to be desired. He had designed his long wheel-base, six-wheel coaches specifically to run without oscillation, but they were subject to severe lateral movements at speed, accompanied by what Isambard described to Charles Saunders on 5 August 1842 as 'that dreadful thumping of the wheels when going fast'.

Isambard made every effort to discover the cause of this defect. At stations he was frequently observed crawling about under the carriages as he searched. He took four years to find it and in the same letter to Saunders added: 'After a great deal of trouble and very close examination I have discovered the cause – an inequality in the thickness of the tyre which throws the wheel out of balance.' These days when car wheels are balanced routinely when new tyres are fitted we are familiar with this problem, but it was new to him.

Isambard also discovered at this point that the lateral movement 'which has quite shaken our carriages to pieces' was caused by the journals of axles having worn longer while their brass bearings were up to an inch too short so that the journal could move laterally within the bearing. 'No mechanical would have done that,' Isambard told Saunders. He went on to say that 'the railway carriage requires engineering superintendence as much as locomotives'. The carriages were built by stage-coach builders and were operated on the GWR under the superintendence of the Clarke brothers, Seymour and Frederick, both very intelligent men but neither of them with a single day's experience in a workshop.

Isambard recommended on 5 August 1842:

all wheels, axles, springs, oil boxes, buffers, heavy iron-work and bolts should be made (or examined, if delivered under contract) at Swindon. I have seen carriages get repaired first at one end [of the line] and then the other and have seen contradictory remedies – what the physicians call 'incompatible medicines' applied. They get terribly patched up and a great deal of work is expended and not very profitably.

So the Carriage & Wagon Department of the GWR, at Swindon, came into being.

As the railway increased in size and complexity Isambard did his best to retain total control over all departments. A less obsessive man would have been glad to hand over some of his responsibilities to a co-equal engineer – such as Gooch – but Isambard regarded the GWR as his own creation and the basis of his high standing with the public, and strongly disapproved of Gooch's growing 'empire'. He felt the need to keep him in check not only because he was a rival for power within the organisation but because he often behaved in an un-Brunellian – and therefore 'ungentlemanly' – manner.

There was the great 'pupil controversy'. Isambard took on a very few pupils each of whom paid a fee for the privilege. These boys were given no formal instruction but had to learn from what experience they could gather by making themselves useful. When they did some useful work Isambard paid them something from his own pocket.

He never 'charged them to the Company'. On 4 September 1842 he noticed his pupil Dazely riding on Company's service in a 1st class carriage with another lad who appeared to be out for a free ride. On inquiring, Isambard discovered that the stranger was one of several of Gooch's pupils, riding for pleasure on a pass issued by Gooch. Isambard was appalled. Not only was the lad 'idling' he was issued with a free ticket *and* he was 'charged to the Company' – that is, was in receipt of GWR wages.

On 5 September Isambard wrote a long letter to Gooch, rebuking him for acting 'improperly' and putting him firmly in his place as a subordinate. He had taken on fee-paying pupils without Isambard's permission, he had then paid them wages from GWR funds and he had issued free passes for them to idle their time away. Furthermore, Gooch had recently given a free pass to Captain W.S. Moorsom and his entire family:

> This is contrary to the regulations and if these irregularities came to the notice of the Directors there would be an expression of their opinions very disagreeable to you. In future, remember that you have no authority to give passes except to forward workmen along the line.

Erection of an engine house and repair shops began at Swindon in 1841, the buildings designed under Isambard's direction with Gooch's advice as to the most convenient internal layout to adopt. Where staffing and machinery were concerned Gooch made his own decisions. He gave pay rises and ordered machinery, including a fire engine for workshops without reference to Isambard. However, Gooch did not ensure that his purchases were entered in the 'Acquisitions' ledger. Isambard discovered this, was suspicious of the motives behind such slackness, and on 9 December 1842 wrote to Gooch 'in the most positive and earnest manner' to 'insist upon every regulation being carried out to the fullest extent. Let it be clearly understood that no expense shall be incurred without a written order from me. No cheques for any expense irregularly incurred after this date will be paid. I shall request Mr Saunders to have no accounts paid *except from my signature.*'

Isambard often found Gooch's money-making schemes distasteful, none more so than the matter of the colliery. In 1854 Gooch recommended that the GWR Directors buy Gyfeillon colliery as a supply of locomotive fuel. This was done and Gooch was put in charge of the operation which enabled him to sell coal to himself – as the contractor, with his partners Evans and Geach – for the supply of fuel to the South Devon Railway. He then had built for himself a steam-powered barge which he placed in the nominal ownership of his friend William Minet. This barge Gooch then hired to himself, as colliery operator, to carry coal across the Bristol Channel to the South Devon Railway to feed his coke ovens there.

In 1856 the Directors of the GWR, concerned at the lack of mineral traffic, asked Gooch to buy a colliery near Ruabon. They promised that if Gooch put the entire output on GWR rails the Company would give him a cheap rate. Thus Gooch became a colliery owner and a privileged customer of the GWR whilst acting as their employee. Isambard was disgusted by all this and wrote to Gooch with some bitterness: 'I entirely disapprove of it but as I shall not be consulted I shall not have the opportunity to express my opinion. I cannot believe that public opinion will sanction the anomaly of an Officer of the Company engaged in a trade which depends upon acts of the Company.'

It is noteworthy that by this time Isambard was no longer privy to all the Company's deliberations as had once been the case.

In spite of Gooch's very special relationship with the Directors Isambard did his best to keep the Locomotive Superintendent under his control, and Gooch was obliged to ask Isambard's permission when he wanted to give any of his own men a pay rise. Isambard agreed to an increase for Archibald Sturrock, Swindon Works Manager, and then wrote him a patronising homily on his, Sturrock's, increased obligations to the Company:

I have great pleasure in recommending to the Directors the increase they have made in your salary. I need hardly say that it was at the suggestion of Mr Gooch and you owe it to him, to the Directors and to myself to exert yourself in the best possible manner. Do not think that I think it necessary to remind you of any such obligation but the responsibilities of your duties are very serious and I felt that to pass over so natural an occasion for remarking on them would be to make light of a serious subject. I believe and trust that you will continue to feel it a pleasure to devote your best exertions to the cause we are all embarked in.

That Isambard could adopt such a condescending tone toward a first-class locomotive engineer and a colleague is evidence of a strong streak of arrogance in his nature. Sturrock was then thirty and went on to become Locomotive Superintendent of the Great Northern Railway. No matter how brilliantly capable Sturrock was, to Isambard he was a servant, admittedly a superior one, but subject nonetheless to Isambard's dictate.

14

Wrath and Pettifoggery

On 14 March 1839 the London Committee approved Brunel's drawings for Reading station. What he had planned is not known but when, on 11 April, the Committee saw the estimated cost of the place they scrapped the drawings and sent warnings to their Bristol colleagues to make a check on Isambard's proposals for architectural spending. The London Committee was very concerned to keep a tight control of costs in general, and it had to keep a hard rein on Isambard in particular. Thus, the station buildings actually erected at Reading, and opened to the public on 30 March 1840, were cheap and ugly – Isambard's revenge, one cannot help thinking, on parsimony.

Isambard's technique of designing anything was to make sketches in his 10 × 8 in. book of lined, squared paper. He drew, crossed out, and drew again until he had what he wanted and this he gave to an assistant to work into a plan which was then returned to Isambard for his criticisms and alterations. Eventually a full set of plans could be engraved on a steel plate and printed for the use of the contractor who would erect the building. An example of how Isambard worked with and directed an architectural assistant is contained in a letter he wrote to William Westmacott on 2 April 1839. It concerns proposed buildings for Bristol Temple Meads station:

> No 1 is exactly what I wanted and I think will make a very pretty elevation. I should like to see the turrets less heavy at the top so as not to form so striking a part of the architecture – more as I have sketched the right-hand one. With this slight alteration I would like to see it worked out in a little more detail. I should wish the two towers to differ as much as

they do in the sketch, the left-hand one being by far the most important
. . . I should like to try also the effect of a general elevation in which the
north entrance 'A' of the GWR and the entrance 'B' of the Exeter Railway
would be the principal features connected by a range of buildings broken
by archway 'C'. This would be a fine range of buildings of 310 ft frontage
and the two extremities might be somewhat enriched.

The existing front of the 'Old Station' at Temple Meads and the
fireplaces within are a joint production of Brunel and Westmacott.

Isambard had to make all his detailed arrangements days in
advance by letter and his daily difficulties of communication are
well illustrated by the following letter, which he wrote to Charles
Lawrence, his Resident Engineer for the Cirencester area, on 28
December 1838:

> I was at Bath last night and inquired but found no letter from you, neither
> have I found one here from you dated later than 25th. [Lawrence was
> working on Christmas Day.] I am therefore at a loss to know how best
> to meet you with the plans etc. I will send them down in the care of
> somebody by tomorrow's coach to you at Cirencester. If anything should
> prevent my sending them in the morning I will send them by the Mail and
> I will also send them to Salisbury. My clerk [John Bennett] will go to
> the White Hart at Salisbury and remain there till 5 o'clock and will then
> go to Mr Swain's house at Wilton where he lives. He will wait in Mr
> Swain's office or leave word there where he is. He shall go by my name
> and will inquire for you.

The line from Swindon to Cirencester and Cheltenham met difficulties both in financing and construction. There was a contretemps
at Purton when the contractor found he was digging through rock
where it was thought that only clay existed, thus forcing a re-
negotiation of his price. There were also great geological difficulties
at the short and long tunnels at Sapperton, in total one mile long.
Most unfortunately, the railway had to run through land at Kemble
owned by Robert Gordon – 'Squire' Gordon – who professed utter
loathing for the railway and did his utmost to prevent it passing.
Isambard despised Gordon and dismissed him as 'a man that can
be bought'. He was indeed 'bought' – for £7500, 1 per cent of the
authorised capital of the Cheltenham & Great Western Union
Railway Company. This sum was paid in respect of 'damage to be sus-
tained'. The wrangling with Gordon lasted at least two years. In fact
Gordon was never reconciled to the railway running through his land
and was able to prevent a proper station being built on it during his

lifetime, but his last objection to the line itself was removed when it was taken further away from his house than had first been planned. Where it passed directly in front of his windows – although a distance of several hundred yards – it was placed in a covered way made specifically to hide the trains from view.

What cannot be placed on an account sheet is the debilitating effect on Isambard's nervous system and physical health of working 20 hours a day – sometimes when he was ill – in order to get his rails through to Bristol or Gloucester and South Wales. Isambard 'led from the front', he never put himself above the dirt and grime of daily railway operation. On 13 June 1839, at Paddington, one of his posting carriages – the 'Extra 1st Class' – broke a spring. Isambard was nearby and at once went to make a temporary repair. According to Gibbs, this entailed 'tying up the spring' and while carrying out this rather risky procedure Isambard hurt himself sufficiently to be sent home in a cab.

He took no time off work for his birthday. The previous year, on 9 April 1838, for example, he had had to write to a contractor called Hemming, working on the Bristol & Exeter line: 'Sir, you have not paid Mr Oldham [another contractor] as you promised me you would. I obtained that engine for you upon terms and at a time when you could not, by assuring Mr Oldham of prompt payment. He now claims his cash and I must insist that you bring your cheque for £950 7s 6d to the Bristol office next Thursday.'

One week later Hemming complained to Isambard of the 'harsh treatment' he was receiving from William Gravatt, Brunel's close friend since the Thames Tunnel days. Gravatt had surveyed some of the B&ER route for Isambard and had been Resident Engineer of the Bristol to Bridgwater section from the start of works in February 1837. He attacked all problems with great vigour – including the contractors if the occasion arose. Around 15 April he had verbally attacked Hemming and the latter complained to Isambard that Gravatt had 'such a decided feeling of hostility' towards him that he did not feel safe in his hands. Hemming also wrote to John Badham, B&ER Company Secretary, asking to be relieved of his contract.

This was a serious matter – the steady progress of Isambard's great work was in jeopardy. He moved with practised skill, persuaded Hemming to withdraw his resignation, persuaded Badham not to mention Gravatt's behaviour or Hemming's letter to the Directors, and then set about re-educating Gravatt. He wrote him a lengthy letter which had all the overtones of a father instructing an erring son. (One wonders if such Brunellian letters reflect the style of those Isambard had once received from his own father.)

William Gravatt was Isambard's own age, at least his equal as a scientist and a very old friend. None of this counted when the future of the Company was at stake. Brunel's letter to Gravatt, on 15 April 1839, was not only a fairly humiliating one for the recipient, it was also an exposition of Isambard's attitude of 'enlightened self-interest' towards other people. Except for a handful of very close ones, his 'friends' were only there to be used – but used with consideration. Isambard explained his principle:

> The interests of the Company require that he [Hemming] should be handled with the *utmost tenderness* – his losses become the Company's in fact. If he is inconvenienced by orders difficult to obey, or by the lack of money . . . the Company suffers. He is the horse we have in harness and upon which we depend and whatever his vices or whatever our rights to treat him as we choose it is in our interest not to over-drive him or starve him and to be contented with his utmost – even if that falls short of that which has been contracted for. [Isambard's tone then becomes personal and bitter.]
>
> I do not think that you or your assistants have been sufficiently aware of the harassing nature of a contractor's business. The fact is – Gravatt – you and your assistants, though you might work hard, like a comfortable life of comparative irresponsibility and do not know what real anxiety is. When you have tasted one-tenth of what has been my share you will feel how essential it must be for the management of expensive contracts that the contractor should have his mind at ease and that he should be able to calculate with confidence on all payments and upon the fairness of those whose decisions govern those payments.

Having thus relieved his frustrations a little, Isambard gave lengthy instructions as to how Gravatt and his assistants were to conduct themselves in future, and ordered Gravatt to come to 18 Duke Street and to apologise to Hemming in his own presence.

The work was life and honour for Isambard and woe-betide anyone who got in the way. He would defend the lowliest clerk if necessary – the clerks were as much a part of his empire as Box Tunnel and were not to be interfered with. When a Director complained to Charles Saunders that he had seen a pair of boxing gloves hanging from the desk of a certain clerk, Saunders passed the complaint on to Brunel who replied:

I do not know why a gentlemanly and industrious young man like 'X' should have his trifling actions remarked upon unless the observer gave him credit for a much more gentle temper than that which I possess . . . if any man had taken upon himself to remark upon my having gone to the pantomime, which I always do at Christmas, no respect for Directors would have restrained me. I will do my best to keep my team in order but I cannot do it if the Master sits beside me and amuses himself by touching them up with the whip.

So far from being a potential ally of Trade Unions, Isambard was opposed to them as an interference with market forces, but he had enough sense to see that his skilled men had to be defended from the stupidities of the financiers who were the overlords of all, Isambard included. One of the most trusted and well liked of all his assistants was Michael Lane, the bricklayer from the Thames Tunnel days who, in 1838, was most ably supervising the construction of Monkwearmouth Dock. Lane's capabilities as an engineer and the clarity of his reports enabled Isambard to direct operations by letter, to be Engineer of the scheme while not going near the site for months on end. So much trust did Isambard put in Lane that it would be fair, since Isambard would never have admitted it, to say that the Monkwearmouth Dock was a Brunel/Lane construction.

Isambard brought Lane down to supervise the construction of the Bath viaducts early in 1839 but in April the Directors of the dock company asked if they could have him back. Obviously, Lane was a very valuable man. Isambard was exceedingly reluctant to let him go but felt so warmly towards him that he would not stand in the way of his advancement. In a letter to the dock company Directors he begged them to keep their promises to Lane: 'I hope any expectations of future advantage he may have formed will be as fully realised as I feel sure yours will be by his usefulness.'

The line from Reading to Steventon was opened on 1 June 1840. The Resident Engineer for the Reading/Swindon section was J.H. Gandell, an architect whose drawing office seems to have been far away at Wolverton, north of Bletchley. He was responsible for some detail design, including a bridge over the Wilts & Berks Canal west of Uffington and for the various culverts required between Reading and Swindon. He also had an influence on the architecture of the Board Room House and the Superintendent's house at Steventon, working within the general outline sketched by Brunel.

Gandell seems to have taken on the job of Resident Engineer of the Reading/Swindon section without taking on full employee status under Isambard. He worked from his independent, Wolverton, office and all correspondence to him from Isambard went there. This apparently ambiguous status led to some arguments. Isambard decided that Gandell was charging too much for his services and thought he saw the cause of this in 'over-manning' in Gandell's office. Isambard wrote on 14 April 1839, ordering Gandell to reduce his staff and in particular to sack Freeman: 'Freeman was formerly with me at Duke Street but was too expensive. You must get rid of him and reduce your establishment very considerably. The best way would be to give one month's notice to all except one draughtsman, one assistant, a clerk and a messenger, a staff holder and chairman.' Gandell was probably not a full 'servant of the Company' because he replied with some pointed remarks about tyranny!

Isambard in turn responded, on the 17th, denying this 'tyranny': 'The expression I used cannot be supposed to mean any more than exactly what I meant – that your expenditure was inadmissible. I am not disposed to cavil on terms and if I gave you pain I regret it but you are wrong in applying to me the term "too imperative". *I wish to express my very decided opinion and therefore you must not complain* of my being "too imperative" or "tyrannical".' Gandell asked if he could retain Freeman if he paid him himself but Isambard had very decided opinions about Freeman and wrote: 'As to your doing such a foolish thing as paying Freeman yourself you will oblige me very much by . . . giving him fair notice.' Isambard seems to have been determined to get rid of poor Freeman and that does seem to be tolerably tyrannical since it was Freeman's employment he objected to, not the amount of wages he received.

Isambard was very keen on 'model' housing for working people and was many years ahead of his time in this respect. He had designed or was designing such housing at many stations along the line, including 300 houses at 'New Swindon'. At Steventon a long row of workmen's cottages was built, parallel to the down line and immediately west of the station, while on the north side were a tall, Jacobean-style house to accommodate the Company board room and close-by an Elizabethan-style house, with an oversailing first floor, for the Superintendent and his family.

A letter from Brunel to Gandell dated 23 April 1840 orders him to enlarge the Superintendent's house 'because Mr Bell with a wife and a dozen children cannot live in the house *I* had proposed'. This might imply that Gandell designed the enlarged house and another letter seems to bear this out. When the plans for the Superintendent's house were finalised and lithographed, Isambard discovered that they had been printed 'left for right of the plan of the elevation *preferred by you* and it is to be built *reversed*'. Gandell resigned as Resident Engineer and architectural assistant on 11 February 1840, received a good reference from Isambard and became Contractor for the construction of the various dwellings at Steventon station whilst S.&C. Rigby built the station, goods shed and engine-house buildings.

When walking through the workshops of the Bristol locomotive constructors Stothert & Slaughter in September 1840, Isambard saw a cracked cylinder fitted to an engine destined for the Great Western. He ordered the foreman to remove the cylinder and break it to bits immediately. He then wrote a blistering letter to the Directors of Stothert & Slaughter:

> The flaw was so large that it could not escape the attention of the most careless observer . . . I do not believe that a workman would have thought of using it in the most contemptible, worst mannered shop in England – except with fraudulent intention – yet I find such a thing in that which you profess to put perfection of workmanship and materials and upon the success of which the reputation of your house depends. . . . your foremen are utterly neglectful . . . they are so grossly ignorant as to suppose that they could succeed in defrauding the Company . . . your workmen are spoilt, they have learned that they may scamp their work. All confidence on my part is completely destroyed and I should neglect my duty to the Company if I did not now withdraw the order.

Throughout 1840 he busied himself with every detail of the railway – whether of civil or mechanical engineering, or architectural design. He sketched the designs and arranged for architects and engineering assistants to finalise them, covering every detail right down to the decoration he required across the front of the 'Elizabethan' fireplaces in the Bristol and Bath stations. Not all of Isambard's architectural staff were as efficient as the 'outsider', William Westmacott. Isambard was vexed beyond endurance by one employee, called Fripp, over a period of not less than sixteen months. Fripp had allowed contractors to get away with 'scandalous workmanship' and he was late in finishing the drawings for Keynsham station. These, Isambard told him, were 'sketches, not deserving the name "drawing". I am sorry to say that I have had several occasions lately to think you negligent and lazy. You must be very much more industrious, laborious and constant, pay attention to the work and be much quicker in everything I require to be done if you wish to gain any credit in your present employment.'

Fripp drew down on his head the most furiously wrathful letters Brunel ever wrote. Throughout 1840, when Isambard was deep into designing the world's largest iron hull for the SS *Great Britain* and re-designing Francis Pettit Smith's propeller, the complaints continued. On 12 October, Isambard was seized with, apparently, a fit of teeth-grinding rage. He must have written in the white heat of his anger. He did not even start with the usual greeting but wrote merely:

> Fripp, Plain gentlemanly language seems to have no effect upon you. I must try stronger language and stronger methods. You are a cursed, lazy, inattentive, apathetic vagabond and if you continue to neglect my instructions I shall send you about your business. I have frequently told you, amongst other absurd, untidy habits, that of making drawings on the backs of others is inconvenient. By your cursed neglect of that you have wasted more of my time than your whole life is worth. Looking for the altered drawings you were to make of several things at the station and which I have just found – they won't do. I must see you on Wednesday. Let me have no more of this provoking conduct or of the abominable and criminal laziness with which you suffer contractors to patch and scamp their work.

Several months later the luckless Fripp was *still* infuriating Isambard. On 21 April 1841, nearly eight months after Bath station had opened, Isambard wrote another 'Fripp' letter:

> A long time ago I gave you instructions respecting certain details in the rooms at Bath station. Notwithstanding this I have to attend to every detail myself. I am heartily sick of employing you to do anything that, if I had ten minutes to spare, I would do myself. If you go over to Bath on Friday and can be ready with the outlines of the finished rooms you may still save me some trouble – if you wish to do so. If not *pray keep out of my way or I will certainly do you a mischief* you have tried my patience so completely.

Isambard was apparently threatening to hit him – but yet not dismiss him. The tone of all the 'Fripp' letters is one of such exasperation that I wonder whether Isambard was *unable* to dismiss him. The name Fripp was very powerful in Bristol. There were two Fripps on the City Council: William Fripp, an anti-Papist Tory, and C.B. Fripp, a Liberal, who was a Director of both the B&ER and the GWR – with special responsibility for architecture. Something seems to have shielded the idle Fripp from Brunel's usual retribution – dismissal.

Isambard's long-running dispute with the contractors McIntosh came to a crisis in 1840. Hugh and David McIntosh had done a lot to help Brunel out of difficult situations by taking on extra work when they did not really need it. His treatment of them was more than a little ungrateful. The arguments over payments dated back to 1837 and by 1840 £100,000 was contested and withheld. In a letter to George Frere in May 1840, Isambard remarked that he and Frere both knew that McIntosh was carrying out masonry work 'at a losing price'. This must have been the coursed rubble work in which Isambard forced such a high standard that it came out as ashlar. It must be said that he did increase some prices that he thought were too low but the price reductions far outweighed the increases. He took the McIntoshes' bills for work done and simply re-wrote them – downwards.

In answering complaints Isambard employed all the 'stone-walling' tactics so dear to those who owe money and are determined not to pay. Letters from McIntosh were not answered from one month to the next and of all the people who had to deal with Isambard, David McIntosh was the only one – as far as existing records show – who had difficulty in arranging face-to-face meetings. On 22 January 1840 he wrote to Isambard: 'I regret I am not to see you this evening as you proposed or I might have heard from you the grounds on which you require I should yield my claim to be paid for the ballasting of the embankment in 3B under a contract already existing.'

The capable Scotsman was not to be disarmed by Isambard's charm, or by his abuse of the archaic legal system of the day. McIntosh pursued his rights vigorously and there can be no doubt that Isambard found this attitude most distasteful. The ramifications are complicated but a flavour of the proceedings may be given. When the Directors inquired why it was taking so long for McIntosh to sign a contract, Isambard replied that McIntosh was 'hanging back' and implied some ulterior motive. When David McIntosh learned of this he wrote a sharp, Brunellian-sarcastic note to Isambard on 22 January 1840:

> I am amused with your offer of £100 payment for the certificate [for work satisfactorily completed] on 2B. I am told by the gentleman from the Company's office in Bristol that it should be £145 19s 8d which is in any case unsatisfactory to me and I can assure you this and other similar

certificates are much more likely to account for my want of confidence and my 'hanging back' than anything that the Directors can charge me with. . . . I am confident that I am acting . . . with a liberality of feeling . . . which I do not experience in return. If 'hanging back' is to be a test of ill will let the Directors know the state of my account [Isambard's non-payment of monies owed] for *there* is the 'hanging back'. . . . As it is the usual custom with the Great Western Railway to say something to the prejudice of the parties written to, I thought it as well to follow your own people's precedent.

Isambard had reduced the 'bottom line' on Contract 9L by about £2500 to £10,000 – and then refused to pay even that. Isambard told the GWR's Solicitor, Stevens, on 21 July 1840, 'when he pressed me to make a certificate for payment on 9L, I pressed him for the accounts of 3L'. Isambard was obsessed by this linking of two completely separate contracts – he had made up his mind that this was the way he wanted to do it and nothing could move him. Hugh McIntosh protested that 3L was nothing to do with him, that his son had taken on that work under his own name and that Isambard should settle the 9L account without delay. Isambard simply reiterated his demand – to settle both accounts together – and in the meantime he settled neither.

Hugh also complained that Isambard and the Company were refusing to return the bond of £2000 which he had deposited with the Company as security for the successful completion of 9L. Hugh had written to Isambard for the return of £2000 on 25 May 1840 and was informed by Isambard that 'there was no objection to the money being paid and it would be paid on Thursday'. But when, on the following Thursday, McIntosh applied to Charles Saunders for the money he was told that no certificate had been forwarded neither had Isambard expressed any wish that it should be paid. Saunders also told McIntosh that the GWR Board had issued a Minute ordering Isambard not to advance any more money, on account, to him.

Hugh McIntosh was doubly alarmed. First, the £2000 was not 'an advance on account' but money belonging to him and due to him under the terms of the contract. Secondly, if the Directors of the GWR could issue orders to Isambard regarding issues of money to McIntosh then Isambard was not a free and independent arbitrator between the parties but an agent of the Great Western Company. In fact the Directors' Minute was an infringement of the contract between them and Hugh McIntosh.

David McIntosh managed to obtain an interview with Isambard on 3 June 1840 at 9 a.m. He asked Brunel to authorise payments for work performed as long ago as 1837 as well as on 9L and to return his father's £2000 bond. Isambard trotted out the same old prevarication: 'You send me the account for 3L and I will pay that along with 9L.'

On 30 June, after research into the accounts and correspondence, Hugh wrote to Isambard giving a résumé of the sorry tale up to that time and concluded:

> We have arrived at the position: The Directors hold themselves as superior to your decisions and you are therefore not a free agent . . . unable to proceed as an Arbitrator and I am driven to the necessity of acting upon the clause of reference in the contract and I name as my referee to meet you upon the account now delivered Mr George Leather of Leeds, civil engineer. May I therefore beg that you will at your earliest convenience make arrangements with him for the speedy termination of these long-standing matters?

To this Isambard replied, the same day, with a short note saying it was all a misunderstanding: 'Mr David McIntosh must have misunderstood and unintentionally misrepresented what passed between us.' He arrogantly dismissed the main and very important point of the letter – to arrange for arbitration – with this: 'As to the latter part of your letter referring to an arbitration, I have not time this morning to reply to you on the subject.' Isambard was well aware, at that time, that Hugh McIntosh was blind and suffering considerably from ill-health because he wrote as much to the GWR's solicitor, Stevens.

Six weeks elapsed before Isambard found time to reply to McIntosh but on 11 July he took time to write to Stevens. Isambard admitted that Hugh McIntosh was owed money on 9L but said that he was withholding payment 'until the account for 3L "the next contiguous contract" is presented'. Isambard then wrote this: 'He has never advanced the argument that they were different contracts and it has never occurred to me.' The first half of that was untrue and the last part would have been an admission of amazing stupidity had it been true. Isambard concluded his letter to Stevens by admitting that he had not been keeping the Directors informed about the McIntosh affair and asking for advice on how to act.

Stevens replied on 24 July. First he assured Isambard that 'In all matters relating to the Contract you are independent of the

Company. It was agreed between Mr Hugh McIntosh and the Company that it should be so,' but then he warned Isambard that 'Mr McIntosh's accounts cannot be mixed up with the accounts of his son.' Stevens suggested that he examine the accounts to see if the matters in dispute came within Isambard's arbitration. All disputed items should, he said, be removed and placed in a separate account and if, on balancing this fresh account, there was found to be a balance in favour of Hugh McIntosh 'he will be entitled to receive it . . . and the Company will be bound by your decision.'

Having received this eminently fair advice, Isambard took no further action for several weeks. He was at this time under tremendous pressure. The line was opening in successive stages – from Reading to Steventon on 1 June and on to Faringdon Road on 20 July, with the Bristol to Bath opening set for August and a vast amount of earthwork – and the Box Tunnel – in between. The unhappy McIntoshes, who had done so much to realise these triumphs of Isambard's designing genius, could safely be ignored with plenty of plausible excuses. On 30 July a short note from Hugh McIntosh, 'desiring a reply to my letter of 30 June' ended with the following furiously frustrated stab: 'If it is your intention to avoid any direct answer, it might be as well to say so.'

It was not until 12 August, two weeks before the Bath/Bristol opening that Isambard replied to Hugh McIntosh's letters of 25 May and 30 June. He expressed regret at the delay, due to his 'very pressing engagements', reassured McIntosh that he was empowered to act as Arbitrator and insisted that he wanted to settle the account of 9L – but only when he had seen the accounts of 3L. 'I have repeatedly urged Mr D. McIntosh to send me the accounts for 3L,' he wrote imperiously, 'as there was a very similar question to be settled in both contracts and I desired to go into both at the same time. I have never yet received these accounts and at our last meeting I again urged him and expressed my surprise at his appearing to withhold these accounts and stated that I *expected them to be sent in before I finally closed the account of 9L.*'

With his certainty of his own infallibility, coupled to his vested interest in keeping down the Company's costs, he was a most unsuitable person to act as Arbitrator. Isambard believed he was in an impregnable position. His letter had the tone of sweet reasonableness but it was in fact pig-headed and stubborn. He was out to get his own way – and that as cheaply as possible. He was acting unreasonably, for while he accepted Stevens's advice that legally he was the Arbitrator between McIntosh and the Company, he ignored his solicitor's advice regarding the improper mixing up the affairs of separate individuals.

On 14 August Hugh McIntosh wrote to say that he could not believe that he was under any misapprehension as regards Isambard's intentions and pointed out that, on 25 May, Isambard had written to say that the bond of £2000 would be returned – 'and up to the present hour I have not received the money'. From this fact Hugh McIntosh concluded that 'the Company have evidently disputed your right [to arbitrate] and hold themselves superior to your decisions'.

Turning to the question of the money owed on contract 9L McIntosh wrote:

> It appeared after your investigation that a sum of £10,000 is due to me which you will not certify, alleging as the ground for refusal, the non-delivery of another, independent account arising out of another contract. This cannot be for a good or friendly purpose but rather, if I may infer from your bearing towards me through your Agents, this reservation was for the purpose of intimidation upon the investigation of further accounts. As for going into the account, already item by item investigated by you, it would surely not be business. I assure you I would most gladly alter my opinions as you require but before I do so the facts must be altered to justify the change.

Five weeks later, on 22 September, Isambard replied to McIntosh's long letter, full of very precise complaints and demands, with the same prevarication – to send the accounts of 3L before those of 9L could be settled. But by that time, blind Hugh McIntosh was dead.

His argument with Isambard and the GWR was taken up by his executor, the lawyer Timothy Tyrell, who bombarded him with requests for payment and was met by silence. On 24 December 1840 Tyrell wrote to Saunders: 'Will you favour me with the determination of the Board as to my letter? I am very unwilling to construe their silence as the same want of courtesy I have experienced from their Engineer.' On 19 November 1841, Tyrell was obliged to declare full-scale, legal war with the following note to Brunel:

> Sir, Not having had any reply to my letter on Contracts 3L and 9L I am now obliged to treat your silence as a refusal to do that which the Great Western Railway by their several contracts requires should be done by you to enable my client, the Executors of Mr Hugh McIntosh, to proceed against them at Law. I will not trust myself to comment on

the fact of a great Company ordering their Agent to withhold the means whereby to try in a Court of Law a Contractor's right to be paid for his work . . . this must be left to Counsel.

Tyrell could not resist the luxury of telling Isambard what he thought of him and on 22 November wrote him a very angry letter. Curiously enough, Isambard was able to reply at once to Tyrell's letter, using the language of lofty innocence. Faced with anger, Isambard would assume an aspect of angelic righteousness which must have infuriated his opponent:

> I should prefer doing no more than acknowledging the receipt of such undignified effusions which surprise me in a man of your professional standing – presumptions as to the causes that might possibly influence my conduct, guess at my motives – appears to me in the form of exclamations which do not admit of a reply and I notice them now merely because it forms a style of correspondence so unusual that I fear what interpretation might be placed upon the silence which I should otherwise wish to observe.

Isambard stalled with a stubbornness that would have delighted the hearts of those expert exponents of pettifoggery and procrastination – the Whitehall bureaucrats and Admiralty officials – and he, Tyrell and David McIntosh were all dead by the time justice had been done. On 28 June 1865 the Vice-Chancellor of England ordered the GWR to pay the McIntosh estate £100,000 with 20 years' accrued interest and also to pay costs. This final reckoning came when the GWR was financially embarrassed and less than one year before they were pushed to the brink of bankruptcy by the failure of their banker Overend, Gurney. This then was the case which the Company's official historian, E.T. MacDermot brushed off with a joke about 'Jarndyce and Jarndyce'.

At Box Tunnel, George Burge laboured under a similar dictatorship to that suffered by the McIntoshes. One ton each of gunpowder and of candles were consumed each week while 1200 men hacked the rock and 100 horses dragged away the spoil. Steam-powered fans did their little best to draw off the sulphurous fumes of the explosive and underpowered pumps struggled to prevent the workings from flooding. The work went on sometimes rapidly by day and night, sometimes slowly and sometimes not at all. The crucial factor was the contractor – not only his financial ability to press the work forward but his engineering skill, his skill as a manager and his sheer strength of mind to press the enormously heavy work onwards, year after year.

The delays caused by flooding, unexpected quicksands and extra-hard rock, prevented Burge from making progress at the rate laid down by his contract – which rate could have been no more than guesswork anyhow when the contract was drawn up – but unless the contracted progress, measured fortnightly, was made Isambard withheld payment. William Glennie was responsible for measuring the completed work, there were endless arguments as to the accuracy of Glennie's measurements, and meanwhile Isambard would pay only what he decided was right – he was the Arbitrator.

Burge and his navvies struggled through another winter of bitter cold in that dank, dripping man-made cave, reeking with the fumes of gunpowder, but they could not make progress at the contracted rate so Isambard was still refusing to certify payment while fulminating at the delay. On 2 April he wrote his most angry letter, beginning with a curt 'Sir' and including many choice lines of abuse of which this is the most splenetic: 'While you are wasting so much valuable time at shaft No 6 in a bungling attempt to make the present machinery do that for which it is totally unfit, you are neglecting to drive the heading between shafts 5 and 6 which would have shown some intention of providing against similar difficulties next winter. Whilst such a lack of management continues I shall not recommend to the Directors any further payment.'

Isambard did not, it will be noticed, dismiss the man he accused of bungling mismanagement, and in the end he had to speed the work in the only possible way – by paying the rate for the job including bonuses for extra rapid work to the foremen and their gangs. Burge patiently bore the insults and he and his navvies struggled on. Early in 1841, Isambard persuaded Burge to throw in every hand and hoof he could muster and 4000 men with 300 horses are reported to have taken part in the great 'battle' to finish the tunnel for an August opening – and 'battle' it was, for at least 100 men died at work there during the five years of construction. The huge hole was finally hacked through the ridge in March or April 1841.

Before leaving the subject of Box Tunnel, a well-known myth should be corrected. The legend is that on 9 April, Brunel's birthday, an observer on the track, looking through the tunnel from the west end, would see the sun rise and fill the bore as it cleared the horizon and long before it cleared the top of Box Hill. This is not true.

In the four years from 1832 to 1836 the rising sun missed passing across the tunnel mouth on Brunel's birthday by a minimum of 24 minutes of arc in 1835 and a maximum of 41 minutes in 1832 and 1836. The sun's track varies in a four-year cycle and its declination has to be less than 6 degrees 54 minutes to cross the tunnel bore. The data necessary to make the 'birthday' alignment was available in the nautical almanacs of his time and he could have made it if he had wanted to. But his fame would be decided by the degree of perfection with which he planned the whole railway, not by astronomical gimmick, to achieve which would have spoiled the otherwise straight approaches to the tunnel. The rising sun and the tunnel mouth coincide only on 6/7 April and 5/6 September. The disc of the sun covered the bore at 6.35 a.m. on 6 April 1996 and this will be repeated at the same time and date in the year 2000.

On Monday 31 May 1841, Sir Frederick Smith inspected and passed as safe for public use the line from Hay Lane (3 miles west of Swindon) to Chippenham and from Swindon to Cirencester, although Chippenham and Swindon stations were no more than platforms at that stage and passengers were coming and going in their thousands through a building site. The Great Western was short of cash, and the cost of the line was rising towards three times Isambard's original estimate, so the contractor, Rigby, who was building all the stations from Steventon to Corsham, was persuaded to build, to Isambard's design, Swindon station and the workmen's 'model' village of New Swindon at his own expense. In return he was to get the rents from the cottages and a 99-year lease on the refreshment rooms at the station. The GWR agreed to stop every train for 10 minutes for this purpose – the trains would have to stop for at least that length of time in any case to change engines and to off-load and re-load luggage and passengers – but in the future this became a great bar to the GWR's progress.

The Bristol to Bridgwater section of Isambard's Bristol & Exeter line, with William Gravatt as Resident Engineer, was opened on 14 June 1841, and it was announced that the Bath to Chippenham section of the GWR would open on the 30th. Sir Frederick Smith inspected the section on the 28th but found so many details incomplete that it took Isambard's personal guarantee that the line would be worked with every precaution to persuade the Inspector to allow the opening as advertised.

There was no public ceremony for the opening, throughout, of rail communication between London and Bridgwater on 30 June 1841. The first train through Box Tunnel that day was an 'inspection special', hauled by *Meridan*, driven by Cuthbert Davison with Brunel on the footplate. Half a mile inside the candle-lit Box Tunnel they were stopped by navvies – the up line track was incomplete. Isambard promptly organised a crew and in the flickering light they slewed the up track into the down and created a set of points. The first public train was the 7 a.m. from Bristol. The first down train to pass through was the 8 a.m. from Paddington carrying the Directors and their friends. When they reached Bridgwater they had travelled 151 miles in $5\frac{1}{2}$ hours, in relative comfort, a distance which would have taken 15 or 20 hours of bone-shaking misery in a stage coach. After the earlier success of his SS *Great Western*, the first of Isambard's dreams had come true, the finest piece of railway engineering in Britain was complete – well, almost – at a cost of £6,282,000, $2\frac{1}{2}$ times his original estimate.

III

Bridges and Ships

15

Isambard's Bridges

Isambard was at his most resourceful as a builder of bridges. He had been concerned with what became known as the Hungerford Suspension Bridge as far back as 1835. On Boxing Night that year he had written of this, in his diary: 'I have condescended to be Engineer to this but I shan't give myself much trouble about it. If done, however, it all adds to my stock of irons.' It was a strange attitude to adopt. Granted, it was only a footbridge, a description which on paper does not conjure up the glamour of a major engineering work, but it was to span the wide Thames in the middle of London and would make life easier for tens of thousands of Londoners, many of whom would surely give silent thanks daily to the designer. If that did not make him a 'household word' nothing would.

He began to design it in 1841, in the midst of all his difficulties with Box Tunnel and the opening of the GWR and B&ER. The mathematical calculations were a matter of logic and probably the easiest part; the most difficult problems arose from the unpredictability of human nature – the never-ending problems of raising funds, the weaknesses of contractors, his assistants and the Board of Directors, which on this occasion included his brother-in-law Ben Hawes. The contractor for the construction of the bridge was William Chadwick who had successfully realised Isambard's superb bridge at Maidenhead, but on the Hungerford Bridge Chadwick was far behind schedule and on 22 February 1845 Isambard resorted to threats and bluff to encourage him to get on with the job:

The Directors have determined upon opening the bridge on Easter Monday [24 March; in fact no opening date had been considered] and I am determined that they shall not be disappointed. All the works must proceed much – very much – faster and unless every part is pushed on vigorously I shall take the work into my own hands. . . . I am determined to have the bridge ready for the 22nd [March] and I shall hold you responsible for any expenses I may be driven to incur in completing the works which is *so much behind* the contract time.

Chadwick replied the same day, promising that he would complete the bridge by '24th of next month'. On 24 February Isambard wrote to the Board of Directors an optimistic note which began: 'The time is, I am happy to say, now arrived when I can report to you that the works of the bridge are in that state that *admits of the fixing* of the day of opening to the public.' On 1 March 1845 Isambard reminded Chadwick of his promise with one of his 'stern yet friendly' notes: 'You can push work as well as any man when you choose and I will once again trust in you to do so. Pray do not disappoint me. I shall be watching each day's progress.' Considering the several other heavy and complicated works Isambard was directing, this last was a rather empty threat and Isambard was indeed disappointed. The bridge was opened on 1 May 1845.

There was no need for Isambard to feel condescending towards it. There were three spans, two side-spans each of 343 ft and a central span of 676 ft. Two piers rose out of the river. They were of brick and were based on foundations covering a large area so as to spread the load widely and avoid undue settlement. From each pier rose four solid brick pillars, 7 ft 3 in. square to a height of about 55 ft. Isambard designed a light, brick filling to join the pillars and piercing these with round-headed 'windows' created the effect of Italian campaniles with tiled roofs.

Through the towers were threaded the suspension chains. So that the two river towers would not be affected by any horizontal pull from the chains and that only a vertical pressure could come upon them from the movement of the chains under load, Isambard laid the chains over a saddle resting on rollers running on a flat, cast-iron bed, a device he – or his father – had designed for the Clifton Bridge. At each of the land abutments the chains passed over a fixed saddle, down to achorages below ground. Isambard designed the disposition of the brickwork in the land towers so that it would resist the horizontal thrust from the chains.

There were four chains, two on each side one above the other. Isambard spent considerable time on experiments to find the best shape for his links so that they would have no weakness at any particular spot. Each link was 24 ft long and 7 in. deep, with a hole (or 'eye') at each end through which passed a 'pin' to join it to the next. The thickness of each link varied according to the strain that would be placed upon it; those links nearest the centre being thinner than those at the towers, thus economising the use of metal and making the bridge as light as possible.

Like almost all his bridges the Hungerford was a great success. At 11 a.m. on 1 May, 200 engineers and other specialists were ushered on to it for a tour of inspection and from noon until dusk 25,000 people paid their halfpenny toll and gave the bridge a rigorous load-testing by standing in hundreds on the central span, enjoying the view.

A year later Isambard still had not been paid for this splendid bridge and he wrote angrily to his brother-in-law:

My Dear Hawes, I do not understand why the Hungerford Suspension Bridge Company don't pay me what they owe me. If they have asked me 'in prima paupers' to give them time, I might, but a company paying 8% has no more right to defer their just debt to me than I have to my tradesmen. Money is worth 4% to me and I have lost £60 or £80 already and, joking apart, I cannot consent to losing any more. I will lend it to the company, if they like, for a 12-month at 4% and I beg to offer it to them.

The Bristol & Exeter Railway was opened from Bridgwater across swampy King's Sedgemoor to Taunton on 1 July 1842. Although the distance was barely 11¼ miles and the land was practically level throughout, Isambard had been faced with two difficult problems – the crossing of the tidal River Parrett about a mile south of Bridgwater station, and the crossing of the Chard Canal a short distance west of the village of Creech St Michael.

The bridge over the River Parrett was begun in 1838 under the Resident Engineer, William Gravatt, and was completed in 1841. It was founded in the soft, alluvial mud of Sedgemoor and here, for once most surprisingly, Isambard miscalculated a bridge. He designed a single, brick arch of 100-ft span yet, because the railway was so close to the ground, the rise of the arch, from its springing at the abutment to its crown, could be only 12 ft. Had he approached the crossing on rising embankments he could have built an arch with a better shape but he did not want to forgo his perfectly level track and thus built his 'flattest' arch. The result was that the out-thrust from the arch gradually shifted the abutments in the soft ground.

This really was a case of the wooden centering holding up the arch and a great local outcry ensued because the scaffolding was obstructing navigation. The centering remained in place until the end of 1843 when the masonry arch was dismantled and another composed of several ribs of laminated timber was erected. All that work was done without interfering with the train service. The relatively light timber had no ill effect on the abutments and the bridge remained in use until 1904.

The B&ER followed closely the course of the Bridgwater & Taunton Canal but found the branch canal to Chard directly across its path at Creech. Here, Isambard was forced to give up his perfectly level track to burrow at 1 in 300 under the waterway. A brick invert or trough was constructed, 660 yds long, to take the railway, while the canal crossed above the tracks, at right angles, through an aqueduct.

Early in 1844 he became Engineer of the broad-gauge South Wales Railway (the Welsh extension of the GWR envisaged by Isambard in 1834–5). The SWR, authorised by Parliament in 1845, was 211 miles long, almost twice as long as the original GWR main line which had cost nearly £6$\frac{1}{2}$ m., yet Isambard estimated that only £2,800,000 was required to build it, including a 1$\frac{1}{2}$-mile ship canal, five swing-bridges, several tunnels, large viaducts, the 600-ft Wye Bridge at Chepstow and a new harbour on Fishguard Bay. GWR trains from Swindon joined the Bristol & Gloucester Railway at Standish Junction, on the east side of the Severn, 7 miles south of Gloucester. The cheapest and most obvious course would have been to make the SWR an extension of the GWR from Gloucester, crossing the Severn by an ordinary bridge, but Isambard objected to the detour up to Gloucester and proposed to build a new station at Standish and a very expensive branch line from there to the far side of the Severn. This line would have crossed the Berkeley Canal by a swing-bridge and would have bridged the 1100-yds-wide Severn on a high bridge at Hock Cliff just south of the Arlingham peninsula.

The Admiralty objected to a bridge over the Severn at that spot, even though the Berkeley Canal enabled shipping to reach Gloucester docks without using the river at Hock Cliff, so Isambard proposed another canal, $1\frac{1}{2}$ miles long, through the isthmus of the Arlingham peninsula, and proposed to carry the railway across this by yet another swing-bridge. All this expense to save the detour through Gloucester! Having crossed the river, the line would then go via Chepstow, Cardiff, Swansea and Carmarthen to Goodwick, connecting there with a steam ferry service to Waterford. From Waterford, railways engineered by Isambard would fan out to Cork and Dublin.

I wonder why Isambard made such an obvious under-estimation of the cost and why everyone concerned was happy to accept it. Lack of finance could lead only to difficulties later. Admiralty opposition to the Hock Cliff Bridge over the Severn forced Isambard to start the SWR from Gloucester, which must have saved £200,000, but the SWR was still under-capitalised.

On the South Devon and on the South Wales Railways Isambard made considerable use of timber for his viaducts, developing techniques used at Sonning and on the Swindon/Gloucester line. By using timber he constructed bridges quickly and cheaply when money was limited. Against this it might be said that he bequeathed an expensive programme of renewals to later years, but his reasoning was that they were pioneer bridges, to enable the new railways to operate as quickly as possible. The bridges could be replaced later, after the company had started to earn money.

There were nine timber viaducts on the 7 miles between Frampton and Stroud, all carrying a double-track broad-gauge railway. Two of them had particularly wide spans: the Bourne Viaduct, built in 1842 over the Stroudwater Canal, had a 66-ft span and the St Mary's a 74-ft. There were six masonry piers, three on each side of the water, and from each of these rose, at a shallow angle, a heavy timber beam, meeting its fellow, end-on, at the centre of the span about 3 ft above the rails. Wrought-iron tie-rods passed across the water, from one pier to the other, to complete the triangulation.

The horizontal beams carrying the track were supported by these beams, which were 'in compression' and acted as an arch or 'King Truss'. Below the horizontal beams was the additional bracing of a 'Queen Truss'. The Stroud Valley bridges lasted not less than twenty-seven years and some much longer, so the railway company obtained excellent value from Isambard's design.

The South Devon viaducts of 1846 consisted of masonry piers 8 ft square at the base, 6 ft square at rail level, which supported the

KING TRUSS

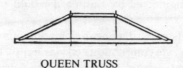

QUEEN TRUSS

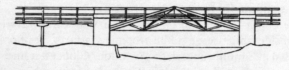

Bourne Viaduct

horizontal timbers carrying the rails. There were five large viaducts built on this plan, at Glaze, Bittaford, Blatchford, Slade, and the largest of all at Ivybridge. This had eleven spans each of 61 ft and carried the rails 104 ft above the valley floor. All these were built for the light loads of the atmospheric system and the horizontal bearers were sufficiently supported by struts socketed into the masonry piers. Before locomotives could run over them, all the viaducts had to be strengthened by the addition of a 'Queen Trussed' timber parapet. Isambard built an identical span at Bristol and tested it to destruction before erecting the design on the viaducts. Thus strengthened, the spans lasted twenty years until the increasing weight of locomotives and the cost of maintenance obliged the Engineer to introduce wrought-iron girders across the spans, hidden within the Brunellian timbers.

Isambard moved from the design of the Stroud Valley viaducts of 1842 to the South Devon and Italian viaducts of 1847–8 and in 1848–9 to the problems posed by deep valleys and wide river estuaries on the South Wales Railway at Chepstow, Newport and Landore. Here again he designed timber viaducts and it is interesting to recall that he also proposed such a bridge across the Tamar at Saltash. The

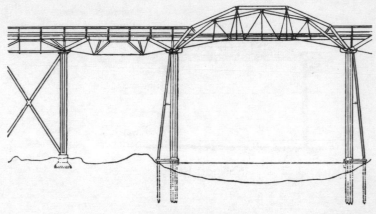

Landore Viaduct

greatest of these timber viaducts were the ones over the River Usk outside Newport and over the Landore Valley approaching Swansea. The Landore Viaduct was 580 yds long with thirty-seven spans. The piers were variously of timber, masonry, or timber and masonry, depending on the strength of the foundation available – Isambard took great care in all his piers, timber or masonry, that he had a very wide base to distribute the weight of the pier.

The Landore Viaduct included a 100-ft span over the river. The 30-ft-wide track-bed was carried on beams supported by a double framework of timbers, an arch within an arch, one on each side of the track and braced transversely against the tendency to fall inwards under load. Isambard constructed with wood what we would expect to see in riveted iron girders. The 1200-ft Usk Viaduct, at Newport, had eleven spans, all in timber, with a 100-ft-span central section. This was destroyed by fire during construction on 31 May 1848, whereupon Isambard rebuilt it using wrought-iron bow-string trusses similar to those he had just designed for his Thames bridge on the Windsor branch.

Most railway engineers were then making considerable use of cast-iron beams in bridges. Isambard was an exception. He did not trust the material as a beam and used it only rarely. Robert Stephenson placed a bridge across the River Dee which was composed of cast-iron beams, bolted together to give the required span. It was the worst possible way to use the material. On 24 May 1847, the Dee Bridge

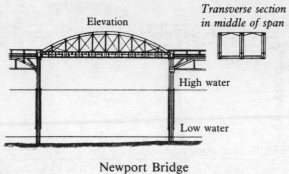

Elevation

Transverse section in middle of span

High water

Low water

Newport Bridge

collapsed when a train was passing over it and for a time it seemed likely that Stephenson would be charged with manslaughter. A Royal Commission was set up on 27 August 1847, charged with 'Inquiring into the conditions to be observed by Engineers in the Application of Iron in structures exposed to violent concussions . . .' and in March 1848 Isambard was asked to attend the Commission to give evidence.

Isambard was totally opposed to legislation to regulate building or engineering techniques and on 13 March he replied that he would attend – but only under protest:

> I regret that the Commissioners should have done me the honour of requesting 'my opinion upon the inquiry referred to them'. . . . If the Commission is to inquire into the conditions 'to be observed' it is to be presumed that they will . . . lay down rules to be hereafter observed in the construction of bridges. In other words [they will] *embarrass and shackle the progress of improvements of tomorrow by recording and registering as law the prejudices and errors of today.*

He refused to condemn the use of cast-iron beams, even though he did not use them himself, because, he said, 'Who will venture to say – *if the direction of improvement is left free* – that means may not be found of ensuring a sound casting . . . of a perfectly homogeneous mixture of the best metal?'

Isambard, before the Commission, spoke of the principles which ought to underly the use of rivets in holding metal plates together: 'I believe that in riveting plates together where they will be exposed to tension, the rivets should not be considered as pins to be exposed to

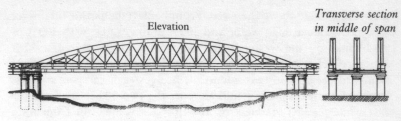

Elevation

Transverse section in middle of span

Windsor Bridge

a cross strain . . . but as clamps which compress the plates powerfully together . . . laying hold of the surface as in a vice. . . . I believe there is hardly any limit to . . . the entire strength of the plates.' William Fairbairn was the pioneer of this technique but Isambard was also early on the trail. He spoke from his experience on the hull of the SS *Great Britain* and from the work he was then carrying out on the new bridges over the Usk at Newport and over the Thames near Windsor.

The Windsor Bridge, opened with the branch line on 8 October 1849, was his first essay into the use of riveted wrought iron for bridges. To support the Windsor trusses, six cast-iron tubes, each 6 ft in diameter, one for each end of each truss, were forced into the ground by placing weights on the top rim and excavating gravel from the interior until the required depth was reached. They were then filled with concrete. The trusses were built at Bristol in 1849 and were load-tested there with $1\frac{1}{2}$ tons per foot-run before re-erection at Windsor.

The bridge spanned 202 ft and was (still is) formed by three parallel trusses designed to carry two lines of 7-ft rails, though now carrying only a single-track, standard-gauge railway. The central truss is twice the strength of the outer trusses because it acts as a support for both.

The floor of the Windsor Bridge was formed with timbers, not placed at right angles to the rails but obliquely, in order that the two wheels on the same axle of an engine would not bear on the same cross-beams at the same moment. By this clever detail, Isambard reduced the maximum load each cross-beam had to support and made the beams lighter and cheaper.

At the same time he was working on the Chepstow Bridge. At the River Wye crossing near Chepstow, the South Wales Railway came from Gloucester in a cutting through a limestone cliff, opening to a sheer drop 100 ft above the river. From bank to bank this tidal river was 600 ft wide at high water and 300 ft at low water, with 300 ft of mud-banks on the western side. The Admiralty required a 50-ft clearance below the bridge at high water over a width of 300 ft. Isambard decided on two, identical, bridges each carrying a single track. Mid-stream piers would support the two 300-ft spans to the cliff while parallel viaducts of 100-ft spans would run from mid-stream to the western, Chepstow bank.

Work began in spring 1849, simultaneously with the construction of the Windsor Bridge and the present Paddington station and while Isambard was directing exploratory work under the bed of the River Tamar, at Saltash, searching for strong foundations for the central pier of what became known as the Royal Albert Bridge. At Chepstow he sank the cast-iron piers by the usual weighting and excavating method till they encountered a rock foundation below 30 ft of mud. The tubes were then filled with concrete to form a strong support for the viaduct. For the mid-stream pier he sank six 8-ft cylinders in a double row, upon which he set 7-ft and finally 6-ft-diameter cylinders.

These cylinders, sunk in 7-ft lengths, bolted together, did not go down without difficulty. The tide was constantly flowing strongly, rising or falling 40 ft with only a few minutes of slack water between ebb and flow. Water and mud was forced into the tubes from below, and when a clay packing was insufficient to stem the flow the tube or tubes had to be sealed and filled with compressed air to keep the ground water out. One of the main piers cracked as it was forced through stony ground but was repaired underground and forced down to the bed-rock. The piers had all been sunk by June 1851.

The 300-ft-long spans over the mud bank were formed with continuous wrought-iron girders, 7 ft 6 in. deep, to form the sides of a trough 15 ft 8 in. wide through which the track passed. Each of the parallel 300-ft spans crossing the navigable waterway was supported by suspension chains anchored to 50-ft towers at each end, the inwards drag of the chains being opposed by the intervention of tubes which were, to quote Isambard, 'arched slightly for the sake of appearance'.

Each tube was 9 ft diameter, made from riveted boiler plate varying from $\frac{5}{8}$ to $\frac{3}{4}$ in. thick, supported at intervals by internal diaphragms and was 312 ft long. They were very light at 138 tons each, designed merely to withstand the compression forces exerted by the inwards pull of the chains. They were not self-supporting but were held up by verticals at two points. The chains passed through the verticals and bore against them.

The wrought-iron links forming the suspension chains were unusually long – 20 ft – and were rolled in a single piece, complete with specially shaped ends, without any welding, after Isambard had gone to the rolling mill and shown the workmen how they could achieve this hitherto impossible task. Isambard varied the weight of the links according to their place on the bridge, designing them to be $\frac{3}{4}$ to $\frac{11}{16}$ in. thick and 10 in. deep. Each chain was formed in alternating widths, 12 and 14 links, and they were pinned to the outer roadway girder at four points.

The suspension chains were forced to incline outwards from their anchorage on the 9-ft-diameter tube to their connections on the 15 ft 8 in.-wide trough below. The chains therefore passed through the rigidly riveted vertical struts awkwardly, downwards and sideways, with a corresponding problem of friction when the bridge moved on its chains as a load first hit it at one end and then rolled across. This was the inevitable result of using the suspension principle. To mitigate the effects of it Isambard introduced strong 'X' bracing between the vertical struts, iron rollers, and bronze rubbing strips between the vertical struts and the chain.

Each truss was to be 50 ft deep – $\frac{1}{6}$ of its length – and its total weight was only 460 tons compared with Stephenson's 1000 tons for a span 100 ft longer. Isambard tested a truss on the riverbank with a load of 770 tons overall, $2\frac{1}{4}$ tons per foot-run, and finding it behaved satisfactorily he prepared to launch it across the river.

The first of the two tubes for the Chepstow Bridge, that for the down line, was launched and raised on 8 April 1852. The 312-ft iron tube had been built parallel to the river, upstream of the site, and was manoeuvred into its launching position at right angles to the river between the piers of the 'mud-flat' spans. It was then mounted on railborne trolleys and pushed forward until the riverward end projected over the water when a pontoon of six barges was placed underneath. It was then a simple matter to shove the whole contraption out across the river.

Isambard had pre-planned the entire operation, every movement and, with the very able assistance of his chief drawing office assistant, R.P. Brereton, and Captain Claxton, the work proceeded without a

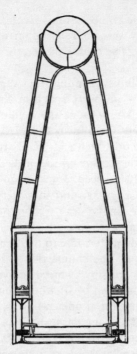

Truss of Chepstow Bridge

hitch. They started to push the tube across at 9 a.m. close to high water and at 9.45 it had reached the far side. The flood tide had hoisted the tube 40 ft but slack water was only of a few minutes' duration so without any delay chains were attached from the midstream and clifftop towers to each end of the tube and by the end of the day it had been hoisted into position.

The downside bridge was opened as a single track on 14 July 1852 and when the upside was completed, on 18 April 1853, Isambard had scored his greatest triumph to date – a masterpiece of economical design. He had had to sink large cast-iron piers well below water-level in a river with the second highest tidal rise and fall in the world. Stephenson's Conway Bridge, for example, carried a double track, 4 ft 8½ in.-gauge railway across a 400-ft gap, without the need to sink difficult foundations, at a cost of £145,190. Isambard, by contrast, carried a double-track, 7-ft-gauge railway across a 600-ft gap, 50 ft above high water – and he did it for only £77,000.

16

SS *Great Britain*

Once the SS *Great Western* proved successful Isambard was commissioned to design a sister ship. An ordinary naval architect with an eye on commercial success would have brought out something slightly larger but closely following the successful design – but not Isambard. For him that would have been a waste of a golden opportunity for *advancement*. At first he planned a wooden hull of 2000 tons but found it next to impossible to make it strong enough either to withstand the Atlantic or the strains imposed by the large engine it would require. Had he been a naval architect, and not a civil engineer, he would not have considered timber but would have gone direct to using iron. He would have known that the *Aaron Manby*, the first iron hull to go to sea, had been launched in 1821 and had been trading successfully ever since.

In October 1838, Isambard happened to see a small, iron-hulled paddle-steamer, the *Rainbow*, come into the Floating Harbour. Excited, he asked Captain Claxton and William Patterson to sail in the *Rainbow* to Antwerp and report on her sea-worthiness. Their report was very favourable and this, together with Isambard's own calculations and comparisons with wooden hulls, was presented to the Directors of the Great Western Steam-Ship Company. They, too, were impressed and in November 1838, a building committee, formed of Isambard and Thomas Guppy, set about designing an iron hull for a ship of over 3000 tons.

They had no precedent to guide them since a typical iron hull of that time was about 600 tons. Not only did they have to design from scratch, they also had to plan the shipyard and the machinery that could make such an enormous hull since it was far beyond the existing capabilities of any Bristol yard. This problem alone would surely have been enough for any engineer but it was only one of many with which Isambard saddled himself. However, it must be remembered that Guppy played a large part in the work, especially as Isambard was so thoroughly engaged at that time in his defence of himself and the broad gauge against the Liverpool Party and most of the GWR Board.

Four hulls were drawn between November 1838 and June 1839, and on 19 July 1839 the keel girders for a 3444-ton, iron-hulled paddle-steamer to be called the SS *Great Britain* were laid down in Patterson's yard, Bristol. It was to be 5 ft 6 in. wider than the lock-gates of the Cumberland Basin, which gave access from the Float to the tidal Avon, but Isambard was assured of the Docks Board's intention to widen the lock and designed the hull on the understanding that the work would be completed in good time.

Isambard wanted to have the engines designed and built by that most expert of marine engine constructors, Maudslay Son & Field. Maudslay's price was the highest and the Great Western Steam-Ship Company was attracted to the lowest price, offered by one Francis Humphreys who had patented an especially compact engine. The price was so low that the firm who held the manufacturing rights on Humphreys' engine did not want the expense of tooling-up to build just one huge engine at a loss and were willing to allow the Steam-Ship Company to tool-up to build the engine for themselves. This they proceeded to do – against Isambard's advice – with Francis Humphreys in charge.

In May 1840 the SS *Archimedes* came into Bristol Dock. She was driven by a screw propeller, invented and patented by Francis Pettit Smith. Brunel was at once attracted by this brilliant idea. Again, it must be a measure of Isambard's intense preoccupations that although the *Archimedes* had been launched in November 1838, he apparently did not know of this new, efficient means of propulsion until he saw it on the Float in May 1840. Then, typically, he swiftly adopted the idea with single-minded enthusiasm.

Thomas Guppy sailed in the *Archimedes* to Liverpool and although there were faults in the shape of her hull which would normally have retarded her progress, thanks to the screw propeller she made a good rate of knots without excessive fuel consumption. Isambard and

Guppy were impressed and persuaded the Great Western Steam-Ship Company's Directors to suspend work on the SS *Great Britain* for three months while the SS *Archimedes* steamed trials in the Bristol Channel. Several propellers of varying pitch and diameter, modified by Brunel according to experience, were used until a final specification for the *Great Britain*'s propeller was reached.

Guppy described it as comprising:

> six wrought-iron arms, formed by placing and riveting together four distinct forgings or centre-pieces, with arms welded to them, each of which is 6 in. thick. Upon the extremities of these are riveted palms of plate iron which are 4 ft $4\frac{1}{2}$ in. long on their circumferential edge, by 2 ft 9 in. height and $\frac{7}{8}$ in. thick. The diameter is 15 ft 6 in. and the pitch or helix of one revolution is 25 ft which equals an angle of 28 degrees. Its weight is 77 cwt.

Isambard then recommended that the SS *Great Britain* be rebuilt as a screw-propelled ship and the Company agreed.

By this time the iron hull was built up to the level of the paddle-boxes which were just being formed but Isambard ordered the hull to be re-built – flush-sided. He intended to fit the largest hull in the world with a novel method of propulsion – which would require novel engines. This was what Isambard relished. He was making a great leap forward in technology – he was taking an enormous gamble – and he was going to make his name even better known than ever.

Humphreys had experienced great difficulty in scaling-up his patent engine. The crank-shaft would be so large that there was no hammer in the world big enough to forge it. Humphreys mentioned his problem to James Nasmyth who had, in half an hour, on a single sheet of paper, designed the steam-hammer which would do the job and, proliferating in thousands, would make Nasmyth's fortune. But there were still plenty of other problems for Humphreys and in trying to solve them, he worked himself into a state of nervous exhaustion. It was at this moment that Isambard came along and ordered him to scrap his low-speed, paddle-wheel engine and start again on the plans for an engine to work a screw propeller. Such an engine had either to reciprocate at high speed or work through gearing to achieve 'high revs' at the propeller. The strain proved too much and Humphreys died a few days later.

About mid-May Isambard was in Bristol where the hull of his SS *Great Britain* was nearly ready for launching. It was by a very large margin the biggest ship in the world, measuring 289 ft × 50 ft 6 in. × 32 ft 6 in., and displacing 3618 tons. The hull was constructed to have great strength but, rather surprisingly, it did not have good lines. Although the bows were to some extent hollow, the hull did not follow the wave-line principles laid down some years earlier by John Scott Russell. Ten longitudinal girders, 3 ft 3 in. deep, lay parallel to the keel girder. To the top and underside of these were riveted inner and outer plates forming a deck and a keel. The SS *Great Britain* was also fitted with five transverse water-tight bulkheads up to the level of the main deck, that nearest the bows being the strongest.

This cellular principle of construction, which Isambard later developed into an axiom of naval architecture, was also used by Robert Stephenson to give strength to his tubular girders over the River Conway and the Menai Strait. While the Brunel/Guppy design was a forerunner as regards size, it was not quite the first in the matter of design principles, since John Scott Russell had experimented with longitudinal girders and transverse and longitudinal bulkheads since 1835, and his wave-line-hulled steamer *Flambeau*, of 1839, was built with longitudinal girders in the bottom.

The SS *Great Britain* had Isambard's own design of 'balanced rudder' and the two foremost funnels, between the boiler and the main deck, were each encased by a water-jacket so that the boiler-feed water could be heated by waste heat from the furnaces. This system, patented by the Scottish naval architect Robert Napier in 1842, insulated the passenger accommodation from the radiated heat of the funnels and prevented any chance of a fire such as that on the SS *Great Western*.

Following the death of Francis Humphreys, Isambard and Guppy set out to design the new engines themselves. The outcome was a pair of inverted 'V' twins, each pair driving on one crankpin of the overhead crankshaft.

The engine could turn the crankshaft only at 18 rpm, and in order to get the propeller to revolve at high speed gearing was required. Isambard's solution can be described briefly as follows. On the 17 ft long, 28 in. diameter main shaft was a toothed drum 18 ft diameter and 38 in. long. Below this, on the secondary shaft to the propeller, was another toothed drum, 6 ft diameter and 38 in. long. Around both drums were four sets of case-hardened chains. The gear ratio was nearly 2.95 to 1 and at a crankshaft speed of 18 rpm the propeller turned at about 53 rpm.

Projecting forward of the drum, the secondary shaft carried a 2-ft-diameter disc of gunmetal which pushed against a cast-iron face to transmit the effort of the screw to the body of the ship. This bearing, in common with the crankshaft and crankpin bearings, was lubricated very successfully with water pumped through internal ways. The shaft passed through a bearing close to the stern post, through a watertight seal in the stern post to an outside bearing where the propeller turned.

On 19 July 1843 a special train from Paddington, with Gooch driving and Brunel riding with him, carried to Bristol the Prince Consort and a representative selection of the aristocratic and engineering establishment, including the inventor and patentee of the screw propeller, Francis Pettit Smith. At Bristol Temple Meads they were greeted by the band of the Life Guards and cheering crowds were held back by police and units of the regular army.

The guests went directly to a banquet before assembling for the launching ceremony. According to *The Times*: 'The Prince took his place on the platform erected for the occasion and the *Great Britain* was towed out of the dock in which she floated.' One would have expected the Prince to *do* something, having mounted the platform, but on this *The Times* is silent. The august personages inspected the ship and then took their train home, again with Gooch and Brunel on the engine. They left around 4 p.m., climbed the two steep inclines to Swindon without fuss and on the 77 miles downhill to London reached 78 mph, arriving at Paddington in 180 minutes from Bristol inclusive of stops, an average of 44.3 mph.

Out on the Float the ship was fitted with her engines and boilers and was ready to steam away in late 1843 or early 1844. But she was prevented from doing so by a wonderful bureaucratic muddle. The Cumberland Lock had not been widened. An Act of Parliament was required to authorise the alterations and 1843 turned into 1844 without that Act being passed. The ship was trapped and the Dock Company refused to alter the locks 'in fear of the liabilities it might incur if, by permitting any disturbance of their works not provided for by Act of Parliament, any injurious consequence should ensue to the port.'

It was December 1844 before the sluggish authorities of Bristol Docks finally gave permission for the Great Western Steam-Ship Company to remove masonry in the Cumberland Basin locks and to remove a footbridge across the lock in order that the SS *Great Britain* could gain access to the open sea. Isambard directed this work and had completed the temporary widening by the 10th. At 6.30 a.m. on 11 December 1844 the ship was towed to the first lock-gate by two steam-tugs with a third at the stern. A high tide was necessary to lift the hull high in the lock but an east wind was blowing strongly which restricted the height of the rising tide.

At 6.45 a.m., 15 minutes before the highest water, the entrance gate to the Cumberland Basin from the Float was opened and the tugs began to move her in. At 7 a.m. the tide was as high as it was going to rise but was 2 ft lower than expected owing to the east wind. Isambard had widened the lock walls to accommodate the breadth of the ship riding 2 ft higher in the water than the actual tide allowed. It was very doubtful whether she would get through or not, but he and Claxton took the chance and the tugs inched her into the lock.

When she was three-quarters of her length in her sides touched the walls. The collision never amounted to more than a scrape, it was spotted at once and the stern tug pulled her back into the Floating Harbour. The real panic was that if they did not get her out on the following morning's tide she would be stuck on the Float for months until the equinoxial spring high tides. Frantic work to widen the lock went on all that day till at 7 a.m. on the 12th the SS *Great Britain* successfully passed the lock on the last spring tide of the season and was towed down-river to King Road on the Bristol Channel. This saga, together with the expense of building the shipyard and engines, raised the cost of the ship from the original estimate of £76,000 to about £176,000.

In January 1845, some trial voyages were made. The Brunel/Pettit-Smith screw pushed the 3618-ton ship along at 12 knots with 18 rpm on the crankshaft, the boiler pressure only an inefficient 2.5 lb psi. The 'slip' or efficiency of the propeller was 9.5 per cent, i.e. it was turning at $13\frac{1}{4}$ knots to produce a forward speed of 12 knots. At 9.30 a.m. on Thursday 23 January the ship steamed away to London for fitting-out to take passengers. For 20 hours she steamed head-on into a gale and heavy seas with most of the tides against her, but still she arrived at Blackwall at 3.30 p.m. on 26 January without any ill effect.

Isambard Kingdom Brunel portrayed by his brother-in-law John Horsley. On the table is the plan of the Great Western Railway prepared for Parliament

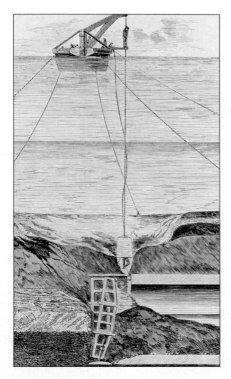

The collapsed Thames Tunnel daringly examined from a diving bell. It is easy to see how Pinckney fell out; yet Isambard took his mother down in the bell

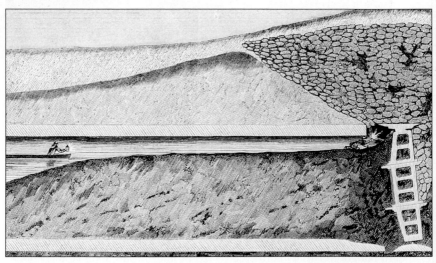

Isambard, having crawled over the silt, examines the damage to the frames

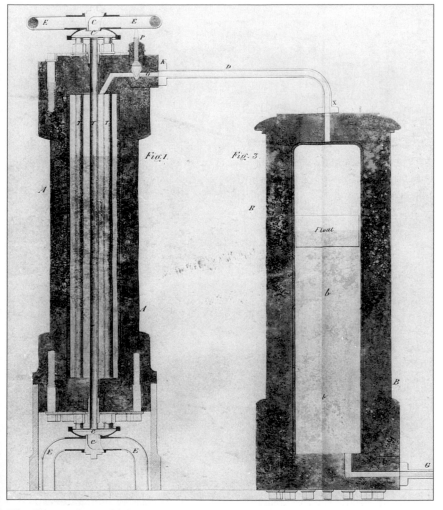

The Gaz engine, which cost Isambard ten years of fruitless labour

A Brunellian standard design for a wayside station on the Great Western
Railway, this one still in use at Culham

A Brunellian pub, suitably disguised as a country house in miniature, at
Steventon, headquarters of the Great Western Railway

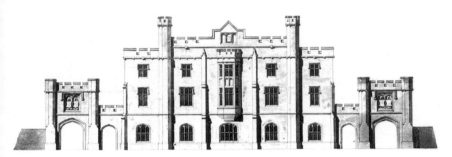

Bristol Station's Temple Gate front

Isambard's classical design for the end of Box Tunnel visible to the public

The South Devon atmospheric railway at Exeter St Thomas Station, with the troublesome longitudinal slot clearly visible along the tube between the rails

Starcross from the jetty, showing Isambard's Italianate SDAR pumping station, its chimney disguised as a campanile

The *Great Western*'s first voyage to New York, begun on 4 April 1838

The *Great Britain* aground in Dundrum Bay, with the brushwood barrier nearly complete

Isambard's private office at 18 Duke Street

A Midsummer Night's Dream by Edwin Landseer, from a series on Shakespearian themes Isambard commissioned for Duke Street

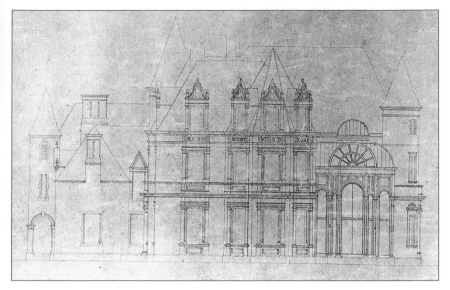

An architect's drawing for Isambard's unrealized mansion, Watcombe Park

The view from the terrace as Isambard intended it

One of Isambard's famous timber trestle viaducts in Cornwall, so fragile-seeming they terrified the passengers

A rush job: this temporary plywood bridge at Bath lasted 38 years

The grand leap at Maidenhead Bridge

Chepstow Bridge carried the railway off a 120-ft cliff 600 ft over the River Wye

The Royal Albert Bridge, Saltash, under construction: the Cornish span
raised, the Devon span waiting

The Royal Albert Bridge in full glory

John Scott Russell, Henry Wakefield, Isambard and Lord Derby anxiously watch an attempt to launch the *Great Eastern*

Isambard by the chains of the stern checking drum of the *Great Eastern*

The same drum with its crew before the first attempt to launch

Awaiting high tide before the final attempt

The *Great Eastern* under way at last. No larger ship was launched for forty years

The last photograph of Isambard Kingdom Brunel, taken on 2 September 1859 aboard the *Great Eastern*. Moments later he collapsed

17

The Holed Saucepan

After being fitted out in a manner becoming the largest transatlantic liner and blessed by a visit from Queen Victoria and Prince Albert, the SS *Great Britain* began her maiden voyage to New York on 26 July 1845, somewhat under-laden, with approximately fifty passengers and 600 tons of cargo. She was a wonderful ship and made the crossing in the unprecedented time of 14 days 21 hours. But, as Isambard often feared, it was too good to last. On 22 September 1846, the SS *Great Britain* steamed away from Liverpool for New York carrying Captain Claxton and 180 passengers, with Captain Hosken as Master. Some hours later, in pitch darkness and pouring rain, Hosken lost track of where he was. He was unaware of a new lighthouse made operational a few months previously, and, assuming this to be the Calf of Man light he had been looking for, made a course alteration accordingly and ran aground on rocks to the accompaniment of a terrible sound of rending metal and the frightened screams of those on board.

The crew tried to lighten her by throwing overboard tons of coal but they could not get her off the reef and when day broke, the tide had gone out and they saw they were lying in lonely Dundrum Bay, where the Mountains of Mourne sweep down to the sea. Captain Claxton hoped to float her off on an especially high tide due on the 28th but a terrible gale sprang up in the meantime bringing thousands of tons of water crashing down on the hull with a force that not even this ship could have withstood for long. He set sail on her and drove her further on to the beach. After that, William Patterson arrived, followed by a succession of expert ship salvagers, but none of them could see a way out. Isambard was so bogged down with his work on half a dozen railways, on bridge designs, on the atmospheric railway and his parliamentary work that he could not spare the time to go to Dundrum. So there the *Great Britain* lay, pounded by the waves of the Irish Sea.

Captain Hosken sent Isambard an accurate drawing of the scene and he could see from it that the ship's back was not broken, nor was she damaged in anything but a superficial way; yet the Company gave her up for lost. Owing to his commitments in England Isambard, to his fury, was impotent to save his SS *Great Britain* – the world's largest, most modern, propeller-driven steamship – so when Hammond did not carry out some of his instructions in November 1846, he came in handy as a whipping boy:

> My Dear Sir, My intention was that you should repair the 'A' shed . . . but my intentions were to be very unimportant. Joking apart, I must say that I deferred writing because I understood you were unwell and I did not wish to worry you but now I must speak seriously. After a *very unpleasant discussion* a few weeks ago, I gave orders for 6 of our new ballast wagons to be given to the South Devon Railway and to be sent down at once. I have been told they have not been sent but some inadequate substitutes. Now, if this is so – which I still wish to doubt – I will be *very much displeased*. I intend that it should be at once determined for my future guidance, whether I am or am not Master. I shall not receive attention to my orders from others if it is understood that Mr Hammond is my Master whilst I may be theirs. While I put it in this shape I feel sure that it will appear ridiculous even to you but if my orders – repeated and urged angrily and positively – are to be ridiculously neglected it seems to me to amount very much the same thing as if I were not the Master whereas I certainly intend to remain so.

In that letter, Isambard also referred to 'those who are weak enough to have feelings of obstinacy' which sounds odd coming from one of the most obstinate men of his day. Hammond died a few weeks after receiving this letter.

The following month, December 1846, Isambard was at last able to visit the *Great Britain*. There it lay, a grim, black hulk under a dismal winter-grey sky, written off, without even the hope of salvage, exposed to the relentless sea with no sign of the breakwaters with which Claxton and the other experts had tried to protect it. Not even that massively constructed hull would survive the sea, intact, throughout a whole winter.

Isambard now confronted perhaps the greatest test of his courage, his most daunting challenge, since the Thames Tunnel. His obstinacy, his phenomenal determination and courage rose in a wave higher than anything the Irish Sea could produce. Everyone else had given up but *he* was not going to be beaten. Without waiting for authorisation from the Company on the matter of cost, he sprang into action.

The earlier attempts at protecting the ship depended on break-waters being built, which were then washed away. Isambard used the ship herself as a breakwater – there was no doubt that she would not move. He envisaged a mass of brushwood and thin spars, bound together into faggots and skewered with iron rods to make a wall as thick as he liked to break the force of the waves. The faggots would be placed under the stern and along her length on the sea side, rising half-way up her hull, lashed in position by chains all around her and weighted down with iron blocks and sandbags. These measures would protect her until the weather moderated in the following spring. Then she could be repaired and re-floated. The ship lay close to the estate of Lord Roden and from that demesne Isambard ordered the necessary wood and labour, showed how he wanted the faggots constructed, and dashed back to London leaving Captain Hosken in charge.

When he got home he wrote a long, scolding, letter to his friend Captain Claxton:

> I was grieved to see this fine ship lying unprotected, abandoned by all those who ought to know her value and who ought to have protected her instead of being humbugged by schemers and underwriters. . . . £4000 or £5000 would repair all the damage done [but she] is left lying like a useless saucepan kicking about on the most exposed shore that you can imagine with no more effort or skill applied to protect the property than the said saucepan would have received on Brighton beach . . . as to the state of the ship she is as straight and sound as she ever was . . . it is beautiful to look at and really, how she can be talked of in the way she has been – even by you – I cannot understand. It is positively cruel . . . like talking away the character of a young woman without any grounds whatever.

Isambard went on to list the relatively slight damage to the hull in a quiet tone of voice which then rose to a crescendo of indignation as the sheer absurdity of the situation struck him:

> The ship is perfect except that . . . the bottom is knocked in holes in several places . . . a vessel still in perfect condition, left to the tender mercies of an awfully exposed shore for weeks while a parcel of quacks are amusing you with schemes for getting her off, she in the meantime

going to pieces. . . . What are we doing? What are we wasting precious time about? The steed is being quietly stolen while we are discussing the relative merits of a Bramah or a Chubb's lock to be put on at some future time. It really is shocking!

Claxton went to Dundrum to supervise the building of the faggot wall but as fast as faggots were planted against the ship the sea washed them away. Christopher Claxton was himself a man of courage and resource but, in a letter to Isambard, he confessed himself beaten. Isambard wrote back:

You have failed, I think . . . from that which causes nine-tenths of all the failures in this world – from not doing quite enough. I would only impress upon you one principle of action which I have always found very successful, which is to stick obstinately to one plan (until I believe it wrong) and to devote all my scheming to that one plan . . . to stick to one point of attack, however defended and if the force brought up is not suffi-cient to bring ten times as much. . . . so with the faggots – if a 6-bundle faggot won't reach out of the water, try a 20-bundle one – if hundred-weights won't keep it down, try tons.

Throughout the spring of 1847 Claxton showed Brunellian deter-mination. The sand was excavated, the vast mass of brushwood and small timber was removed, somehow he managed to drive massive timbers under her keel at low tides so as to get working space beneath. The 'holed saucepan' was roughly repaired and the water within pumped out. Then on the highest tides she was warped towards the sea and, on 27 August, the SS *Great Britain* floated out over the reef which had punctured her hull almost a year previously. After further difficulties she was towed a few days later, on the verge of sinking, to a berth in the Coburg Dock, Liverpool.

The great ship never again returned to top-rank duties but her loss was no fault of Isambard's; she had, indeed, been a huge success as a piece of naval architecture. Isambard's work on the development of ships' propellers and iron hulls had not gone entirely unnoticed by the Admiralty and as early as February 1841 their Lordships called upon Isambard to carry out a series of experiments on screw propellers for the Royal Navy. Isambard agreed to do so 'on the express understand-ing that the work be conducted by me without any other interference than the direct orders of the [Navy] Board'. This was agreed, Isambard designed the engine, Maudslay's made it and only then did Isambard discover that the Admiralty had omitted to build the hull to house it.

The Admiralty administration was split into two camps: those for Isambard and the modernisation of the Royal Navy and those against, the Surveyor-General being one of the die-hards. It was objected that the presence of a driving force at the rear-most part of the ship would render the hull hopelessly unstable and unbalanced. Isambard pointed out that, though the screw was undoubtedly at the stern, its thrust was communicated to 'midships' through the drive shaft and was thus powerfully conducive to stability. Because it was underwater it was far less vulnerable to damage from enemy fire than paddle-wheels were. Clear thinking and decisive action did not appeal to some at the Admiralty – Isambard wanted to stir up activity and get things done. He was a very unpopular man.

Isambard spent some time during 1841 at Southampton with Captain Claxton, carrying out trials with the paddle-steamer *Polyphemus* for later comparison with a screw-propelled ship. He was then offered HMS *Acheron* for conversion to screw propulsion. The hull shape was totally unsuitable, so Isambard refused the offer whereupon the Admiralty ignored him. After several months of unanswered letters to the Admiralty, Isambard wrote his resignation. At that point the Admiralty called him in for an explanation.

The impression Isambard gained from his interview was that nothing was known of him at all, that they thought he was some crazy inventor with a bee in his bonnet about screw propellers. He had to explain that he was trying to make comparative trials at the behest of the Navy Board. With fresh orders – in writing – and with the sloop HMS *Rattler* for conversion to screw propulsion, Isambard attempted a fresh start. The engine, the geared chain-drive to the shaft and the propeller were designed by him but he played no part in their installation or the later trials. Had he done so he would not have permitted unscientific and childish experiments such as one where the *Rattler* was tied, stern to stern, with a naval paddle-steamer for a 'tug-of-war'. With both ships steaming 'full ahead' it was found that the *Rattler* dragged the other backwards at 2.8 knots. Even Queen Victoria was fed with false information in an effort to ridicule his designs. On 28 April 1845, Isambard wrote to Claxton: 'I know nothing as to any or what screw is making but I fancy that something was said the other day to the Queen about one of these models being that which I intended to apply – and if it was the model I saw, I altogether disapprove of it.' The model referred to must be the one featured in this anecdote which Isambard used to enjoy relating.

He was summoned to the presence of the First Sea Lord, Sir George Cockburn, and found him in a state of trembling rage. On his desk was a scale model of a sail-driven warship such as Nelson would have been proud of – except that the elegant stern had been cut away most inelegantly to make room for a clumsy propeller. The model carried a label stating: *Mr Brunel's Mode of Applying the Screw to Her Majesty's Ships*. The First Sea Lord pointed to the vandalised vessel and roared at Isambard, 'Do you mean to suppose that we shall cut up Her Majesty's ships after this fashion, sir?' Isambard was doubly charming because he could truthfully disclaim all knowledge. Sir George sent messengers to find out who had sent the model and while he and Isambard waited the latter boldly scratched off the slanderous label with his pen-knife.

In May 1845, the Admiralty wrote to Isambard asking for a report on his conclusions from the trials. Isambard replied with a caustic letter:

> I soon ceased, practically, to have any control over these experiments – nor has any other *one* person. . . . I consider that four valuable years have been wasted and that private individuals and the French government possess more accurate information than you do. Latterly no further reference was made to me, I have heard nothing more of the *Rattler*, her fitting out for sea and I have never been applied to make any reports, indeed, from the unsatisfactory course pursued I should have no proper materials for making any.

In 1845, twenty Royal Navy ships were fitted with the screw and from then on the propeller superseded paddle-wheels on warships and merchant ships alike. The screw propeller was invented by Francis Pettit Smith but it was Isambard's use of it on the huge SS *Great Britain* that had forced the Admiralty to take notice. He never asked for payment for his research and development – simply because he was so disgusted with the bureaucratic types with whom he had to deal. The Admiralty Establishment 'picked Isambard's brain' and then ignored him, denying him the public honour of having introduced this highly effective means of propulsion to both the Royal Navy and the Merchant Navy.

18

Engineering Knight-Errant

It is curious that Isambard believed himself to be a most prudent and cautious engineer when he could be swept off his feet by an idea and was quite capable of altering his plans, without regard to expense, in the middle of a project if he thought he saw a better way of doing things. In September 1844 Isambard, Daniel Gooch and many other eminent engineers were present at Kingstown (now Dun Laoghaire) to witness a demonstration of Clegg & Samuda's atmospheric train on the $1\frac{3}{4}$-mile-long, single-track, Dalkey & Kingstown Railway which connected Kingstown harbour with the Dublin & Dalkey Railway. The piston carriage hauled its two-coach load smoothly and silently up the 1 in 120 rising gradient, reaching a maximum speed of 28 mph.

Isambard was very impressed. He saw it as a new form of motive power, something he had been looking for ever since he began his youthful experiments with the Gaz engine. Gooch, not for the first time, found himself diametrically opposed to Brunel's thinking on mechanical engineering and wrote: 'I could not understand how Mr Brunel could be so misled. He had so much faith in his being able to improve it that he shut his eyes to the consequences of failure.'

The atmospheric system of propulsion was patented by Samuel Clegg and Jacob Samuda on 3 January 1838. Clegg was trained as an engineer and was a principal pioneer of the gas lighting industry. Samuda was a brilliant marine engineer and shipbuilder. The Clegg & Samuda atmospheric system consisted of a cast-iron tube which was laid between rails and sealed by airtight valves at each end. A piston, attached to the floor of a piston carriage, was pushed past the valve into the tube. A stationary steam-engine on the lineside had previously pumped air out of the tube, creating a partial vacuum ahead of the piston so that the greater pressure of the atmosphere behind the piston forced it through the tube and drew the carriage along.

The piston was attached to the underside of the floor of the carriage by a vertical metal plate, and the tube between the rails had a $2\frac{1}{2}$-in.-wide slot along its top, along which this vertical plate passed. The slot was made airtight by a strip of metal riveted to a leather hinge, the former resting in a sticky composition to act as sealant. As the plate moved along the slot it lifted the seal which then fell back under the weight of the metal plate to re-seal the tube.

At a time when steam locomotives sometimes showered the passengers with hot water and always sent out a steady rain of cinders, this was a clean and silent transportation system. Several European governments were advised by their experts that the system was practical for major trunk routes and the British Prime Minister, Sir Robert Peel, urged the railway companies to consider converting to the atmospheric principle since it was clean and silent and would allow railways to be laid cheaply on steep gradients. Robert Stephenson, who was opposed to it, said it was analogous to rope-haulage and conceded that, if it had any application at all, then it would be for short, suburban lines such as the $3\frac{1}{2}$-mile Blackwall Railway or for assisting trains on inclines, such as his rope-worked Camden incline out of Euston. George Stephenson called it 'a great humbug'.

The South Devon Railway Company Act obtained its Royal Assent on 4 July 1844 and shortly afterwards the Directors received a proposal from Clegg & Samuda that the atmospheric system should be installed on their line. The matter was referred to Isambard and he replied on 9 August with an exceptionally bold letter:

> The question is not new to me. I have frequently considered it. Any part I should take in examining into the system will be purely from the desire – which I always feel – to forward good inventions and when I have formed a decided opinion no fear of the consequences shall prevent my expressing it.

Isambard then opened his case with some outrageous assumptions:

> I shall *assume* – and I am not aware that it is disputed by anybody – that stationary power, if freed from the weight . . . of a rope must be

cheaper . . . and is more susceptible to producing much higher speeds than locomotive power.

In the next sentence he contradicted himself regarding the lack of dispute by stating:

> I am aware that this opinion is directly opposed to that of Mr Robert Stephenson and others who have published elaborate statements with explanations and calculations . . .

His use of the word 'elaborate' might be intended to be derogatory and the 'others' who disputed his assumptions included his own Locomotive Superintendent, Daniel Gooch, who was sure he could run the Kingstown line cheaper with a locomotive. Isambard was so biased in favour of the atmospheric as to warn against

> mathematical calculations, dependent as they are upon an unattained precision, which are as likely to lead far from the truth as not. By the same mode of calculation did Dr Lardner arrive at all those results regarding steam navigation and the speed on railways which have since proved so erroneous.

While Isambard criticised Lardner's erroneous conclusions regarding speed on railways he made a Lardneresque assumption himself when he stated that stationary steam power was always cheaper than locomotive power. The most experienced mechanical engineers had told him that the system was impractical yet Isambard, the civil engineer, asked to be allowed to ignore the insuperable problems in the interests of experiment. He insisted that he had been 'cautious and without bias' in his investigations of the Dalkey line yet he came to the most incautious conclusion:

> The mere mechanical difficulties can be overcome. The experiment has entirely succeeded, a system of machinery which at the first attempt works without interruption, constantly for many months may be said to be free of mechanical objections.

But what was this machinery doing? Once an hour between 8 a.m. and 6 p.m., a train was lifted up to Dalkey from Kingstown. To create the necessary vacuum in the tube, the stationary engine pumped for an average of five minutes. The train ran back by gravity to Kingstown. In eleven months from March 1844, when the line opened, the stationary engines failed seven times and closed the line for a day on each occasion. Isambard stated, 'No locomotive line that

I have been connected with has been equally free from accidents.' But an engine failure on the GWR did not close down the whole system for a day.

Traction on an atmospheric railway did not depend on the adhesion of a heavy locomotive to the rails so he could economise on earthworks by allowing steep gradients. These gradients, he said, would be too steep for locomotives to climb except slowly whereas the atmospheric trains would ascend at a high speed. But he did not provide sufficient pumping power for this. Bridges and viaducts could be built less substantially and the cost of locomotives and their tenders would also be saved but instead he had the cost of miles of piping, a lot of under-used pumping engines, and their 'houses'. He even claimed that the cuttings and embankments of an atmospheric railway would be far less liable to 'slipping' owing to the absence of the heavy locomotive and the 'hammer blow' from its unbalanced rotating parts; yet he must have known that rain, frost and soft foundations were far more likely to move hundreds of tons of earth than the 'hammer blow' inflicted by a 20-ton locomotive.

He told the SDR Directors that the line could be built, complete with all engine houses and rolling stock for the same cost as the track-bed alone of a double-track, loco-hauled railway and concluded with these fateful words:

> I have no hesitation in taking upon myself the full and entire responsibility for recommending the adoption of the atmospheric system on the South Devon Railway and of recommending as a consequence that the line and works should be constructed for a single line only.

His recommendation was accepted unanimously by the SDR Directors although the Directors of the GWR protested, reminding the SDR that they had agreed to subscribe to the company on condition that it was locomotive hauled on double track. To condemn Isambard for his espousal of the atmospheric system is not to be wise after the event. His own friends on the GWR warned him against it. But he had formed 'a decided opinion' about an attractive theory and nothing less than the loss of vast sums of other people's money would convince him he was wrong. It must be said, however, that he put some of his own money into the venture, as was ever his policy when he was Engineer of a scheme.

Daniel Gooch and Robert Stephenson were sure the atmospheric system was useless for a main line railway. Lt-Colonel Sir Frederick

Smith, RE, Government Inspector of Railways, and Peter Barlow, Professor of Mathematics at Woolwich Military Academy, were equally certain that any savings in cost due to minimal earthwork construction would be lost by the cost of the pipes, the engine houses and engines they contained; these engines would be very expensive since they would be standing idle for most of the day and were, in fact, less efficient in the use of fuel than a similar engine operating a rope-haulage system. Professor Barlow and Lt-Colonel Smith had reported their findings to Parliament in 1842 and doubtless ranked among the 'others' in Isambard's report to the SDR Directors. He was adept at bending arguments to suit circumstances.

Safety from head-on collisions on a single-track atmospheric line was guaranteed but this safety was fairly well assured on locomotive-hauled lines, either by the simple expedient of a wooden 'train staff' (a baton without which no train could use the line) – which was then waiting to be invented by some really practical railwayman – or else by the Cooke-Wheatstone electric telegraph, which was given its first trial on the GWR in 1838 but which Isambard had allowed to fall into disrepair by late 1840. Isambard did not give electrical devices the attention they deserved. To the Parliamentary Select Committee on the atmospheric system, on 4 April 1845, he stated:

> The telegraph not being used for the purpose of communicating the cause, if a stoppage occurs on the GWR, the notice of that stoppage can only be conveyed by the passing of another train along the other line of rails, therefore, they remain there frequently a considerable period before notice is conveyed to any of the principal stations.

This was an astonishingly complacent admission of inefficiency when the advantages of electric communication were well known. In 1839, Charles Saunders, GWR Company Secretary, had acknowledged such advantages to a Parliamentary Select Committee.

Isambard pointed out that the more trains run on an atmospheric railway the cheaper the cost of the stationary power became, but the whole truth was that *unless* the trains were frequent the cost of stationary power was higher than that obtained from locomotives. The best application of an atmospheric railway was to an 'urban commuter' line, where frequent, well-loaded trains could be run, yet Isambard not only intended to install 52 miles of atmospheric railway over some of the most sparsely populated country in England, he also suggested that the low cost of construction would make them ideally suited to rural Ireland!

Tractive effort depended upon the diameter of the piston and the degree of vacuum ahead of it so as to make most use of the atmospheric pressure behind it. Isambard used despised mathematical calculations to discover the correct dimensions assuming a certain weight of train and a certain required speed. But what would happen when train loads developed beyond the capacity of the tube to haul them? The existing tubes and pumps would have to be scrapped and larger plant installed. Isambard knew this but still clung to his 'decided opinions'.

He was drawn to the atmospheric as inexorably as the piston was driven along the tube. He saw what a reputation he would achieve if only he could make it operate. The insurmountable difficulties were as nothing beside his mountainous desire to be the man who made this smooth-running, clean and silent system work.

On 4 April 1845, he was called before a Select Committee to give evidence on the atmospheric system. He answered 339 questions. One of the first was from the Chairman, the Hon. Bingham Baring: 'I suppose you have set out in your own mind the manner in which the line will be constructed?' A reasonable supposition but Isambard calmly admitted that he had no clear idea of how the job would be carried out:

> To a certain extent but not entirely. The whole system of working a line with the atmospheric apparatus requires a great deal of consideration and requires many new contrivances and I do not think I have at all completed, to my own satisfaction, all the details. . . . I think I see my way clearly to effect them but I should still hope to effect many improvements.

Asked how he would surmount the steep inclines west of Newton he replied, 'I propose to have different sized pipes or possibly to have double pipes.'

The Chairman asked how he proposed to make one piston fit the large- and the small-diameter pipes, to which Isambard replied: 'I am prepared with several ways of doing it but have not yet made up my mind. All these schemes are floating in my head. I do not know which I may adopt when the time comes.' The Chairman asked how he proposed to control the trains' descent on the very steep gradients. 'I have not yet determined,' replied Isambard, '"sufficient unto the day is the evil thereof".'

This 'suck it and see' attitude was to cost his shareholders their savings.

One of the undoubted advantages of the atmospheric system was that there would be no large, smoky, and unsightly engine sheds. Bingham Baring asked him: 'The stations will be cleaner under those circumstances?' On this Isambard could be emphatic: 'Yes, I think the stations and the railway will be very superior in general comfort and luxury. I think the stations will be very much prettier than they are at present.'

The Editor of the *Railway Times* wrote of him at this time:

> We do not take him for either a rogue or a fool but an enthusiast, blinded by the light of his own genius, an engineering knight-errant, always on the lookout for magic caves to be penetrated and enchanted rivers to be crossed, never so happy as when engaged 'regardless of cost' in conquering some, to ordinary mortals, impossibility.

As a knight-errant Isambard attacked only the biggest dragons and rescued only the most beautiful maidens. Electricity in 1845 was an ugly infant, a row of batteries, foaming and fuming with evil smells. Others had the foresight and were even then conducting experiments on electric traction – albeit battery powered. The infinite potential of 'galvanic magnetism' made no appeal to his artistic, glory-seeking, soul. It was a great pity that Isambard did not take electricity seriously – that really would have been foresight.

Isambard was singularly vague in his dealings with the South Devon Railway proprietors. In February 1846 he told the shareholders' meeting that the slow progress they complained of in completing the Exeter/Newton* section was due to his desire to 'profit by the experience of the Croydon Railway'. He was not telling the truth and, indeed, the only economy he made on the South Devon was an economy of truth.

William Cubitt's atmospheric Croydon Railway began trials in August 1845 and opened to the public on 19 January 1846 using a 15-in.-diameter tube. Isambard started tube-laying on the Exeter/Newton section – using a 13-in.-diameter tube – early in 1845, without waiting to 'profit from the Croydon Railway's experience'. In December 1845, he decided to follow William Cubitt's example on the Croydon Railway. The 13-in. tube was scrapped, and a 15-in. tube

* Not called Newton Abbot until 1877.

installed at a loss of approximately £31,000 to the SDR.

The larger tube meant an increase in volume so that the pumping engines, still on the drawing board, would not be powerful enough. The obvious solution was to increase the size of the engines under design but instead he told Maudslay and Boulton & Watt to design auxiliary engines to augment the capacity of the original machines. Thus each engine house had to be enlarged to accommodate two engines instead of one, and building and maintenance costs were for two, rather than one engine.

On 16 May 1846 he reassured the SDR Directors that the airtight valve on the Croydon Railway's tube was working well. This was not true. The valve had started to break up on 2 May and on 20 May the Croydon line was closed while the entire valve was renewed. The line was not re-opened until 13 July. As Isambard's declared intention was to use the Croydon Railway's experience, he ought to have known of the increasing problems on the line and ought not to have reassured the SDR Directors. If he really had been unaware of developments on the Croydon line, then he had failed in his duty in giving his reassurance of 16 May.

The Exeter to Teignmouth section of the SDR opened on 30 May 1846 and was worked by Gooch-designed locomotives while the installation of the vacuum tube and its leather/metal valve continued. On 16 August 1847 an experimental service of atmospheric trains, not carrying passengers, began running between Exeter and Teignmouth. On 27 August, Isambard reported complete success: the trains were punctual and even had time in hand. He blamed the three-year delay in bringing about this happy state of affairs on the manufacturers of the pumping engines: 'The engines have proved sources of continued and most vexatious delays both in the unexpected length of time occupied in their erection and in subsequent correction of defects in minor parts . . .'

We are indebted to Charles Hadfield for publishing this letter from G.& J. Rennie, 28 May 1847, answering Isambard's criticisms:

In reply to that part of your letter complaining that you are waiting for our Engines, we beg to say that these engines were ready for delivery agreeably to our contract, nearly two years since and that subsequently we have met with such repeated interruptions for the want of engine houses and other preparations being ready to receive them that it has been impossible to proceed faster. Even now the engines at Teignmouth are ready to start but there are no coals to work them.

Isambard could not be everywhere at once but in the case of the SDR, which was becoming embarrassing, he absented himself as much as possible and had to be *ordered* to attend Board meetings. He was so busy with his vast spread of works, so busy finding out the exact architectural detail of Florentine churches, so busy interfering with Gooch's management and writing fatherly sermons to his assistants, that he neglected important aspects of his work and, when criticised, he had the unpleasant habit of blaming someone else. Yet, when the SDR, like the GWR nine years earlier, begged him to appoint a deputy to attend the line and the Board meetings he refused – it might have meant sharing the glory.

Two public atmospheric trains ran between Exeter and Teignmouth from 13 September 1847. From 10 January 1848 all SDR passenger trains, and some freight, between Exeter and Newton, were 'on the pipe' and from 23 February all trains ran behind a piston carriage. They were, for a while, a tremendous novelty. Isambard Brunel jun., in his biography of his father, wrote: 'The new mode of traction was universally approved of. The motion of the train, relieved of the impulsive action of the locomotive, was singularly smooth and agreeable and the passengers were freed from the annoyance of coke dust and the sulphurous smell from the engine's chimney.' Such annoyances could have been substantially reduced, if not cured, very cheaply, by tight couplings and closed carriages.

On test, high speeds were achieved with unprofitably small loads: 68 mph with 28 tons and 35 mph with 100 tons but the start-to-stop time for a service passenger train, from Newton to Exeter, 20 miles with four intermediate stops, was 55 minutes. The very low average speed was due to having to wait at stations for the arrival of the other trains, off the single line, and for each train then to be drawn forward by horse or auxiliary piston until its piston was engaged in the next section of tube. In making an advantage of the fact that the atmospheric could be worked with perfect safety as a single track, Isambard had thrown away the main advantage he claimed for it – speed. There was no possibility of reversing on the atmospheric system, so all goods trucks and passenger carriages were shunted either by man or horse power.

The hinge of the airtight valve and the ring around the piston were of leather, simply the wrong material for the job – as had been the experience at Croydon, although it created no difficulties on the Dalkey line, perhaps because the trains ran much more slowly there and the valve was not subject to such rough treatment.

A large body of men had to be employed on the South Devon, continuously rubbing a sticky sealant on to the valve to make it air-tight. This sealant became useless after exposure to the air, and an alternative compound, using cod oil and soap which remained soft, was sucked into the tube along with the natural oils in the leather, which itself was dried and cracked by the sun and wind. The iron plate, rusted by sea-water, broke away from its rivets, while tannin in the wet leather reacted chemically with the iron and caused the leather to decompose. Air then leaked into the pipe through torn leather so that the pumps had to work harder and burned too much fuel. In freezing conditions wet leather became rock hard and trains could not pass.

Isambard Brunel jun. wrote, 'These difficulties were not only such as had not been anticipated – but such as no one was justified in anticipating.' Yet they had been the Croydon's experience a year before.

On 26 February 1848 the valve was disintegrating rapidly but Isambard reported to the shareholders:

> Notwithstanding numerous difficulties, I think we are in a fair way shortly of overcoming the mechanical defects and bringing the whole apparatus into regular and efficient, practical working and as soon as we can obtain good and efficient telegraphic communication between engine houses and thus ensure proper regularity in the working of the engines we shall be enabled to test for economy of working. At present this is almost impossible owing to the want of the telegraph compelling us to keep the engines constantly at work for which the boiler power was not intended.

It was air leakage that caused the engines to be over-driven but Isambard blamed the electric telegraph to distract attention from the disintegrating valve, the 'Achilles' heel' of the system, for which he had no remedy. Isambard had ordered the installation of the telegraph circuit through the pumping stations in January 1847 but it was not operational until August 1848 so he could not accuse it of inefficiency in February of that year. In fact the inefficiency was Isambard's in not ensuring that the telegraph was promptly installed.

Between October 1847 and June 1848 a constant struggle was waged to keep the valve in working order. Just over 2 miles of it was completely replaced and miles more patched up while Isambard kept well away from the scene. It was not he who sounded the alarm over the decay of the valve but a member of the public who wrote a letter to the Directors. A committee was appointed to look into the complaints on 23 May 1848 and this report was before the Board on 20 June. It stated that 'there was an unexpected, rapid and continuing destruction going on in the leather' which occasioned 'serious weekly expense in repairs'. The South Devon Railway returned a profit of around £5000 each half-year, from May 1846, under full or partial locomotive haulage but when the accounts for the half-year ending 30 June 1848 were published, it was seen that, under full atmospheric running, a loss of £2487 was suffered. The cost of full atmospheric working was 37d per train-mile against 16d for locomotive haulage.

The valve was on a 12-month guarantee from Clegg & Samuda so the Directors sent them the £1018 repair bill and on 30 June wrote to Isambard, asking what ideas he had to prevent the destruction of the valve. Isambard ignored the SDR Directors, which might be taken to show that he was 'avoiding a commitment which was becoming embarrassing', to borrow a phrase which Rolt would apply to John Scott Russell. On 18 July the SDR's Atmospheric Committee, which included the Chairman of the GWR, Charles Russell, demanded to interview Isambard, at Duke Street, on 1 August. He received them in a subdued mood and blamed Clegg & Samuda for the shortcomings of the system.

He noted that Clegg & Samuda believed that their valve could be made to work 'if properly attended to from the first' but he concluded, 'I do not think I could rely on the result.' Isambard believed that a better valve could be made using galvanised iron to prevent rusting and the rotting of the leather – but in any case the entire valve would have to be replaced. He also noted that the pumping engines were not powerful enough, which was certainly his fault, and would have to be improved at further cost. After all this outlay, he promised that the operating costs would be reduced. The Directors listened to his suggestions, asked for a written report and departed sadder but wiser men.

Isambard's tone, in his written report, delivered on 19 August, was gloomy and depressed, a far cry from the brash, or rash, enthusiasm with which he had urged the adoption of the system four years before. Gone were the 'decided opinions' he usually expressed – indeed, he had 'great difficulty' in expressing any opinion 'with respect to the future working of the apparatus between Exeter and Newton' and he 'could not anticipate the possibility of any inducement to continue the system beyond Newton'. He also admitted, for the first time, that inconvenient fact which he had known about for at least four years – that there could be no increase of power 'without renewal of the pipes and pumps'.

He concluded with the fateful words: 'From the foregoing observations it will be evident that I cannot consider the result of our experience of the working between Exeter and Newton such as to induce one to recommend the extension of the system.' Isambard's tidal wave of enthusiasm for a beautiful theory had cost the South Devon Railway shareholders approaching £500,000. The Directors, with the exception of the Chairman, Thomas Gill, MP, were sick of the constant expenses and a resolution was adopted that the line should go over to locomotive haulage as from Sunday 10 September 1848 until such time as Clegg & Samuda agreed to repair and guarantee the airtight valve. All that remained was for the shareholders to be told. The meeting was convened at Plymouth on 29 August when Isambard was to stand up and tell these shareholders, whose money he had lost, that he had been wrong.

Rolt has praised Isambard for his 'high courage and unfaltering decision' in abandoning the atmospheric. Isambard had no choice but to abandon the experiment; he had faltered in making the decision for years, and 'courage' did not come into it. The proprietors did not think Isambard courageous. One angry shareholder at the 29 August meeting stated:

> On the system which was now to be abandoned, the Company had already expended some £400,000. Mr Brunel had received warnings from engineers at least as eminent as himself but still recklessly entered upon an expenditure, not at his own expense but at that of others, the expense of persons of small means, widows and others who had invested all their savings and who could ill afford his playing in such a manner with their property.

Isambard's biographer son has written:

> Critics have erred greatly in representing him as a man who, in order to accomplish some vast design, thought but little of the distress which follows want of success in commercial enterprises. So far from this being true . . . his chief thoughts were for those who would suffer through the failure of his plans.

Bearing in mind Isambard's whole-hearted support for free-market capitalism and his passionate belief in the freedom of every individual to follow his own life's plan without hindrance, it is difficult to believe that he lost any sleep over the fate of unsuccessful investors. Kind-hearted though he could sometimes be, he had his priorities ruthlessly worked out and his business quite definitely came first. Those who invested – including himself – took their chance. But he did make one small, private, gesture of contribution. He waived his fee on the South Devon until the railway had been opened on 2 April 1849 throughout to Plymouth as a locomotive-hauled railway.

19

Double Standards

In February 1846, Edwin Chadwick, a great and virtuous Victorian who, like J.S. Mill, advocated governmental provision of basic public works such as education, clean water, proper sewage disposal, humane working hours and hygienic conditions in factories and prisons, sent Isambard his proposals for laws to protect the railway navvies from the harsh conditions imposed on them by self-seeking employers – and invited Isambard's comments.

Isambard was keen to right all the wrongs suffered by the navvies, and any other working person – but only if the remedies remained as *gifts* to the workmen and were not made into legal *obligations*. In his reply to Chadwick on 7 March, Isambard agreed as to the problems besetting the lives of railway navvies and their families. He and the Directors of the companies he worked for 'had made more exertions than you appear to think Directors generally do. Indeed, this is a common error into which . . . redressers of wrongs frequently fall – that of supposing that parties connected with the grievances *and with opportunity of profiting from them* do not anxiously endeavour to remedy them. I should be most happy to join in any well-directed attempt to remedy these very great and crying evils – if proper exertions are directed at the roots of the evil.'

But what were 'well-directed . . . proper exertions'? Isambard was sure of one thing – they were only to be undertaken voluntarily. 'I am convinced that any *legislative interference* in the shape of penalties, upon those parties whose *friendly and cordial* assistance can alone afford any chance of success, will only aggravate the mischief without removing any of the original causes. Penalties . . . can always be evaded . . . and the endeavour to evade them will recreate the original causes of the evil.' A conservative at heart, Isambard was saying that nothing could be done to put right 'very great and crying evils' except to rely on the 'friendly and cordial' feelings of employers who were profiting from those same abuses.

Isambard listed the evils affecting navvies as: the truck system – when a contractor paid his men in food and drink rather than money; irregularity of payment of the men; excessive sub-letting of contracts. He professed such detestation of the truck system that he was actually agreeable to a law forbidding it. All his contracts, he said, contained a clause absolutely forbidding the contractor to pay his men in anything but the coin of the realm and further insisting that the navvies were to be paid at least once a fortnight. In fact the Brunellian clause, if it existed, did nothing to bring about regular payment, nor did it abolish the truck system on Brunellian railways when a contractor short of cash, frequently due to Isambard's withholding of payments, could not pay his men.

The third 'great evil' – 'sub-contracting to excess' – often left men without pay. Ordinary workmen formed a group of, say, six, and gave the main contractor their price for a piece of work. One of the six acted as ganger and was paid by the main contractor. The men, faced with heavy competition, offered to complete a job for an unrealistically low price, or came up against unexpected difficulties which consumed their funds whilst no progress was made. To quote Isambard: 'Frequently he [the sub-contractor] decamps, defrauding the other men, rendering them reckless and teaching them to be rascals in their turn. The Gang is broken up and the men in debt leave the place to seek work elsewhere – thus aggravating the unsettled, roving and consequently reckless habits of the men.'

Isambard asserted that 'none of these original circumstances can be prevented by law', but might be diminished and to some extent eliminated by 'the encouragement of responsible contractors'. 'The latter class of men', he said, 'were not to be harassed by penalties which are in principle unjust.' Where were these 'responsible contractors' to be found? In ten years of construction Isambard had difficulty in finding half a dozen such firms – and one of those he was harassing and defrauding of tens of thousands of pounds at the very moment he was writing to Chadwick. One 'great evil' which neither Chadwick nor Isambard listed was that of an Engineer who thought he could do no wrong.

Employees in 1846 had no redress if, during their employment, they were injured; nor could their families demand compensation if they were killed. Chadwick suggested that the employer should be liable in law to compensate a workman or his dependents for injuries received at work. Isambard found this idea quite alarming and attacked it as 'unfair to the employer' tending to encourage 'men of low character who would succeed in evading the law'. He became, at times, just daft on the subject and suggested that evasion of the law would take the form of contractors refusing to employ married workmen – for then there would be no surviving dependents to compensate – and even became so over-excited as to assert that compensation for injuries would encourage workmen to risk loss of limbs for the sake of pensions.

He suggested the formation of 'a sort of association of railway engineers, directors and philanthropists such as yourself *working without any fixed rule* who would, each in their respective spheres, endeavour gradually to introduce improvements and to this end would correspond with each other . . . even eventually promoting the education of the workmen.' One wonders how long the navvies would have had to wait for these voluntary correspondence societies to bring about improvements when, as Isambard had written, many of the correspondents were profiting from those same grievances.

Such a voluntary corresponding society would have minimal costs – a great advantage – and Isambard was 'sure' that those costs would be 'most cheerfully and most liberally met by the Companies'. Isambard, a prolific writer of letters, thought this was 'an excellent scheme' and warned Chadwick that he would 'resist on principle anything like legislative interference just as I would resist the introduction of a disease'. Thus the cruel reality of Isambard's principles. He would dispense largesse to the deserving poor as and when he felt like it.

In April 1848 a revolutionary situation existed in several European capitals and fear of revolution also gripped the government in London. Isambard signed on as a special constable for his district to protect life and property from a non-existent mob and in the midst of directing the works of half a dozen railways he received instruction in how to render rioters unconscious with his government-issue truncheon:

On encountering a Rebel . . . stand firm . . . and holding the staff at point very firmly in your right hand, advance upon your enemy and give a vigorous thrust at the third button of his waistcoat – counting from the bottom of that garment. If the blow be . . . vigorous it will double-up your opponent and present his head and neck in the most favourable position for receiving a slashing cut . . .'

What had to be done if the scurrilous rioters had removed their waistcoats, or if they were too poor to own such garments, was not explained.

No rioters appeared and, disappointed at the lack of excitement, Isambard went with Ben Hawes to Paris, not as one might have thought to assist the National Guard in putting down the revolution but, to quote his grand-daughter, Lady Celia Noble, 'for the pleasure of seeing the famous barricades . . . crowned with the red flag and defended by women as vehement in republican ardour as the men'. Isambard saw street fighting and was present when the mob stormed and sacked the Tuileries palace. According to Lady Noble: 'This gave Isambard the opportunity of purchasing many French pieces to add to the Majolicas, bronzes, etc., he had brought from Italy.' Thus loaded down with *objets d'art* – which they knew must be looted – Isambard and Ben Hawes returned to London to take up their patrols as constables, entrusted with protecting property and keeping the peace.

Isambard had surveyed the route for the Oxford, Worcester & Wolverhampton Railway during 1844 and a rough time he had. The Chipping Campden Town Trust held, or holds, a truncheon which is inscribed: *1844 Campden Glos. Defeat of Issambard Brunel – Oxford Worcester and Wolverhampton*. The truncheon had been wielded – ironically for 'Issambard' – by a special constable, one of several raised by a landowner, Sir John Fox, for the express purpose of excluding Brunel or any of his employees from Fox land, and stopping the survey.

The OWWR Bill received the Royal Assent and became an Act of Parliament on 4 August 1845, whereupon Isambard was paid £6500. Construction began and Isambard's estimate was soon seen to be, as usual, over-optimistic. The OWWR Directors needed more money and, to encourage would-be investors, they asked the GWR to guarantee 4 per cent on whatever sum it took to build the line. The GWR Directors agreed to pay 4 per cent on a sum not exceeding £2½ m. but the OWWR Chairman, Francis Rufford, misled his shareholders into thinking that the GWR was guaranteeing 4 per cent on an unlimited sum and they were stupid enough to believe him. The wrangling between the two companies became increasingly bitter, Isambard's position as Engineer to both companies became impossible and in March 1852 he resigned but continued to take responsibility for works he had started.

These included the Mickleton (or Chipping Campden) Tunnel where, since 1846, a Mr Williams of Liverpool and Robert Mudge-Marchant, Isambard's second cousin, had been contractors with £10,000 of 'plant' – wagons, timber and machinery which they had purchased from the original contractor. Isambard was his usual dictatorial self as regards payment – or non-payment – for work done and in June 1851 Williams and Mudge-Marchant stopped work due to being owed £34,000 by the OWWR.

In July the OWWR Directors ordered Isambard to evict Mudge-Marchant from the site – and to seize his equipment to compensate the OWWR for £6300 which, the Company said, Williams and Mudge-Marchant owed them. Mudge-Marchant set his men to guard the equipment and for a week desultory bouts of fisticuffs took place between employees of the rival contractors while Isambard, his sense of law and order completely overcome by his indignation at Mudge-Marchant's defiance of Brunellian orders, built up an army of navvies at Banbury. Isambard's *other* set of morals were once more to the fore.

On the evening of 17 July 1851, Isambard, Robert Vardon, his Resident Engineer from Banbury, and Mr Hobler, Isambard's legal adviser, set out in the 'Flying Hearse' (his famous britschka) at the head of hundreds of navvies for the long march to Mickleton Tunnel. Mudge-Marchant, being advised by his spies that the Brunellian army would fall upon him at about 3 a.m. the following day, at once raised barricades to prevent access to the site and sent for the Chipping Campden magistrates, Kettle and Ashwin. These worthies arrived with the local constabulary – all three of them – armed with cutlasses.

When Isambard arrived on the scene he was rebuked – but not arrested – by the magistrates for inciting a riot and causing a breach of the peace. Isambard, forgetting that he had, on two occasions in the past, been sworn in as a special constable to prevent rioting, refused to withdraw. Hobler engaged the magistrates in a war of words, and the navvies, to relieve boredom during the conference, began fighting each other.

Isambard demanded that Mudge-Marchant give up the ground. Mudge-Marchant refused, the navvies became even more excited and one man produced a brace of pistols only to be knocked to the ground. The situation was by then one of 'tumultuous assembly', due largely to Brunel's action, and Ashwin had twice to bawl the statutory words of the Riot Act, commanding the unruly crowd to disperse, before Isambard called off his navvies.

Isambard returned soon after dawn with a small body of men hoping to surprise Mudge-Marchant but he was on guard. Fighting broke out but the magistrates were still on site. They invoked the Riot Act once more and Isambard retired to make fresh plans. He regretted departing from his principle of overwhelming force and sent for reinforcements from Cheltenham, Warwick and Moreton-in-the-Marsh. Ashwin, on hearing about this late that evening, set off for the works. On his way he met a large body of Brunellian infantry who asked him the way to the tunnel. He sent them off in the opposite direction. At the tunnel, in the small hours of the 19th, he found Isambard sitting in his carriage, a veritable Napoleon, surrounded by his mounted officers and a large crowd of foot-soldiers or navvies. He was waiting for his reinforcements to converge from all sides; the last thing he expected to appear was a magistrate.

The men were already fighting and Ashwin spoke so urgently to Isambard of his responsibility for the affray and resultant injuries, that Brunel repented and was again sworn in as a special constable to keep the peace. But by then General Brunel's troops were pouring in from the west and north, until 3000 men were in the field. Desultory fighting took place throughout the day but with Isambard's assistance a general engagement was prevented. Bones were broken but no one was killed – the accounts of injuries were grossly exaggerated by the creative journalism of the *Illustrated London News*. At 6 p.m. Mudge-Marchant could see his position was hopeless and surrendered on Isambard's promise of an arbitrated settlement.

Isambard's impromptu manoeuvres at the 'Battle of Mickleton Tunnel' have been given exaggerated praise by Rolt as 'a highly organised military operation, perfectly timed and executed'. In fact, he carried out an illegal show of brute force. He had incited 3000 men into a riotous assembly. If the law had been enforced impartially he would have been arrested, tried and, if found guilty, transported to a penal colony in Australia. But Isambard was too illustrious a gentleman for such a fate.

It is also surprising that the workmen should have so willingly fought each other, inflicting and receiving broken limbs in defence of their respective employers who frequently omitted to pay them. In the case of Mudge-Marchant's men, they were often paid with truck system vouchers which were negotiable only at the contractor's tommy-shop. So much for Isambard's claim, to Chadwick, that the truck system was prohibited on his works. The system was used throughout the years of construction of the tunnel.

Robert Mudge-Marchant was declared bankrupt on 29 November 1851. He wrote to Isambard what must have been an abusive letter, to which Isambard replied, with a hypocritical display of affection, on 16 February 1852:

> Marchant, I can't make out . . . why, with such feelings as you profess to entertain, you address me at all. You go into partnership with a man who has no capital but borrowed money and who is involved in an unfortunate contract and you are ruined. How could it be otherwise? And then you abuse the only man who ever did or does care sixpence for your welfare. You now talk of *forgiving* this man. . . . This is cant. Your excessively irritable temper, your imprudence, I can stand, but not your cant. As long as you wish to abuse me, have the goodness to do it in some other way than writing to me as I shall return the letters unread.

The arbitration took place in October 1852 under Sir William Cubitt and Robert Stephenson who took the only practical course open to them – of upholding the OWWR's decision to remove Williams and Mudge-Marchant while awarding them compensation for the loss of their contract.

20

'Stark, staring, wildly mad'

In 1844 that great bubble of credit known as the 'Railway Mania' was growing. The main trunk railways had proved to be a good investment and thousands of simpletons believed that any projected railway would create a good return. Ordinary folk invested their life savings while unscrupulous financiers – such as George Hudson – raised large sums of credit to launch railway projects which were inherently unsound or, in many cases, were merely 'paper railways' never to be built but useful to manipulate the stock market. Money for good schemes – such as Isambard's – became hard to find. He himself despised all speculators and wrote about them in very strong language.

On his return from a visit to his Italian projects, in 1844, he wrote this to an unknown individual: 'Dear Sir, I returned only this afternoon and am endeavouring – but very ineffectually as yet – to comprehend the present extraordinary state of railway matters when everybody around seems mad – stark, staring, wildly mad. The only sane course for a sane man is to get out and keep quiet . . . I do not intend to go mad and I soon should at the rate the others are going.'

As Engineer to the Bristol & Gloucester Railway he cautioned his Directors against unsafe trading practices. They were waging a price war with other carriers and he wrote to them in February 1844: 'Bristol is not Liverpool and if you carried for nothing you could not make a larger trade than you could at moderate prices . . . railway people are *all mad* – excuse my saying it – the B&G amongst them and when the public learn that you have been carrying an enormous trade at a loss, like cheap linen drapers, there will be a dreadful reaction.'

His life was, he complained frequently to close friends, 'a dreadful scramble' but he continued to take on more work. Of the innumerable letters he wrote at night from his Duke Street desk or in some wayside hotel at the end of an exhausting day, the one he penned to Sam Wells of the Bedford Levels Corporation on 11 April 1845 gives a vivid impression of the pace at which he lived his life and the huge distances he covered:

> It occurs to me to mention a point which may influence the Board in requesting my attendance, the subject of my professional charges. I think it better if there can be no possibility of disappointment. I have long since given up any mode of travelling, when off the railway, except in my own carriage. When I tell you that I shall probably come up from Bristol to London on Sunday night, that I go to Exeter on Monday night, return on Tuesday night to go to Ely (if I go) on Wednesday and return to London on Thursday night, you will not be surprised that, to enable me to lead such a life I am obliged to adopt every means for diminishing fatigue. I mention this that no misunderstanding may arise as I hate extravagance as much as those who have to pay for it. If I come to Ely I would want to get away to Wisbech and then to Peterborough by daylight and make full use of the day.

The Corporation employed him as their adviser in cases where railway companies wanted to bridge the 100-ft Drain and other Fenland waterways – another iron in his fire, along with his English and Italian railways.

The Piedmontese government – which Isambard insisted on calling by its pre-Napoleonic title, the Sardinian government – was looking for the cheapest tender for a railway from the port of Genoa up through the Apennines to Turin via Alessandria. Isambard had been back and forth, surveying the route and negotiating with government officials. He was also negotiating to become the Engineer of the Maria Antonia Railway from Florence to Pistoia. In 1845 he had installed Herschel Babbage, son of his close friend, the mathematician Charles Babbage, as his Resident Engineer in Italy and directed him through a steady stream of letters. Isambard's memory was Napoleonic for he maintained a postal supervision of a dozen engineers at widely differing works and not only gave directions on construction but also smoothed out the frequent personality clashes which arose between engineer and contractor or between brother engineers.

Employing Herschel Babbage lost Isambard a contract and his continued employment may have been a rare example of Isambard employing a man purely for friendship's sake. Herschel, it seems, was not as soberly industrious as Isambard would have liked. He became involved with Directors of the Modena/Ancona Railway called Bonfil and Jackson, who had a rival Genoa/Turin line and who attempted to prevent Isambard's scheme by the simple expedient of removing Herschel by offering him £1500 a year to go and work on their Modena/Ancona line.

Herschel was under no obligation to Isambard – other than that of one friend to another – and, market forces being what they were, £1500 was quite an amount. Isambard was not prepared to enter into an auction for Herschel's services as he had capable men at Duke Street who could replace him, but he saw through the plot and warned Herschel, describing Jackson as 'a clever, spirited man who has made Birkenhead a rival to Liverpool'. Bonfil was sinister, 'a clever – a very clever, Neapolitan speculator'. He told Herschel: 'If Bonfil should wish you to go to Ancona – mind you get your money in advance . . . keep me well informed of your movements.'

By early June 1845, Isambard had 'arranged everything with the Sardinian government for the construction of the line from Genoa to Alessandria' – but he did not know if he still had a Resident Engineer. He wrote to Herschel on 10 June, 'assuming you have made up your mind to be my assistant . . .' and continuing, full of instructions for driving a tunnel near Ponte Decimo*: 'I think of bringing Brereton over for you at the tunnel. He has had more experience than any man I have and as I suppose he will take his wife he will be a great addition to your circle which I should think is a small one.'

Isambard's object in introducing a highly respectable married lady into Herschel's circle seems to have been intended to calm Herschel's unfettered bachelor existence, for Isambard's letter continued: 'You must now cast off quickly all the effects of your tedious, expecting life and set down to work soberly and seriously. . . . I imagine you will find it difficult to get rid of your peculiar, unsettled habits . . . it requires an effort . . . I expect you to work seriously.' Herschel took fright at these fatherly exhortations to sobriety and the relinquishing of his intriguingly peculiar habits and went to work for Jackson on his rival scheme.

---

* Brunel's spelling; unidentifiable location.

As a result of Herschel Babbage's defection, Isambard was unable to proceed with the construction of the railway, the Piedmontese government grew tired of waiting, and in 1846 gave the job to their newly formed Public Works Department. With that, Jackson and Bonfil dismissed Herschel who returned to Isambard's employment on the Maria Antonia Railway out of Florence. The Babbages must have been very dear friends indeed to Isambard. Herschel Babbage worked hard for Isambard here, however. The Tuscan countryside was in a state of near insurrection but Babbage managed to push the work on; indeed, one would never know from the letters that there was any unrest at all. On 15 April 1846 Isambard concluded a letter of instructions to Herschel with this:

> Can you send me some sketches – thank you for those received – of the campaniles in the country. These are prettier, I think, than those at Genoa, Novi or St Julian in the Plains of Marengo(?). This style, light, tall, elegant, I have a vivid recollection of them yet there is nothing like them in any of your sketches.
> P.S. In England, architects when they build Italian, affect a sort of tiling thus — . Now I have no recollection of any such. I only recollect a mass of half-round tile all close together without any flat ones. Let me know if you can find any of the former or whether my recollection is correct.

Isambard's interest was not simply academic, he was designing the buildings to house the pumping engines for his atmospheric system on the South Devon and felt that the Italianate style would be very effective on the warm, red-sandstone Devon scene. The 'details of ornament of the church of Santa Maria Novella, such as the corbels and tower', probably found a place in one of the pumping houses he designed. His architectural taste was impeccable and his generating stations for the South Devon atmospheric, the beautiful campanile disguising the chimney, were the best part of the whole system.

Isambard's generous and forgiving attitude towards Herschel Babbage was a good example of why his friends loved him so much but this circle of friends was very small. Usually, when a choice had to be made between a friend and the Company, the friend was sacrificed. When Lord Granville Somerset, who had done a very great deal to push the Great Western Railway Act through Parliament in 1835, asked Isambard to find a job for a young friend, His Lordship could not be refused, but Isambard's usual policy towards requests that he use his influence was very different. On 19 March 1843, for example, a Mr Pearce wrote asking Isambard to 'put a word in' to the GWR Directors on behalf of a young man, and received the following reply:

> You can easily imagine that there are 100 applicants for every crumb that falls from the scanty meals of railway employers and I can assure you that I have no patronage nor is any exercised by anybody. All applicants are received, examined, accepted or rejected like samples of merchandise without any interest being used or useful.

Isambard's Bristol Division Resident Engineer, George Frere, who had been responsible, under Brunel, for the entire construction of the line from Box to Bristol for six years, left GWR service in August 1841, whether voluntarily or under dismissal is not known. On 23 April 1844, Frere wrote to Isambard asking for a job on the South Devon Railway. Isambard took five weeks to reply and when he did he rebuked his old friend for making comments about 'matters which are not strictly confined to business'. Isambard went on:

> You want employment, we are friends of long standing and, of course, if I can do what you want consistently with what I think is right, I will. The matter is not a simple one. I have to think who will do the work best, I must take care that those who employ me are satisfied with those I employ and I must be as just as I can to those who have been working for me. I am aware of the bachelor school, this will always be a difficulty to be considered. If and when the opportunity occurs when I want simply an engineer and a man implicitly to be relied on then there is no one I should be more glad to have than you.

So much for George Frere, to whom, between 1835 and 1841, Isambard had written hundreds of friendly, supervisory letters and from whom, the whole record shows, he had always received satisfaction. On 6 January 1846 Isambard met Frere to offer him a job, but the meeting turned out to be a bad-tempered one and Isambard afterwards wrote:

> I thought to propose something agreeable to you and I sought to obtain a person well qualified for the work I had to get done . . . not a single word did you utter to lead me to suppose that you felt in the slightest degree obliged to me for thinking of you. . . . Any third person present yesterday might have supposed that you had called upon me to complain of some illiberality of mine. . . .
> I must not press an appointment on a man who does not feel the ordinary obligation of the employed to the employer. If you do feel

pleasure in accepting the offer then say so and I shall have even more pleasure in having made it.

The air of injured innocence in that letter is similar to that used in the letter Isambard wrote to Robert Mudge-Marchant. There are so many letters of Brunel's and very few from the other side. If only we knew Frere's side of the story. As there is no record of that we have to give him some benefit of doubt and wonder why, if Isambard was being so generous, Frere, who was unemployed, was so rude. Could it be that Isambard, taking advantage of Frere's position, was asking him to work for less than the going rate?

Isambard, then, was engulfed in work of every possible description and, much as he complained of the pace of his life, he was very reluctant indeed to slow down. The reasons for this are clearly shown in a long letter he wrote in August 1848, in the depths of the economic depression following the collapse of the 'railway bubble', to his brother-in-law John Horsley, RA:

> You consulted me as to giving up the school or rather – as I look at it – the salary . . . I am disposed, no doubt, to look at things with a gloomy eye at present but the reason for my doing so must also be a reason for you to do the same. My spirits are particularly broken by the proceedings I have been compelled to adopt. The state of trade and money in England is such that I have for weeks past been obliged to dismiss men and cut salaries to the amount of £10,000. Imagine the extent of pain and misery that I have had to inflict and you can easily understand the anxiety I must feel for anyone who has to give up any certainty, however small.

Since Isambard would no more countenance legislation to regulate the greed of individuals than he would agree to the 'introduction of a disease' and since the depression was caused, by his own admission, by greedy, 'illiberal' persons, who were 'stark, staring, wildly mad', his grief for those he was dismissing could, perhaps, be considered crocodile tears. In the midst of these economies he was engaged in purchasing for himself a large tract of land at Watcombe, near Torquay.

After considerable outpourings wherein – it seems to me – he luxuriates in his power over men with large families, he suddenly changes the subject:

> I do not think I would give up £250 a year unless I was certain I could replace it. Do you feel confident that when you leave your employment you will *slavishly* occupy the time you will thus gain? Your profession is

one that admits of great industry but does not compel it. I believe that *compulsion even to irksomeness* induces wholesome habits. If you give up the school let me entreat you to *slave*. . . . I feel this strongly because I believe that I am naturally idle and all my life is one of *slaving and compulsion*. You and many others may think my life a pleasant one because I am of a happy disposition but from morning to night, from one end of the year to the other, *it is the life of a slave*. I am never my own master and I always have an overwhelming quantity of work which *must be done* by certain days.

There is, I feel, real anguish in that completely unguarded lapse into his deeply private feelings. Not only does he admit how miserable he is, having finally succeeded in becoming the Great Engineer, but he also betrays an enormous sense of insecurity. If he stops 'slaving' his 'natural idleness', a little blue devil from his adolescence, will come and carry him off to the land where 'mediocre successes' live. So he is chased by devils and cannot rest. What price ambition?

21

Brunel – Paterfamilias

Mary bore Isambard three children: the elder boy, Isambard, was born on 18 May 1837; Henry Marc in 1842; and Florence Mary in 1846 or 1847. The first son was born with a crippled leg. According to Lady Celia Noble, 'Mary's pride was deeply mortified. A simple operation would have put matters right but Mary shared the popular horror of surgery,' she 'seemed to find consolation, to the end of her days, in the boast, "I would never let the surgeon's knife touch him".'

Brunel's responsibility for directing the construction of a large part of the industrial infrastructure of Great Britain prevented him from seeing as much of his children as he might have liked but in all too rare periods of relaxation he was a charming, delightful companion. He loved children and enjoyed the clowning that entertained them. He enjoyed the absurdity of pantomime and always tried to visit the Christmas performances – even before he had children old enough to accompany him. His children's nurse recalled his 'charging up the stairs to the nursery' to play with them – when he could spare the time – and I wonder at what cost to his own happiness he pursued his ambition of public reputation, wealth and industrial imperialism.

On 3 April 1843 Isambard was at home, 'entertaining some children', and performing his conjuring trick of putting a sovereign in his mouth and taking it out of his ear. The gold coin was in his mouth and, as he spoke to his audience, it inadvertently slipped down his throat. Isambard experienced no discomfort, assumed that he had swallowed it and continued to work and to travel. After two weeks though he began to suffer fits of coughing. He consulted the eminent surgeon Sir Benjamin Brodie on the 18th. Brodie diagnosed the coin as the cause; it was in Isambard's right bronchus. He then withdrew from work.

Next day Isambard bent over a chair and felt the small but heavy coin slip towards the glottis. He stood up and as the coin fell back he went into a spasm of coughing for several minutes. When this subsided he did the same thing again – just to make sure – and got the same result. A table with hinged top was constructed and on the 25th Isambard was strapped to this, face down. He was not, as Rolt has stated, whirled around to throw the coin out by centrifugal force. The hinged section was lifted, bringing his head to the floor, feet uppermost and he was thumped gently between his shoulder blades in the hope of dislodging the coin. All that resulted was an uncontrollable bout of coughing so frightening that the experiment was discontinued.

On 27 April, a tracheotomy was performed by Brodie with the intention of extracting the coin with forceps or, failing that, of making an opening in the windpipe which would prevent the suffocating coughing fit brought on by the inversion technique. The forceps brought on a coughing fit so exhausting that nothing further could be done until 2 May. As a result, Isambard missed the opening of the Bristol & Exeter Railway to the temporary station at Beambridge, $8\frac{1}{2}$ miles west of Taunton. The new attempt on 2 May brought about a coughing fit violent enough to lay him low for eleven days, the wound in his windpipe being kept open throughout that time.

On 13 May Isambard was again strapped to the hinged table-top and raised vertically, head downwards. His back was struck gently and after some ordinary coughing he felt the coin move from the right side of his chest. He wrote to Captain Claxton, later: 'At $4\frac{1}{2}$ [i.e. 4.30] I was safely delivered of my little coin; with hardly an effort it dropped out, as many another has and, I hope, will drop out of my fingers. I am perfectly well and expect to be in Bristol by the end of the week.'

Isambard had so far succeeded in becoming a household word that *The Times* reported regularly on the progress of his treatment. When the coin fell out the news was carried by word of mouth across London. By that eminent man of letters, Thomas Babington Macaulay, who ran along the pavements to the Athenaeum Club shouting, 'It's out! it's out!' So far from thinking him mad, everyone knew exactly what he was excited about. On 16 May 1843 a full account of the whole episode was published in *The Times* at Brunel's request, 'as a guide to future practice'.

At the time of the accident Isambard's parents were living with him at 17 and 18 Duke Street. There were two reasons for this. One was Marc's frail health. He had suffered a heart attack in November 1842 after which he and Sophia had moved from their small house in Park Street, opposite St James's Park, to Isambard's large and opulent house in Duke Street. The second reason was Marc's straitened finances. The Thames Tunnel was opened to the public on 25 March 1843 and Marc was well enough to attend. The assembled throng gave him a vast ovation but the Thames Tunnel Company omitted to pay him the second part of his fee for completing the job. They owed him £5000 and he never received it. Isambard gave financial support to his ageing and ill-treated parents and the richer he became the more help he gave. Unfortunately this did not produce harmony and Isambard's mother Sophia, in particular, found the position of dependency galling and the sight of her daughter-in-law flaunting all the signs of considerable wealth very irritating. Extreme coldness developed and Isambard's accident with the sovereign was the last straw, turning the tense situation into a full-blown family row.

Courteous old Marc Brunel was so far incensed as to make this outspoken entry in his diary on 21 April: 'Intimation given to me and my dearest Sophia that we must leave the house tomorrow though she has not been addressed for 3 weeks! This in consequence of Isambard's particular case of illness. Engaged accordingly in packing up everything to go to a house, No 9, in same street.' On calm reflection Marc crossed this out and we have Lady Noble to thank for deciphering the entry. The Brunels patched up their differences and after Marc's death on 12 December 1849, Sophia spent the rest of her life at 18 Duke Street.

When young Isambard was sent away to boarding school, four weeks before his eighth birthday, his father was down in the West Country preparing for the opening of his Bristol & Exeter Railway from Beambridge to Exeter. The little lad with the crippled leg was understandably puzzled and unhappy at being sent away from his mother, brother and sister, and Mary was unhappy to lose him. His father had no such feelings and when Mary wrote to him to convey her sadness, Isambard replied on 17 April 1844 with a breezy letter:

My Dear Love, Here I am on my way to Exeter. I have every reason to believe that though I may be at home on Thursday I shall be away again on Friday. I hope, dearest, that you are well and happy. You are wrong in supposing that I cannot feel your parting with dear Isambard. I hope the poor little fellow is not very unhappy but it is what all must go through. He had infinitely less cause for pain than most boys in beginning. I made my beginning in ten times worse circumstances. He will soon get over it. Give my love to the dear boy and tell him I have smoked his cigar case twice empty. Adieu, dearest love to Baby, Yours devotedly, IKB

In spite of the affectionate words it was a tolerably dismissive letter. Did Brunel have such a dreadful beginning? Was that any reason for inflicting it on his son? Official beatings and secret bullying were a normal part of school life in those days and a handicapped little boy was a potential victim who particularly needed the security of his family.

As the boy grew older his health became more obviously delicate, and his perfectionist father became evermore disappointed in him. According to Lady Celia Noble, Isambard's letters to his son became 'shy and aloof'. He also wrote to his son ordering him to pay attention to his drill instructor, even ordering him to 'try to walk properly' which, of course, he was quite unable to do. One letter concluded: 'If I could have you under my care for three months, I feel sure I could cure you . . . but you must try and do it for yourself.' As the boy grew older, I imagine that he must also have become shy and self-conscious owing to his much-remarked-upon disability.

In the summer term, 1852, young Isambard was sent to the rough-and-tumble of Harrow School where Charles Vaughan was Headmaster and beatings were daily punishments – ordeals from which Isambard himself had been carefully shielded by his own father. Isambard did not send his son to Harrow because he had a good opinion of the education to be obtained there. Indeed, it appears he had a low opinion of it, and he also knew that boarding at Harrow was somewhat uncomfortable. During 1855 young Isambard was appointed a School Monitor and on 22 November Brunel wrote to him: 'I think I must take you in hand at Christmas for I fear that the quality of your arithmetical knowledge is very queer, whatever the quantity must be and that is probably small. Half a pint of poor small beer a day is not nourishing and cannot be called a malt liquor diet, neither can I imagine Harrow arithmetic to be much better.'

Young Isambard must have complained about conditions at the school because this letter from his father concluded: 'It is very distressing but one must put up with it as if brought up in a country where it is the practice to put out one eye.' Brunel sent his eldest son to Harrow simply because he believed his status as a famous engineer required it. For one who gloried in his own individualism, this was indeed bowing to convention.

To balance the gloomy picture, and to be fair to Harrow, it must be said that the education he received there, however deficient in mathematics, stood young Isambard in good stead. He went up to Oxford in December 1856, gained his BA in 1860, his MA in 1863 and was called to the Bar the same year, going on to become a Doctor of Law in 1870 and Chancellor of the Diocese of Ely from 1871 to 1893.

Brunel regretted the distance between himself and his children although he was never regretful enough to do anything to improve matters. He was trapped by his ambitions. On 20 May 1855, he wrote a poignant note to Isambard for his eighteenth birthday: '. . . and my dear Isambard, although my constant engagements have prevented my seeing so much of my children as I should have wished, yet I hope that you would look upon me as your first friend if you ever got into difficulty . . . pray then, dear boy, while you have a father to whom you might safely . . . confide anything, consult him if ever you have the slightest difficulty; and to you, my dear Isambard, many happy returns of the day.'

Over the line 'while you have a father', his son wrote later 'Alas! Alas!' That same line might imply that his father knew that his health was now in serious decline.

To attend to the wants of Mary and the three children – and himself when he was at home – he employed, according to the 1851 census, a footman, twenty-three-year-old William Lawson; two sisters, Penelope and Mary Ann Bates, aged sixteen and nineteen respectively, as kitchen maids; three housemaids, also in their twenties, a cook and a housekeeper. Besides these there were a governess and two nurses for the children. In 1847 and 1848 he was wealthy enough to complete the extension of the family rooms above the offices in Nos 17 and 18.

The clean lines of his public works were not reproduced in his private rooms. He established drawing rooms, one in each house, panelled – not in oak – but in plaster, painted and 'grained' to look like panelling. On these peculiarly false walls hung mirrors in elaborate gilt frames. Those walls which were not covered by ornate mirrors were draped with crimson velvet or were covered with paintings. The ceiling was just as heavy, with much pendant plasterwork. Sumptuous banquets were eaten in one of these rooms off Dresden china, at a massive table laden with heavy silverware.

In the drawing room above the offices at No 18 there were twenty-four paintings, twenty by Sir Augustus Calcott, RA, Mary's great-uncle, and four by her brother, John Horsley, RA. One of the Calcott paintings was *The English Claude* and on the subject of payment great-uncle Calcott wrote to Isambard, on 5 August 1844, a delight-fully dotty letter in a schoolboy scrawl but with so many indecipher-able words as to make it – sadly – impossible to quote at length. However, in it he says how much he wants – £8000 – 'you see I do not even stipulate guineas but merely confine myself to pounds.' Having given Isambard a fright, he then lays out his terms for pay-ment by instalments at the end of which Isambard must have been very relieved to see that he was being teased. 'The mode of payment I propose', added Calcott, 'is to be by 95 bills commencing 2 August 1844, the second on 2 August 1944 and every succeeding century until the whole 95 have been paid. The price of the frame is Willet's concern . . .'

On 14 December 1847 Isambard invited eleven of the most famous artists of the day so that he could lay before them his grand design for a set of paintings from Shakespearian scenes. The artists included Edwin Landseer, David Roberts and Isambard's brother-in-law John Horsley. The paintings were each to be paid for in hundreds of guineas and all the artists agreed, naturally, to take a commission. On the 27th Isambard sent them all a written specification including a plan of the wall on which the paintings were to hang and the dimen-sions of each man's painting. Isambard managed to leave the choice of subject to the artists, provided it was a scene from a Shakespeare play.

The finished paintings were hung in the drawing room of No 17. David Roberts contributed 'The Three Witches' from *Macbeth* and Edwin Landseer produced the happiest composition of his increas-ingly mad life. Isambard paid him 400 guineas for it. The picture, $31\frac{1}{2} \times 51\frac{1}{2}$ in., illustrates the well-known incident in *A Midsummer Night's Dream* where Titania, Queen of the Fairies, awakes in a woodland glade. While she has been asleep Oberon has squeezed in her eyes herbal juice to make her fall in love with the first person she sees. This is Bottom the weaver. In the picture a young and well-endowed – if rather stout – young Titania is seen reclining against Bottom, her head on his shoulder, a rose in her hand, while he sits slumped against a tree trunk, his donkey's head garlanded in flowers. In the right foreground some fairies ride on white hares and others fly about. It was perfectly in tune with the then fashionable fairy-rustic fantasy cult of a class who saw themselves as thoroughly modern technocrats.

Isambard first saw the landscapes and seascapes of Devon and Cornwall in 1828 when he convalesced in Plymouth – almost certainly with his Kingdom grandparents – after the collapse of the Thames Tunnel. In 1844 he spent weeks surveying in South Devon and Cornwall and decided that somewhere in that region would be the place for him to build his gentlemanly mansion and estate. In September 1847 the 'railway bubble' burst and thousands of individuals and some banking houses went bankrupt. In November hundreds of men were laid off from the Swindon factory. Those still at work paid $3\frac{1}{2}$ per cent of their wages weekly into a fund to support their unemployed workmates: Isambard contributed £100 and Gooch £50.

During that summer, Isambard decided on Watcombe, about 3 miles north of Torquay, as the site for his retirement. There he would build a great house and park, 'draw in my horns and make room for others'. He bought his first piece of land in 1847. Over the years he gradually extended his holding till he owned 136 acres bordering on the sea in the east and centred on the valley of Watcombe, falling southwards from a ridge 500 ft above the sea, and giving views across Babbacombe Bay to the coast beyond. He wanted to build his house just below the ridge, facing south to the sea, with views also to the west over Dartmoor.

On Christmas Eve 1847 Isambard wrote to a Windsor solicitor on railway business and in the course of this letter he asked a rather imperative favour: 'Do you happen to know Mr Nesfield of Eton College? Is he the landscape gardener and if you happen to know him intimately could you learn from him *at once if you would* what is his opinion of one Forsyth, a gardener who refers to him and who is wanted to superintend the formation of a park where all is to be done and where great knowledge of tree cultivation – not fancy gardening – is wanted.'

Isambard's lack of experience of gardening matters was equalled by his enormous enthusiasm, his love of trees and his great artistic sense. This 'Mr Nesfield of Eton' was in fact W.A. Nesfield, the greatest tree expert in Britain, adviser to the London parks and to the Royal Botanic Gardens at Kew. James Forsyth was also a great 'tree man', having among his triumphs the arboretum at Alton Towers. He was also a delightfully eccentric character who drank 'holly tea' and chewed the flowers of the rhubarb plant as a cure for that great complaint of the over-fed Victorians – constipation. Nesfield became adviser to Brunel and Forsyth was head gardener, planting the trees where Isambard directed.

He was hankering after his rural roots and when, in 1849, he rented a villa in Torquay, he named it Haqueville after his ancestral village in Normandy. His happiest times were spent building up his holdings at, and his plans for, Watcombe, planning magnificent vistas of the sea and the moor through glorious lines and clumps of trees. He planned the siting of every shrub and tree and wanted to plant mountain ash 'everywhere I can stick them for the sake of their berries'. In his sketch-books Isambard planned and fantasised, drawing a complicated, richly ornamented house and elaborately geometric, balustraded, south-facing terrace, the design of which was obviously a source of great pleasure to him. Interspersed amongst plans for balustraded terraces, lodge gates, lodge cottages, ornamental gutterings and down-pipes are sketches of local fishing boats and tackle for raising tall poles. He was his own quantity surveyor and, while engaged on his plans for the SS *Great Eastern*, took time off to calculate the materials required for his great house at Watcombe.

It is quite wrong to say, as Rolt has, that Brunel became totally absorbed in the fight to build the *Great Eastern*. Watcombe Park was important to him. He spent as much time as he could there and, even when absent, the evidence of dated drawings for the house or gardens in his sketch-books proves that he frequently gave his mind to it in the midst of his great problems. As late as 22 October 1857, only eleven days before the launch of the *Great Eastern*, he was badgering a landowner called Daniel Woodley to sell some of his ground, offering him £1000 for $5\frac{1}{2}$ acres 'if the offer is accepted at once'.

In the *Gardeners' Chronicle* during 1887 it was stated that the cascade, water garden and rockery he planned and had built at the foot of the combe was 'a place of outstanding beauty' and the lines of trees – which he did not live to see – were described:

With one's back to the evening sun the opposite slope presented as effective an example of leaf colouring as could be imagined: the variety of hues of the evergreens, from the black green of the Austrian pine to the pale tints of the deodars, in contrast with the purple beeches and the light and dark leaves of the other deciduous trees was a good illustration of what may be done when the planter knows what he is about.

Isambard really loved his growing ranks of fine trees, the burgeoning of a park and garden out of the unkempt hillside and he lavished on it all the care and money that he could, creating something for love rather than profit. Thousands of cartloads of peat were carried to the site for the young trees which were planted upright on the steep slopes by means of a levelling device invented by Isambard for the purpose. He also invented special digging tools for various planting and gardening jobs. But it was not at all obvious to contemporary observers that Isambard was the planner of the park, and we also should not forget Mary, his formidably bossy wife.

We are indebted to the historian of Watcombe, Geoffrey Tudor, for uncovering the following glimpse of the Brunels. Arthur James, who married Isambard's daughter Florence, visited the place in about 1858 and briefly described the scene: 'I went with the party to visit the Brunels. Mr Brunel, whom I saw for the first and only time, was a little, businesslike man in seedy dress with a footrule in his hand. Mrs Brunel was planning and setting out the gardens . . .'

Carriage drives were terraced into the hillside and the terraces were supported by cobble stone walls which are still standing today, 140 years later. These drives were routed through the trees to give exquisite views of the park and of the coastline from Tor Bay to the west, Babbacombe below and eastwards to far-off Lyme Bay. To reach the sea-ward views the drive had to cross the Torquay/Teignmouth road as it climbed Watcombe hill and bisected the estate in a deep cutting. Isambard planned a rustic bridge across the cutting using a clever arrangement of interlocking poles to support the roadway 'girders'. He involved his second son, fifteen-year-old Henry, a budding civil engineer, in planning and erecting it but he died before it was completed. The 'Great Bridge at Maidencombe', as it was known to the family, was completed *in memoriam* by Henry, in 1861. Henry went on to work for Sir John Barry in the construction of several important bridges including Tower Bridge in London.

Designed by the foremost country house architect of the day, William Burn, Isambard's mansion would have been sumptuous, in the Loire Valley château style, faced with Northumberland Prudham stone. Water would have been pumped to the house from the foot of the valley, a rise of 250 ft, by a gas engine. He planned to house his staff in ten semi-detached cottages with the money he got from his work for the Great Exhibition but he managed to build only four, nearby in Church Road, Barton, and never got beyond laying the foundations for his own great house.

This is what he had striven for all those years past. To be a great engineer, creating enormous works of the greatest perfection so as to gain public honour and the great wealth necessary to become a gentleman, *un grand seigneur*, surrounded by his well-cared-for workers. He wanted to work with nature to produce the utmost beauty and poured as much time and money as he could into Watcombe Park from 1847 to his death in 1859. When staying at Hacqueville, Isambard and Mary added to the social life of the area, lording it somewhat over the countryfolk but also giving leadership and employment.

He took a leading role in preventing the construction of a gas works on the beach at Babbacombe Bay and when he sent all his Watcombe staff to the Great Exhibition for a week at his own expense he probably was the first employer ever to give employees paid leave. Mary donated the money to build the village school at Barton and he subscribed most of the money required to rebuild St Marychurch village church. The vicar of the parish was known as 'Candlestick' Watson on account of his 'Romish' tendencies and when the rebuilt church re-opened it lacked half its congregation. They had built their own, Low-Church establishment at Forrough Cross.

Whether Isambard's support of the 'Romish' Watson indicates that he, Isambard, was moving towards a ritualistic religious observance in his advancing years is difficult to say. Isambard's dramatic nature may well have enjoyed the Gothic influence of Rome on plain, Protestant worship but then Rome was so 'illiberal' that Isambard would have rejected anything more dogmatic than candlesticks.

The atmospheric system and the Watcombe estate were both Brunellian dreams, the *châteaux d'Espagne* he had been searching for since 1825. The atmospheric was a dream disguised as a commercial venture, Watcombe Park a dream to escape from commercialism. He detested the 'racket' of speculation yet he needed the market if he was to raise money for his great projects. According to his letter to Horsley he suffered torment from guilt caused by the total unpredictability of the market system which he could see needed control, yet he was as opposed to any legislation for that end as he would be to 'the introduction of a disease'. 'It would suit my interests and those of my clients if all railways projected were stopped for several years,' he had written to William Froude. Isambard was a mass of contradictions.

22

The Puppet-Master

There had been several attempts to build a railway from Falmouth to Plymouth, two of them engineered by Captain William Scarfe Moorsom. Gooch, it will be recalled, was rebuked by Isambard for issuing a free pass to Moorsom and his family on the GWR in 1842. Moorsom's first survey came to nought because the Company failed to attract sufficient public support. In August 1843 the Cornish promoters obtained promises of financial assistance from the GWR, and Moorsom was asked to make another survey. While he was engaged in this he was appointed on 30 May 1844 as Engineer of the Southampton & Dorchester Railway – intended as a broad-gauge line to be leased to the GWR. His Cornwall Railway survey was published in September 1844 and proposed a train ferry across the half-mile-wide Tamar, or Hamoaze, at Torpoint and then over the hills to Falmouth. In a route approximately 50 miles long there were to be 26 miles of 1 in 60 gradients, several miles at 1 in 50 and one mile at 1 in 45.

Moorsom intended the line for atmospheric haulage, hence his apparent disregard for heavy gradients. For the train ferry there seems to be no excuse apart from lack of imagination. The plan was shown to Isambard who, craftily perhaps, approved it. When the Cornwall Railway Bill came before the House of Lords, in May 1845, their Lordships disapproved of the train ferry and steep gradients and they threw out the Bill, whereupon Isambard superseded Moorsom as Engineer of the Cornwall Railway. That was, perhaps, what he had intended.

However, this happened at a particularly difficult moment for relations between Brunel and Moorsom. Captain Moorsom's route for the Southampton & Dorchester Railway through the New Forest had aroused such strong objections that, in May 1845, the Directors of the railway asked Isambard, to 'advise them on the proper means to be adopted to obviate the objections which appear to exist on the part of Lord Lincoln and Her Majesty's Commissioners of Woods and Forests'. Isambard was going to show Moorsom how to do his job on two fronts.

The difference of approach between Moorsom and Brunel in Cornwall was the difference between a 'mediocre success' and a man of genius. To describe Isambard's approach as bold and imaginative seems like an understatement. The close, tumbled hills and deep, winding valleys brought out the best in him – his eye for the lie of the land and his unrivalled daring in bridge design. Instead of trying to cross the Hamoaze at water level, at one of its widest parts, Isambard went upstream and proposed a high bridge across a narrower part, at Saltash, and thus saved the steep haul from sea level on to the moors. Beyond St Germans Isambard adopted Moorsom's line but with cunning use of the land, and with viaducts such as only he would have dared to design, so that, apart from a very short stretch of 1 in 57 between Doublebois and Bodmin Road, there were no gradients steeper than 1 in 60 anywhere in the 50 miles from Saltash to Truro.

It was obvious that Moorsom would be annoyed at losing his position as Engineer to the Cornwall Railway and, thinking to soothe his wounded pride, Isambard told the Directors and Moorsom that 'I wish to avail myself of Captain Moorsom's assistance whenever I consider . . . that assistance desirable.' That does not sound like any great favour but Isambard felt he was being generous and told Moorsom: 'I did it . . . with the object of keeping up your connection with the Company and with the best of intentions towards yourself and on your account only.' In return, Isambard hoped to make use of Moorsom's extensive local knowledge: he made his first visit to Plymouth as Engineer of the Cornwall Railway at the end of July and on the 27th wrote to Moorsom saying, 'it would be very desirable if you could accompany me'.

Isambard went down by train to Exeter and thence by 'Flying Hearse' to Plymouth, but Moorsom was still sulking; he did not want his brains picked by Isambard – so he did not turn up. Having spent a couple of days with his assistant Mr Johnson, going over the ground, and then leaving Johnson with his orders, Isambard set out for Turin. When he came home in late September he found a letter from Moorsom angling for a permanent situation on the Cornish Railway or, failing that, asking to be relieved of his duties to take up other work.

Isambard was exasperated. Moorsom had no duties at all on the Cornwall Railway and, on 11 October, Isambard told him to do whatever he liked:

> I will not take on myself the responsibility of inducing you to forgo advantageous connections with other parties by the prospect of engagements on the Cornwall Railway. It would place me in a position which I do not choose to be placed in – of obligation to you instead of the reverse . . . and as you plainly make your acceptance of the offer of other parties dependent on my answer I must . . . urge you to take an independent course and relieve me and the Company of any claims or expectations of yours.

Moorsom had developed the idea that he was employed to make surveys for Isambard and to 'overlook' Johnson. A day or two before Christmas 1845 he sent Isambard his professional account. Isambard was very annoyed and had to carry the annoyance through Christmas Day, the only day in the year on which he did not work. He was back at his desk on Boxing Day and on the 27th he dealt with Moorsom. He must have been seething because the letter exploded into exasperation and indignation from the first word. Isambard was always economical in his use of punctuation and he forgot it almost completely in this letter. I have supplied the punctuation for the sake of clarity:

> My Dear Sir, You are certainly the most extraordinary man I ever became acquainted with. I have written and spoken to you plainly enough . . . to make you understand . . . my position in relation to you . . . and after all that has passed I could never have conceived it possible that your infatuation could have led to assume, or to dream of assuming, such a position as that taken by you and referred to in the items of the account you have sent in against the Cornwall Railway.
>
> I find it utterly impossible to write about it in ordinary language, the whole thing seems so absurd and so inconceivable. How on earth came you ever to imagine that I could ask or that I could permit you to 'make arrangements for my surveys' or to 'overlook my surveyors'? and what makes the matter more unintelligible is that neither Mr Johnson nor

myself are sensible of having received such assistance. . . . As to the 271 miles of section [gradient profiles] Johnson states that he never asked for them, nor used them when they came . . . pray don't oblige me with any more.

As I am upon the subject of sections I must tell you that . . . you have most grossly *fudged* your Parliamentary sections. I can use no other term and the incorrectness of the whole plan and sections was beyond anything I have had experience. . . . I have no wish to quarrel with you, on the contrary I am determined not to do so. . . . but your extraordinary presumption – I must out with the word – is enough to drive away the staunchest friend and I can stand it no longer. You build so very quickly and so loftily upon the smallest foundations that it is dangerous to stand near you. . . . the plainest language is lost on you and I must therefore confine our communications on business to the narrowest possible limits. I remain, yours faithfully, I.K. Brunel

Isambard's original design, for bridging the Tamar or Hamoaze at Saltash, was a series of timber-trusses to carry a double-track bridge 80 ft above high water. This was approved by Act of Parliament in 1845 but the Admiralty wanted a clear space of 100 ft above high water. Fresh Parliamentary powers were required for this, so back to Parliament went Brunel and the Cornwall Railway. One wonders why Isambard did not consult the Admiralty as to the headroom required before spending thousands of pounds on obtaining the 1845 Act.

The new powers were obtained in 1847 and at once he began an exploration of the riverbed, hoping to find at midstream a reef of the 'greenstone trap' that could be seen outcropping on the Saltash shore. This very hard rock would be more suitable as a foundation than the clay slate which predominated in the area. Divers found the rock, exactly where it was required, in midstream.

In 1849 Isambard designed and constructed a 6-ft-diameter, 85-ft-long tube which was floated to midstream and sunk vertically into the mud. Within it the workmen laboriously probed 175 holes over 50 sq.ft down to the rock so that Isambard, or, more likely, R.P. Brereton, could make a map of its surface. Finally the tube was taken down to the rock, which was levelled within the tube and a pillar of masonry constructed several feet high to prove the feasibility of Isambard's plans. Lack of money prevented any further progress.

The Cornwall Railway Directors had difficulty in raising sufficient cash and in April 1852 Isambard reduced the proposed length of the two river spans of the Saltash bridge from 465 to 455 ft and reduced their width to accommodate only a single track. These modifications cut £100,000 off the cost of the bridge and made it possible to start work.

From a foundation on the midstream rock, a column of granite ashlar had to be raised 96 ft to clear the high water mark. On top of this, four octagonal, cast-iron columns were to be raised to support the midstream ends of the wrought-iron main spans, 100 ft above high water. There were to be seventeen 'land spans' resting on masonry piers between 83 ft 6 in. and 69 ft 6 in. apart: eight on the Devon side and nine on the Cornish side, these latter arranged on a sharp curve. The length of the whole bridge was 2200 ft.

In January 1853 Isambard met C.J. Mare, who was rash enough to agree to build this enormous bridge for a mere £162,000, and work got under way at once, starting with raising the masonry piers for the land spans and making a caisson to be used in the construction of the great central pier. Isambard called this his 'Great Cylinder'. It was made up from boiler plates riveted to form a tube 90 ft long. The upper 50 ft was to be 37 ft in diameter, the lower 40 ft to be 35 ft. The upper section was constructed in halves, bolted together longitudinally.

The lower end was a diving bell. A dome was fitted across the cylinder about 15 ft above the bottom edge and an inner wall formed an annular working space 4 ft wide. This inner wall rose to the dome which was pierced by a 10-ft diameter tube. Fixed eccentrically within the 10-ft tube was a 6-ft diameter tube which carried compressed air to the annular space to prevent ingress of water under the inner wall. Within the 10-ft tube were steam pumps to drain water from the central section. The river-bed mud, augmented with piled sandbags, would, it was hoped, prevent water leaks from the outside.

Air pressure had been used before to prevent ingress of water when sinking tubular iron bridge piers, using the pier itself as the pressure vessel but Isambard's 'Great Cylinder' was the first example of a caisson designed specifically for use with compressed air. It was a synthesis of Isambard's ideas and those of his assistants William Glennie and R.P. Brereton. Isambard designed the tube to float not quite horizontally but with what was to be the lower end being one-quarter submerged, and equipped it so that it could be sunk vertically in a controlled manner.

Thanks to the exploratory work carried out in 1848-9, Isambard knew that the rock on which he intended to found his pier sloped to the south-west, so he designed the cylinder with one side 6 ft longer

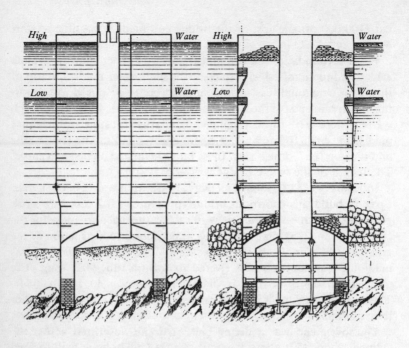

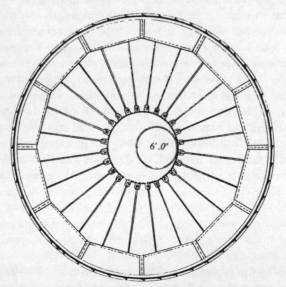

The Saltash 'bell' in plan and elevation

than the other and gave it a sharp edge to enable it to cut through the mud to the rock below. The 'Great Cylinder', a masterpiece of invention, began building on the Devon shore in March 1853, and was ready for launch in May 1854, just as construction work started on the 'Great Ship' at Millwall and on the track-bed of the Cornwall Railway.

The system of floating the 'Great Cylinder', towing it to midstream and sinking it vertically to the river-bed was worked out by Isambard, probably with some advice from Captain Claxton. The great tube was secured between four Brunel-designed iron pontoons and was brought upright by letting more water inside. It was then sunk. The floating and sinking took about two weeks so it is unlikely that Isambard supervised the entire operation but rather left his Resident Engineer, R.P. Brereton, to get on with the work.

The cylinder cut through the river-bed mud to a depth of 13 ft without difficulty, but it landed on a pinnacle of the jagged rock upon which the pier was to be built and heeled over 7 ft 6 in. towards the east. Pig-iron was loaded on to the internal dome on the higher side while air and water-pumps were erected on top of the leaning tower to assist in preventing ingress of water and to pump out what had already leaked in. Thirty men worked within the pressurised annular ring and in the main space to excavate the mud and beds of compacted oyster shells. The cylinder sank steadily and, being weighted on one side, righted itself.

The men then attacked the very hard 'greenstone trap' with hand-held hammers and chisels. In some places they had to go down through 6 ft to reach the required level. Water poured in as the rock was broken open but the men hammered sheets of iron piling into the fissures to stem the flow sufficiently to allow the pumps to master the leak. When admiring Isambard's 'great courage and determination', we should also admire the identical qualities in those unknown workmen – they made 'Isambard's Great Work' possible, as indeed did the highly capable and courageous Resident Engineer, Robert Pearson Brereton.

While this great work was going on below the Tamar, Isambard was faced with the problem of carrying the railway through Cornwall, spanning eight estuaries and thirty-four deep and relatively narrow valleys. The company lacked the funds to build masonry bridges of orthodox design so Isambard adopted the expedient of timber trestles on masonry piers. This design was 'unitary' with all components made to standard sizes and to a repetitive pattern.

He used two types of construction for the piers. The taller (and they rose to 118 ft in the case of the St Pinnock Viaduct) consisted of a stone wall reinforced with tapering buttresses at each end. If the wall were below a certain height he omitted the buttressing. The piers were spaced 66 ft apart and rose to a point 35 ft below rail level. At the top of each pier were bolted cast-iron 'shoes' into which the timber struts were socketed. On the taller buttressed piers he placed a 'shoe' at each end where the buttresses made the widest and so strongest foundation, and on the shorter piers he spaced three 'shoes' equidistant along the top.

From the top of each pier rose four frameworks, each consisting of three Baltic pine struts, to support the three horizontal timber beams which carried the track-bed. Viewed from the side the struts looked as fragile as four fingers of a hand, fanning out from the tall pier. Indeed, so fragile did they appear that many people, in the early days, would not use the railway for fear the timbers might collapse under the weight of a train.

Isambard had developed the wood-preserving techniques of John H. Kyan to a high degree and with pine of very good quality, carefully kyanised, he was able to turn out this brilliantly economical design in order to get an impoverished Company into business. He made the masonry piers as slender as he dared and they were none too strong. Where they were built on curves the lateral thrust set up by a train's flanges against the rails forced some piers sideways. In all of them the Baltic pine struts decayed or became distorted. They required constant inspection and a steady replacement of individual struts which kept ninety men in nine gangs busy for many years.

These Cornish viaducts were fine structures but Isambard would not have agreed with the unreserved praise heaped upon them by some writers, including Rolt. He had no illusions about the difficulties his viaducts would cause the Company and told the Directors that although they were cheap in first cost, they would become an increasing liability and that at the end of ten years they would cost £10,000 a year to maintain. It was for reasons of maintenance cost, not because of a lack of suitable timber, that the trestle viaducts were replaced. The first to go was at Probus, replaced by an embankment in 1871, when there was no shortage of finest Baltic pine. In accordance with Isambard's intention, others were replaced by masonry arches, or embankments, as fast as money could be found. The last

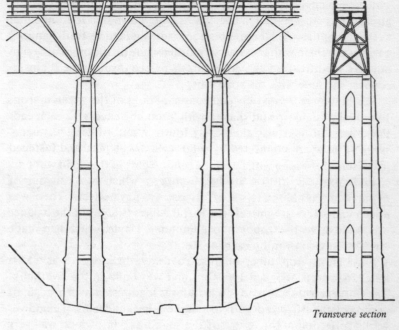

Transverse section

St Pinnock Viaduct

one to go from Cornwall was the Collegewood Viaduct, on the Falmouth branch, in 1934; but the very last Brunellian timber-trestle viaduct in service was on the Dare Valley mineral line, in South Wales, erected about 1853 and, after many replacements of timbers, taken out of use in 1947.

From January 1853 until September 1857, Isambard designed or supervised the erection of the Royal Albert Bridge at Saltash – between his work on the 'Great Ship', raising a riot at Mickleton Tunnel and relaxing occasionally amongst the trees and the blue morning glory flowers at Watcombe.

The Royal Albert was his masterpiece, in which he brought together his experience of riveted wrought iron, of ships, of 'tubular' construction and of the suspension bridge principle. The major improvement on the Royal Albert Bridge over the Wye Bridge was that the tubular compression girder was elliptical, 16 ft 9 in. broad by 12 ft 3 in. tall, which gave it greater resistance to a sideways strain while allowing the chains to hang vertically, in line with the roadway girders they must support. The chains hang down in a festoon equal to the rise of the tubular compression girder and ten vertical 'hangers' connect the chain with the roadway girder while (in the original design but now modified) eleven vertical struts passed through the chains to connect the tube with the roadway.

The chains are in two tiers and consist of links of flat wrought iron, 1 in. thick, 7 in. deep and shaped with 'clamping cheeks' at each end. Each chain of links was alternately fourteen and fifteen links wide, spaced 1 in. apart, connected by solid, cylindrical 'pins' and fastened to the same towers on which rest the tubes. Some of the chain was purchased from the Clifton Bridge Company which had run out of money and was obliged to sell off its assets to pay its debts. There was not enough chain to complete the Royal Albert Bridge but the balance was made up by the Copperhouse Foundry, Hayle, which had made the Clifton chains in the early 1830s.

Each truss – top tube, chains, roadway, bracings – was 455 ft long, 56 ft deep, weighed 1060 tons and was built on the riverbank. The Cornish truss was ready first and was load-tested with a strain of approximately 10 tons per sq. in. on the tube and chains. The downwards deflection at the centre of the span was 5 in., which was very satisfactory, and preparations went ahead to float the truss across the river and position it on the piers for raising.

Docks were cut into the riverbank close to each end of the truss and Brunellian pontoons were floated in beneath it and sunk. A timber framework was placed between the pontoon and the truss. The pontoons were then raised and with the truss resting upon them they were hauled across the 1100-ft-wide river. Traction was provided by winches fixed to barges moored upstream of the central pier, the ropes being passed around pulleys fixed to other moored barges so that they came on to the pontoons at various angles and controlled precisely the progress of the cumbersome truss as it was influenced by wind and tide. It was a demanding operation in which Isambard received a good deal of advice from Captain Claxton, but it was Isambard's show and the minutely detailed arrangements and contingency plans were the perfection of Brunellian stage-management.

Isambard planned to direct the winch operators from a platform on top of the tube by means of red, white or blue flag signals given by a man standing on a platform just over Isambard's head. Each barge had a 'captain' and an 'assistant'. The assistant's task was never to take his eyes off the handsignalman and to pass on the flagged instructions to the captain who would supervise the winchmen. The truss was 'strung' like a puppet, capable of being manoeuvred in any direction. Isambard was puppet-master with 500 'stage hands', including Claxton in charge of the 'fleet' and Brereton as Resident Engineer. The audience numbered thousands.

The launch took place at 1 p.m. on 1 September 1857. When the tide raised the pontoons and lifted the truss clear of the ground, Isambard signalled the relevant winches to haul away and bring the truss out, parallel to the riverbank. The massive structure went gliding out to the centre of the river and was stopped. Ropes were cast off, others attached and the signal given to haul again. The truss swung round, the midstream end pivoting against the stone pier till the Cornish end was alongside its pier. Powerful winches then inched the ends over the stonework, the pontoons were submerged lowering the truss precisely into position, resting on hydraulic jacks.

The jacks, designed by Isambard, had a screw-thread cut in the ram with a locking nut to enable them to be secured at 'full lift' and thus insured against any failure of the hydraulic system. By these means the truss was raised 3 ft at a time and the masonry built up beneath, until the final position 100 ft above high water was reached in July 1858. Isambard, deeply involved at Millwall, supervised one 3-ft 'lift' and then left the works, including the floating and raising of the Devon span, entirely to Brereton.

23

The Great Persuader

The Great Western Railway Company was, for ten years from 1844, engaged in a fierce 'gauge war' with the London & South Western and the London & North Western, both of which tried to prevent the encroachments of the wide gauge on to what they considered their territory. Isambard was responsible not only for planning real railways such as the Berks & Hants, Birmingham & Oxford, or Oxford, Worcester & Wolverhampton; he was also engaged in organising the surveys and marshalling the Parliamentary arguments for routes which were no more than 'paper' railways, tactical movements designed to 'attack' and 'capture' territory ahead of similar incursions by rival companies. The rivalry between these three companies would have existed in any case but the incompatibility of the gauges gave the standard-gauge companies a perfect stick with which to beat the Brunellians.

On 25 June 1845, Richard Cobden MP moved a resolution that a Royal Commission be set up to inquire whether 'in future private Acts, provision ought to be made for securing a uniform gauge and whether it would be . . . practicable to . . . bring railways already constructed or in progress of construction . . . into a uniformity of gauge. . . .' The resolution was passed and a Royal Commission into the 'gauge question' was established. The Commissioners were Sir Frederick Smith RE, late Inspector-General of Railways; George Airy, Astronomer-Royal; and Peter Barlow, Professor of Mathematics at Woolwich Military Academy.

Isambard was planning broad-gauge railways to run into Dorset,

Cornwall, Worcester, Birmingham and beyond, and the narrow-gauge companies were planning counter-attacks to these thrusts. His SS *Great Britain* was being fitted out as a transatlantic passenger liner at Blackwall, but now he set about preparing his case to go before the Gauge Commissioners, and at the same time added to his mountainous workload by taking on the job of Engineer to the Cork & Waterford and the Cornwall Railways. No wonder he was complaining about 'the dreadful scramble in which I am forced to live'. The Royal Commissioners on the Gauge of Railways opened their proceedings on 6 August 1845. The atmosphere of the Inquiry, reading the papers today, gives the feeling of a court, with the Stephensonites coming as Plaintiffs to accuse the Brunellians of heinous offences – such as speeding. Both Robert Stephenson and Joseph Locke attacked the broad gauge for its speed and the Commissioners so pre-judged the case that, without waiting to hear from the Brunellians, they applied to Parliament to make a law restricting speed on railways.

Isambard appeared before the Commissioners on 17 October and attacked them with the utmost vigour. The reasons he gave for adopting the 7-ft gauge were not those he had advanced to the GWR Directors in 1835. Then he had made much of the need to reduce friction by the use of large wheels outside the body of the coach. Such a technique he had found to be impractical and now he told the Commissioners: 'Looking to the speeds which I contemplated and the masses to be moved, it seemed to me that the whole machine was too small for the work to be done. . . . I think the impression grew upon me gradually so that it is difficult to fix the time when I first thought a wide gauge desirable.'

The Commissioners thought he had over-reacted and asked him if he would still use the broad gauge, if he could start from scratch but with all the experience he had since accumulated. Isambard came out with a defiant, fighting reply: 'No. If anything I would go for something over seven feet.' When cornered, Isambard was as pugnacious a bantam-weight as ever entered the ring.

The Commissioners tried to get him on the ropes with a different punch: 'Do you think that any great convenience would result from bringing the whole of the railways of the Kingdom into one gauge?'

Isambard flung himself on to his opponents in a frontal attack: 'I believe most firmly that the public advantage would generally be injured by having one gauge,' he said, and followed that by admitting – and dismissing – the advantage of a uniform gauge:

> There would be an advantage – of course – in similarity of gauge in as much as it would get over the difficulty experienced in changing from one gauge to another but on the other hand I believe that a great deal of progress that has been made on railways has arisen from the fair emulation that exists between the promoters, either of two gauges or of four- or six-wheeled carriages or engines and of all the other varieties. The system of generalising [i.e. standardising] whether the gauge or anything else would do more harm than good.

'As in cramping genius?' asked a Commissioner sarcastically. Isambard was in no way abashed but thrust straight back:

> Yes – and without reference to the genius of persons, it is interfering with that feeling and spirit which brings about all improvements of the day in this country. There can be no question, I believe, in the public mind, that the express trains, if they are an advantage, arise entirely from that question of competition between the two gauges.

Why did Isambard think it was competition of gauge – specifically – which brought about improvement? Speed on the GWR owed nothing to the 7-ft gauge and everything to Isambard's well-laid track and Gooch's fine locomotives hauling six-wheeled, long-wheelbase, carriages. Competition between two companies of the same gauge would have brought about the same improvements given the same designing genius. Isambard's dismissal of standardisation was unfortunate. Gooch's system of standardised locomotive components had conferred upon the GWR an advantage in reduced building and maintenance costs and a constant supply of reliable locomotives with which to run the much-admired GWR express trains.

Because broad-gauge carriages had a greater seating capacity the total 'fleet' was smaller, saving on maintenance. Also, because broad-gauge carriages had a higher seating capacity than those on the standard gauge, GWR trains were relatively short compared to those on the standard gauge and thus they presented a smaller area to the wind and thus required less fuel to move them. Gooch stated that the rolling resistance of a broad-gauge train amounted to 18 lb per ton at 60 mph whereas on the standard gauge the resistance was around 40 lb per ton at the same speed. Gooch's figures were disputed by the standard-gauge establishment – whose champions were George Bidder and John Scott Russell – in an argument which was not concluded until 1848. To settle matters in a practical way in 1845, Isambard suggested a series of locomotive trials between the two gauges. These were arranged for December.

No new locomotives had been built for the GWR since 1842 but Isambard was sure that a Gooch 'Firefly' class was more than a match for any standard-gauge engine. Gooch chose *Ixion*, delivered to the railway in October 1841, to compete against a Stephenson 'Long Boiler', No 54 of the North Midland Railway, built in October 1845. The latter had 6 ft 6 in. driving wheels, 15 × 24 in. cylinders fixed outside the frames, the most powerful boiler yet built with 1023 sq.ft of heating surface and a firegrate of $11\frac{1}{2}$ sq. ft. The engine weighed $24\frac{1}{4}$ tons.

The defects of No 54 had nothing to do with the gauge; it was simply badly designed. Its splendid boiler sat upon a wheelbase of only 12 ft and overhung the rear axle so much as to destabilise the machine. Neither the wheels nor any of the heavy, rotating parts were balanced, so more wobbles were introduced and their effects were made worse by the leverage exerted by the pistons set well outside the longitudinal centre-line of the engine.

The *Ixion* had 7-ft diameter driving wheels, 15 × 18 in. cylinders fixed between the frames, and a boiler 10 in. wider than that on No 54 but with only 699 sq.ft of heating surface; it had a grate area of $13\frac{1}{2}$ sq.ft and weighed 24 tons. *Ixion*'s moving parts were not balanced either but the short boiler was carried within the frames on a 13-ft wheelbase and the inside cylinders were placed to exert the least twisting effect on the frames; a sensible and well-proportioned engine of dimensions that could have been carried on the 4 ft $8\frac{1}{2}$ in. gauge.

To make the best time over the 44 miles from York to Darlington and to use the least fuel whilst so doing, George Bidder used pre-heated water for the engine's boiler and began the timing from a 'flying start'. Such was the partiality of the Commissioners that they allowed this cheating. Little good it did them. Over a road of Brunellian level the best the standard-gaugers could manage was 60 mph with 40 tons. On one run, No 54 leaped and swayed so violently that, reaching 53 mph, it flung itself off the track.

Ixion established its superiority by making three double trips over the 53 miles from Paddington to Didcot without showing the slightest tendency to derailment. With 80 tons the engine cruised at 53 mph on the very slight uphill gradients and returned with the same load at a steady 60 mph. With smaller loads it went even faster. Brakes on these trips consisted of a rudimentary handbrake on the engine's tender and another in the guard's van.

The Gauge Commissioners reported to Parliament early in 1846. They admitted that 'broad-gauge engines possess greater capabilities for speed . . . and the working . . . is economical where very high speeds are required or where the loads require the full power of the engine'. They also had to admit that 'the public are mainly indebted for the present rate of speed and increased accommodation of the carriages to the genius of Mr Brunel [what about Gooch?] and the liberality of the Great Western Railway Company.'

Then came the bad news. The Commissioners were still convinced by the Stephensonite line of argument – that it would be dangerous for the broad gauge to be allowed to run any faster – dangerous for standard-gauge interests? – and that in the transport of freight the standard gauge 'possessed the greater convenience and was more suited to the general traffic of the country'. They also considered that a broad-gauge railway cost more to build and showed no savings over a standard-gauge railway in its annual running costs – in spite of the fact that the broad gauge required a smaller fleet of carriages and wagons.

The technical excellence of Brunel's railway was unquestionable. Presented with the serious shortcomings of the Liverpool & Manchester Railway in 1831, he had arrived at a solution at once dramatic, daring and very eye-catching – the broad gauge. But, quite apart from arguments as to its utility, it was ten years too late. He had introduced a major difficulty: the duality of gauges. That being so, was he wise to press on in the teeth of common-sense objections? He was, without any doubt, a colourful and a daring person, there was a large slice of the great gambler as well as the great engineer in his personality. Did his flamboyant personality, his desire for fame and glory, overcome his engineering sense?

With the exception of John Gray on the Hull & Selby Railway, all locomotive engineers, prior to 1843, were convinced that a very low centre of gravity was necessary if an engine was to run steadily. Designers restricted the diameter of their boilers so as to restrict the height of the main mass of the machine. This was the popular misconception Isambard did not see through. He used the broad gauge in order to use large boilers, slung low between the frames, to keep the centre of gravity low. If he had gone into the matter more deeply, as a man of great foresight and cold logic would have done, then he would have discovered the error, already discovered by John Gray, and could have done all that was required on the standard gauge. Neither Gooch nor his successors Armstrong and Dean found the need to exploit the possibilities of the broad gauge and although Gooch's beautiful 8-ft 'Singles' between 1871 and 1888 were using larger boilers than anything then existing on the standard gauge, they were unable to cope with more than average loads whilst in the same period, on the standard gauge, faster and more powerful engines were running. Good design rather than width of gauge was the answer.

Isambard adopted the broad gauge as the solution to the problem of smooth running because he unquestioningly followed a popular misconception of the engineering establishment of his day, the need for a low centre of gravity. He thereby created another, far larger, problem. But Isambard was pleased with his solution. It was spectacular, it seemed to him and to others to be a great, technological step forward – it was uniquely Brunellian. He dashed onwards, always insisting upon his correctness, attacking the opposition with fierce elegance.

The Commissioners had a difficult decision to make. There could not be two main-line gauges in the country; for the benefit of uninterrupted communication from north to south and east to west, one of them had to go. They 'esteemed the importance of express trains for a relatively small number of people' but 'if it were considered imperative to produce uniformity we recommend [an] alteration of the Broad Gauge to Narrow Gauge, more especially when we take into consideration that the extent of the former is only 274 miles while the latter is not less than 1901 miles'.

Isambard did not understand this talk of 'uniformity' and of a *law* to enforce what was to him nothing more than a measurement – an engineering concept. Under stress of 'attack' he wrote to Charles Saunders a theatrical note, as if he were a general rallying his troops on the night before a battle: 'When the enemy is weak is the time to attack. Pray let us come up to the scratch. We are all hungry and will fight well.'

Burning more midnight oil in his office at 18 Duke Street, he wrote a fifty-page refutation entitled *Observations on the Report of the Gauge Commissioners*. There were plenty of inconsistencies in the report and these he exposed, also exposing a few inconsistencies of his own along the way. He insisted that the inconveniences of the 'breaks of gauge' was the invention of a 'greedy monopoly', this being his favourite *bête noir*. It is ironic that he should have attacked 'monopolies' since he had set out, in 1835, to construct his own monopoly from Paddington to Penzance and West Wales. He would not admit that the breaks of gauge were a nuisance to passengers and made proposals for transferring freight from gauge to gauge by containers. Given the wide range of railway freight, from coal to cattle, not even Gooch believed this idea would work.

Isambard was outraged that the evidence of the standard-gauge witnesses had been accepted without being subjected to any cross-examination and insisted that competition between gauges was essential to scientific progress. He told the Commissioners:

> Any attempt to restrict improvement by annihilating the Broad Gauge would be in the highest degree impolitic and would be a subversion of every principle which has hitherto stimulated science and mechanical skill and would be most unfair and unjust as a punishment to those who have successfully and spiritedly pursued the course of improvement.

A brilliant advocate and an energetic lobbyist of Parliament, he had his *Observations* printed as a pamphlet which he circulated to every Member of Parliament. As a result a 'saving' clause was added to the Gauge Act which became law on 18 August 1846. This established the 4 ft 8½ in. gauge as the sole, legal gauge of Britain (5 ft 3 in. in Ireland) excepting 'any railway constructed or to be constructed containing any special enactment defining the gauge or gauges of such railway'. So Isambard single-handedly persuaded Parliament to allow him to continue building 7-ft-gauge railways. That was, surely, one of his great, unsung, triumphs, though in the long run it would prove a hollow victory.

IV

Great Ship –
or White Elephant?

24

Heading for Disaster

During 1848 Isambard designed a permanent station for Paddington, the construction of which began in 1849. The site for the station was in a cutting which Isambard decided to roof with glass on cast-iron columns. The design was unprecedented and set the style of industrial/railway architecture for many years to come. It pre-dated Paxton's design for the iron and glass 'palace' for the Great Exhibition by at least eighteen months. Without any doubt Isambard's methods at Paddington were seminal for Paxton's design.

The space to be roofed in at Paddington was 700 ft long and 238 ft wide. He designed three semicircular roofs, partly glazed and partly covered with corrugated iron. There was a central span of 102 ft 6 in., flanked by spans of 68 ft and 69 ft 6 in., while two transepts 50 ft wide intersected the length. The glazing was Paxton's patent system, supported by light arches of wrought iron, springing from cast-iron columns which in turn were bolted to massive foundations of brick. Isambard designed a new, wooden, goods station at the same time and in both the goods and the passenger stations he made use of Sir William Armstrong's hydraulic machinery to operate lifts, traversers and winches. He had no time to design embellishments to his brand-new style of industrial architecture and so asked Matthew Digby Wyatt to design them for him.

Prince Albert proposed the idea of a Great Exhibition of Science and Industry in 1849 and a Royal Commission was set up to organise it with Digby Wyatt as Secretary. Among the Royal Commissioners were Isambard's friends, Joseph Paxton and John Scott Russell, who at once invited him on to the Building Committee and appointed him both Chairman of the Jury for 'Civil Engineering, Architecture and Building Contrivances' and a Member of the Committee of the Machinery Section. He must be the only exhibition judge in history to have disapproved of awarding money prizes or medals; he felt that the glory of being in the Exhibition was reward enough. On 11 March 1850 he wrote to Prince Albert to give his views of the Royal intentions:

> I strongly disapprove of any prizes being offered. It is quite unnecessary . . . there are an infinity of shades of merit . . . prizes will be mischievous as conferring undue advantages upon a thing well displayed and well got-up and will be sought for *puffing* purposes [that is, advertising – one of Isambard's pet hates]. The opportunity of exhibition . . . will be quite sufficient to induce all the competition we can desire.

There Isambard spoke as a true craftsman. However, no one took any notice of him.

Isambard was full of advice on what ought to be the spirit of the Exhibition and what ought and ought not to be exhibited. He made a special point of denigrating electricity, although it had been used on railway communications since 1838. He wrote to Russell: 'I think in an English exhibition you should seek to secure that characteristic of which we are most proud . . . that for which we are most distinguished, usefulness . . . for that reason I should omit any mention of electric machines which as yet can only be considered as mere toys.'

In 1853 he was asked to join in a company being formed to exploit a discovery of one Mr Wilkins who had found how to transmit messages by electricity without wires – wireless. His reply, it seems to me, is a very laboured excuse for not joining in a great project. He actually has to apologise for breaking his normally strictly held principles supporting variety and condemning monopoly. He wrote:

> I am a great advocate for competition. The public is suffering from the monopoly now existing. The invention of Mr Wilkins contains much that is beautiful and likely to be eminently useful but I have, much against my inclination, and acting for railway companies, been such an active agent in securing the monopoly of the old Company (Electric Telegraph Co.) and I am so closely connected with its Directors and Engineers being my personal friends that I should be placing myself in a painful position in actively assisting the promotion of a competitor.

None of the 245 designs which the Building Committee received as proposals for the building to house the Exhibition was accepted and as a result the Committee set about producing a design of its own. The result was a long row of permanent, brick buildings with, at the centre, an enormous central dome of iron and glass, 150 ft tall and 200 ft diameter. This was Isambard's contribution, but his exuberant ideas on industrial architecture only made the rest of the design look timid and unimaginative so the whole design was rejected.

Isambard did not approve of the expense of permanent, brick buildings to house a temporary exhibition. He saw that a prefabricated building would not only be cheaper but, if easily assembled iron parts were used, it could be made fantastically dramatic – a fairy palace for technology. It was the Brunellian synthesis of art and engineering, with a touch of fairy fantasy, for he envisaged the future Europe as a fairy-tale place of sweet reason where there would be no more war because nations would be linked by railways and by interdependent industry under the rational rule of reformed politicians and ever-seeking, liberal-minded engineers. There would have been no accountants to spoil matters since Isambard had a gentleman's contempt for anything as sordid as money.

The Building Committee having failed to produce an acceptable plan, Joseph Paxton was invited to submit a design. He produced it in mid-1850. It was entirely of iron and glass and it owed much to the great glass dome in Brunel's rejected plan. The Great Exhibition building was erected in Hyde Park and enclosed one million square feet of grass together with the tall elms that Isambard, aspiring landscaper, and Joseph Paxton, superintendent of the Duke of Devonshire's gardens at Chatsworth, were loath to cut down. This vast iron and glass palace was erected in less than twelve months under the direction of Isambard and Paxton – a feat of construction and supervision unsurpassed to this day.

The Exhibition was opened on 1 May 1851, in the presence of Queen Victoria and Prince Albert, with a large procession of engineers, churchmen, aristocrats and politicians. One would expect the Order of March to reflect the hierarchy of the organisation but somehow Isambard, who did not hold particularly high rank, established himself in solitary state fourth from the front of this noble procession. Well down the line came the Royal Commissioners including the designer, Joseph Paxton, walking with and sharing the honours with John Scott Russell.

It was ten weeks later that Isambard incited 3000 navvies to break the Queen's Peace.

During 1851 Scott Russell and Charles Geach MP, senior partner of the ironworks Beale & Son, a millionaire and Chairman of the Midland Bank, formed the Crystal Palace Company to purchase the Great Exhibition building and to dismantle and re-erect it at Sydenham in south London. Obviously, Geach had a high regard for Russell's character and abilities because he also supported his successful bid to buy his retiring partner's share of the Millwall shipyard they jointly owned.

Also in 1851, Isambard's boyhood friend William Hawes, Chairman of the newly formed Australian Royal Mail Company, asked him to act as that company's Engineer and adviser in the purchase of two fast steamships with which to establish a regular service and exploit the need created by the discovery of gold in Australia. Isambard knew exactly the right man for this job and asked Russell to design a pair of iron-hulled, propeller-driven ships to a general specification which he laid down. They had to be capable of making the voyage with a single stop for coal at Cape Town.

There can be no doubt that Russell and Brunel had a friendship dating back to Bristol in 1836; they knew each other well and respected each other's capabilities. Russell returned Isambard's favour by giving him the task of designing the two enormous water towers required to operate hydraulic machinery in the re-erected Crystal Palace. These were to be 284 ft high each supporting a tank 47 ft diameter by 38 ft high and containing 1200 tons of water. The total weight of each tower and its full tank was something in excess of 3000 tons and this had to stand on a clay hillside. Isambard took the foundations deep into the hill and formed a wide base of concrete upon which a great block of brickwork was formed to ground level. The towers were twelve-sided with two hollow cast-iron columns at each angle and were well braced inside with wrought iron. They stood until demolished by the military in 1940.

In the account which follows of the building of what Isambard called the 'Great Ship' I follow closely, and with his generous approval, the work of George Emmerson, whose biography of John Scott Russell, published in 1977, gives a very complete account of the working arrangements of Russell and Isambard and the later quarrels between them.

Russell's reply to Isambard's request for ships was delivered on

16 February 1852. He had on his drawing board a design for a ship almost as big as the SS *Great Britain*; 288 ft long with a beam of 38 ft. Rolt has quite rightly stated that Isambard had nothing to do with that design but he is incorrect when he states that it 'lacked the great longitudinal strength that distinguished all Brunel's ships'. The *Adelaide* and the *Victoria*, as they were later named, had Russell's innovative, partial iron deck riveted to transverse watertight bulkheads; longitudinal box girders ran the length of the ship and a box girder formed the keel. Isambard recommended the designs to the Australian Royal Mail Company.

Russell's shipyard at Millwall was a well-organised factory with an efficient workforce and these large and novel ships were launched six months after their respective keels were laid. One month from launching the SS *Adelaide* had been fitted-out, and on 12 December 1852 she steamed away for Australia. As Engineer to the Company Isambard had ordered Russell to install a 'balanced rudder' of his, Isambard's, design. Going down Channel the *Adelaide* encountered heavy seas, the Brunellian rudder proved ineffectual, forcing the vessel to return to Millwall where a conventional rudder was fitted. Once Brunel's experimental rudder was replaced the ship performed faultlessly and made the passage to Sydney in sixty days.

The problems of pan-global steam navigation were suitably enormous and made Isambard think hard. On 25 March 1852 he made his first sketch for an 'East India Steamship' and underneath it he wrote, musingly, 'Say 600 ft × 65 ft × 30 ft'. The ship he was creating in his head, in 1852, was so big that nothing larger was to be conceived for half a century. It was intended to steam to Calcutta and back without the expense and delay of coaling *en route*, but difficulties over the relative shallowness of the Diamond Harbour, Calcutta, made Isambard, in 1853, re-think the ship for the Australian run. He increased its hull to 680 ft.

Isambard involved Russell from the outset in what he called the 'Great Ship'. Russell reported that the required ship would displace 20,000 tons and would need an engine capable of 8500 hp for the required speed of 14 knots. As Emmerson explains, no such single engine could be built, twin screws were then out of the question, so it was decided to use screw and paddle-wheel propulsion.

With the expertise of Russell and his shipyard and also that of Maudslay Son & Field and Mr Blake of James Watt & Co, the ship was technically possible but Isambard would have to persuade a sufficient number of very rich men before he would get his hands on the necessary funds. Russell advised him to approach the Directors of the recently formed Eastern Steam Navigation Company who were looking for a pair of ships with which to start their business. The ESN Co. appointed a committee to interview him in mid-July 1852, but on the appointed day Isambard was ill so Russell deputised.

The Committee was in favour but when they put the proposal to the full Board some Directors resigned, perhaps because they knew too much about Isambard's grand designs. Isambard was a great creative engineer but not necessarily a creator of great profits. Isambard regarded every project he engineered as his personal mission. Directors were there to organise and to provide him with the money to carry out his great 'improvements', but when businessmen grew faint-hearted or when money became scarce Isambard would rally them, personally raising funds, sometimes with rash promises, always with bold leadership. Now he was happy to replace the doubters by men with stronger nerves. One of these was Russell's friend and source of vital financial support, Charles Geach. Others included the railway contractors Samuel Peto and Thomas Brassey.

Isambard was appointed Engineer to the ESN Co. in July 1852, and was authorised to start work as soon as 40,000 shares were taken and £120,000 paid up. After a month's illness he threw himself energetically into share canvassing and to set a good example he bought more than 2000 for himself – as did Geach. Peto and Brassey each had 1000; most other investors took 500 but, significantly perhaps, Isambard's friends on the Boards of the Great Western and South Wales Railways could not be persuaded to take more than the minimum of fifty each.

Brunel wrote to the ESN Directors that 'with respect to the form and construction of the vessel nobody, in my opinion, can bring more scientific and practical knowledge to bear than Mr John Scott Russell'. Russell's tender to build, launch and deliver the 'Great Ship' at his Millwall yard was accepted. Isambard wanted him also to design the engines to drive the screw propeller but to avoid what he called 'a strong party attack' he allowed James Watt & Co. to supply an engine to Blake's design. This, apparently, was not a good design but, Isambard said, 'by attending to every detail of Blake's design I can secure all that is desired'.

Russell estimated that he could design and construct the hull, the paddle-wheel engine, the boilers for the paddle and screw engines, fit out the cabins and erect the rigging for £275,200 or £258,000 each if a second ship should be ordered within six months of the first. Rolt accuses Russell of an underhand practice in tendering an unrealistically low price, simply to get the job. If that was so, then it was no more than Isambard had done on several occasions. Isambard obviously would not have agreed with Rolt's assessment since he recommended that Russell's offer be accepted.

Later, Isambard wrote to Russell: 'The wisest and safest plan in striking out a new path is to go straight in the direction we believe to be right, disregarding the small impedimenta which may appear in our way – to design everything in the first instance for the best possible results, without yielding in the least to any prejudice now existing . . . or any fear of the consequences.' That was merely Brunellian rhetoric but if it meant anything at all it meant that Isambard was, as always, going to steam-roller his ideas through all opposition, come what might.

A fire at Russell's works on 10 September 1853 caused more than £150,000 worth of damage, less than half of it covered by insurance. Buildings and plant, plans and work-in-progress were lost. However, the financial support of his wealthy friend Geach made it possible for Russell to continue despite this loss. Isambard drafted the formal contract between Russell and the ESN Co.

Under the terms of this contract Russell was bound to make the detailed designs and submit them to Brunel for 'revision, alteration or adoption'. The concept of the 'Great Ship', and its cellular construction was Isambard's and he was to be in sole command, yet Russell was to be responsible for the vessel's successful construction and launch. Thus Russell, with his Chief Engineer Dickson, the Yard Manager Hepworth and their drawing office staff would work out solutions to complex problems of construction in what was at the time the biggest ship in the world. Isambard would pick over their ideas, overruling, approving, very occasionally improving them, but always delaying, increasing their cost, and publicly gathering to himself great glory. The contract made no provision for the method by which Russell would be paid.

The greatest problem with the 680-ft-long hull of the 'Great Ship' was to provide strength without undue weight. Isambard brought all his undoubted genius as a designer of iron bridges to bear on the problem of hull design but Rolt goes too far by implying that he *invented* the concept of the hull as a bridge girder. Russell had noted in 1840 that wooden steamships, built in America, were constructed as if the hull were a bridge.

Strength was obtained through the cellular hull, a technique first sketched by Isambard in July 1852 and now an axiom of naval architecture. Initially he proposed an inner hull of iron and an outer skin of copper-plated wood to prevent the otherwise inevitable heavy incrustation of marine life. From there it was an easy step to the tremendous strength of a double *iron* hull. The inner one would be made watertight and both would be riveted to longitudinal girders to form the bottom and sides, which, with a main deck of similar construction, formed a cellular box girder very similar to that already used by Robert Stephenson at the Britannia Bridge over the Menai Strait.

The engineering reputation and the personal honesty of John Scott Russell has been shamefully attacked in Rolt's biography of Brunel. Russell is accused of 'bitter enmity' towards Isambard and of trying to sabotage the 'Great Ship'. The facts – and common sense – show this was not true. Russell made a large financial outlay in tooling-up to build this unique vessel and took a large proportion of his pay in ESN Co. shares, so his only hope of recompense was to see her built.

As soon as he had Russell 'signed-on', Isambard showed his dictatorial manner by telling him he would be paid 'railway style' – in monthly instalments according to how much work had been done – and not all the payments were to be in cash but in ESN Co. shares – and provided that all Isambard's demands had been complied with. Thus he could withhold payment on any pretext whatsoever.

Russell explained that ship-builders were paid lump sums at specified intervals and that the ship-owner had claim on all the ship-builder's property in case he failed. Having protested he gave in, confident, Emmerson suggests, that Geach, who was supplying the ironwork, would not let him down financially.

Isambard rejected Russell's plan for a dry dock as impractical and expensive owing to the nature of the ground at Millwall. This dock would have enabled the ship to be simply floated out on to the river but Russell was, as usual, too easy-going with Isambard and instead of insisting on this plan he merely suggested it. Russell, perhaps Britain's foremost naval architect, was so keen to take part in the venture that he submitted himself to the control of Brunel, a civil engineer. He ought to have known how capricious and dictatorial that great man could be.

Isambard decided to reinforce the riverbank with hundreds of timber piles, build a launching ramp down to the water's edge on these and erect the ship on the ramp, parallel to the water. He would then launch it broadside. To avoid the danger of grounding the ship as it fell into the water, Isambard proposed a controlled launch.

Russell was a past-master in the art of launching ships but a controlled launch was unknown to shipbuilding and naturally he was reluctant to go along with Brunel in an unknown and expensive experiment. Isambard, who had virtually no experience of launching ships, ignored Russell's experience and proposed a dramatic leap in the dark instead of taking the undramatic but more certain solution. So much for Rolt's assertion that Isambard 'preferred a pinch of practice to a pound of theory'. To use a Brunellian phrase from 1833: 'How the devil was Russell to build the ship with Brunel tied to his neck?'

25

Jibes and Jealousy

John Scott Russell was a gifted teacher and explainer of ideas. He was a scientist, mathematician, naval architect and leading ship-builder. An easy-going man with distinctly democratic tendencies, very willing to delegate authority to his men, he accepted with a good grace the novelty of his subordinate role, although I suspect that the marine engineers Dickson and Hepworth were resentful of being subjected to a civil engineer – and an overbearing one at that. In three months Russell and his engineers had, as Emmerson describes, very efficiently advanced the drawings for hull and engines and on 29 March 1854 Russell wrote to Brunel: 'I hope that . . . when you consider the very short time since the order was given, you will see that I have not been remiss in taking every step in my power to secure the rapid and satisfactory advancement of the work and I can only express my desire to avail myself of every suggestion that can be made to me of any modes of improving or accelerating the work.'

Isambard was ready with detail alterations for the hull and Russell altered every detail to Isambard's satisfaction although this took extra time and money. The work of scaling up Russell's existing, very successful, four-cylinder, paddle-wheel engines into the largest engine yet built was done by Dickson, with happy suggestions from Isambard, who looked in regularly to advise and criticise. In the light of Isambard's doubtful career as a mechanical engineer this must have been gall and wormwood to Dickson.

Isambard's preoccupation of mind at this time was such that he could not avoid making bad judgements. On 6 June 1854, Isambard allowed the Birmingham & Oxford Junction Railway, of which he was Engineer, to offer for sale the land above the newly made tunnel at Birmingham Snow Hill. The plot was bought by Samuel Briggs who intended to build a three-storey terrace on the site. He sent his plans to Isambard, for his approval, in accordance with the sale contract; Isambard approved the plans on 11 August and Briggs went ahead with the work. He cleared the earth down to the level of the brick arch, under the supervision of John Hewitt, Isambard's Resident Engineer, and the foundations of the terrace were laid on the tunnel brickwork. By 4 November the walls were raised to third-storey level.

At this point, Isambard realised what was happening. The arch was not designed to carry a concentrated weight and he ordered Briggs to 'fill up with concrete the whole space between the arch and the ground floor in order to distribute the weight of the walls'. Briggs refused to go to any expense on the grounds that Isambard had unconditionally approved his plans. Isambard then declared the buildings unsafe and the Company sought an injunction to force Briggs to 'restore the land to the same condition in which it was when excavations commenced'. In return, the Mayor of Birmingham sued for an injunction to restrain the railway company from using the tunnel on the grounds that *it* was unsafe due to the weight of buildings above it, legally erected with the Company's consent.

Isambard's frustrations, personal regrets over his lack of family life, his heavy cares, his lengthy and tedious travels, enormously difficult and varied technical problems, his recurring bouts of painful illness, exacerbated his eccentricities. He did not willingly collaborate with anyone, yet with the 'Great Ship', he had created a project which was beyond even his unaided powers. He had been obliged to ask for help from men more knowledgeable than he and they were developing their own ideas into machines to fit Isambard's specifications. The glory of the 'Great Ship' could not be his alone and this collaboration with Russell, which Isambard refused to admit to himself, was a trap just waiting to be sprung.

The moment arrived when he read an article entitled 'Iron Steam Ships – The Leviathan' in the *Observer* of 13 November 1854. The article, first quoted by Emmerson, contained a few correct technical facts but also a great deal of nonsense. Isambard chose not to notice the nonsense but decided that the article 'had the stamp of authority' and had been written by someone trying to steal his glory. Though the article was unsigned, like many *Observer* articles, its author was, in Isambard's opinion, Russell. But it is my opinion that Isambard was becoming jealous of Russell's large part in the ship. Isambard had always been jealous of his status in the eyes of the world – and therefore he now decided that Russell was jealous of him. When Isambard formed 'decided opinions' it was difficult, if not impossible, to disabuse him of them.

I think it likely that a reporter went to Millwall looking for serious information about the ship, and interviewed some senior people, perhaps Dickson and Hepworth. It is certain that they were proud of their design contribution and were irked by being ordered around by Isambard. I believe they took this opportunity to claim for their office the credit they thought belonged to it. They might have planted the well-placed 'digs' at Brunel along with the factual information or the reporter may have indulged himself at Isambard's expense.

Isambard was justifiably incensed by the line: 'We are not precisely aware to whom the credit of this bold suggestion (of a ship steaming non-stop to Australia) is due.' It must have been well known to the top drawing office staff at Millwall that the idea was Brunel's, and there is equally no doubt that had Russell been asked he would have said so. In his public statements Russell *always* made this clear. The article then stated: 'Mr Brunel, the Engineer of the ESN Co., approved the project and Mr Scott Russell undertook to carry out the design.' This also infuriated Isambard because it minimised his involvement while maximising Russell's. Isambard did far more than merely 'approve' but it is also true that Russell's contract obliged him to design the entire ship except for the screw engines. Given Isambard's obsession with being seen to be in charge, this arrangement was bound to lead to trouble and, I have no doubt, was an ever more bitter draught for Isambard to swallow as time passed, his health deteriorated and his pain increased.

The article was a confused piece of journalism. The reporter succeeded in confusing the SS *Great Britain* of 1847 with the SS *British Queen* of 1839. He stated that the *Great Britain* had sailed from Portsmouth, which was not so. He also stated that the designer of the *British Queen*'s engines, Robert Napier, 'is now associated with the most splendid triumphs in steam locomotion', which was also untrue. The SS *Great Britain* he referred to as 'the largest steamship yet built' but in the next paragraph he accorded this honour to Russell's SS *Himalaya*. He also stated that the SS *Great Britain* had 'recently' been sold to the Belgians for £18,000 after costing £250,000 to build, when in fact it had been sold ten years before having cost £176,000 to build. There were other contradictions and inaccuracies besides.

Had Isambard been fit and well, he would have dismissed this garbled article as he had done others. But instead, although he admitted that not everyone noticed what seemed glaringly obvious to him, he treated it seriously. 'The objectionable points . . . evidently did not strike you,' he wrote to John Yates, Secretary to the ESN Co., and continued: 'I cannot allow it to be stated, apparently on authority, while I have the whole heavy responsibility of its success resting on my shoulders, that I am a mere passive approver of the project of another which in fact originated solely with me and has been worked out by me at great cost of labour and thought devoted to it for not less than three years.'

Isambard had forgotten that while the idea originated with him, a large proportion of 'labour and thought' was being devoted to the subject, on his behalf, by Russell, Dickson and many others. The tragedy was that this silly article, coupled with painful bouts of illness, increased his innate jealousy and made him distrustful of his old friend who was working so hard to build his 'Great Ship'.

On 8 February 1855, Isambard's half-yearly 'Engineer's Report' to the ESN Co. Directors was published in full in *The Times*. This showed Isambard as Engineer in charge of the 'Great Ship' without once mentioning Russell and ought to have soothed away his paranoid suspicions. But he was not soothed and the situation was not improved when in March Prince Albert's secretary wrote to Russell and asked if the Prince could come and see *his* 'Great Ship' during a visit to a floating siege gun which Russell was also building. Russell at once invited Isambard to be present, as Engineer of the ship, but he, being unable to attend, asked Russell to ensure that his, Brunel's, supreme role in the business should be emphasised.

The Prince had himself designed 'floating cupolas' (partly submerged floating gun turrets), on which the Crimean War had focused interest, and when the visit was over, he had spent more time on the gun-ship than on the 'Great Ship'. Russell wrote a report of events to Isambard and took the opportunity of reassuring Isambard:

My Dear Mr Brunel, I took the opportunity of explaining what I supposed he and everyone else knew, that you are the Father of the 'Great Ship' and not I. . . . you may always trust your reputation to me as far as the Big Ship is concerned . . . I have as much reputation as I desire or deserve, I think it much wiser to be just than unjust, I would much rather preserve your friendship that filch your fame . . .

The Crimean War dragged on through 1855 and Isambard took it on himself to suggest to the Admiralty that fortresses along the Russian Baltic coast should be bombarded. He submitted his ideas for a battery of semi-submerged, shot-proof cupolas each carrying a 12-in. breech-loading gun and showed how they could be propelled by underwater steam-jets which could not be damaged by enemy fire. Apart from the steam-jets, there was nothing new in the idea and the Admiralty ignored the suggestion.

Isambard, at that time, was designing wire-wound gun barrels and also a rifle barrel, activities which brought him into friendly co-operation with the armaments manufacturer Sir William Armstrong. Armstrong tried some of Isambard's ideas in experimental gun barrels but found his co-operation far more useful as a 'back door' to the contracts department at the War Office, since Isambard's closest friend, Ben Hawes, was Permanent Under-Secretary of State and wielded considerable influence. In December 1854 Armstrong wrote to Isambard and asked him 'to pull a few strings' for him in the War Office.

The death-rate among British soldiers in the Crimea from wounds, disease and lack of clothing was very high. The advent of the 'war correspondent' ensured that this fact was known to the public and there was an outcry. Besides what he would have learned from William Russell's reports in *The Times*, Isambard was probably made aware of the terrible conditions through conversations with Ben Hawes. Hawes was heavily engaged on two fronts: in assisting the conduct of the war – with extreme inefficiency – and in preventing Florence Nightingale from reforming the Army's medical and quartermaster services – for these reforms required nothing less than the reform of the War Office itself.

In January 1855 Lord Palmerston became Prime Minister with a reformist-minded cabinet. Florence complained in her diary that she had as her ally the reforming Sidney Herbert, as Secretary of State for War answerable to Parliament, and the reactionary Ben Hawes, answerable to no one, preventing improvement. Florence bombarded Hawes with plans for improved hospitals, for edible food and warm clothing for the men but Hawes' skill in blocking reforms and his capacity for raising smoke-screens were recognised as unrivalled by other civil servants.

Florence described Hawes as, 'a Dictator, an Autocrat, irresponsible to Parliament, quite unassailable from any quarter'. In their obsessive personalities, their love of energetic action and their detestation of bureaucracy, Florence and Isambard had everything in common, yet Isambard supported Hawes who, for years, had stood for all that Isambard detested in entrenched, privileged bureaucracy. This is one of the great contradictions of his life.

On 16 February 1855, Isambard was formally requested to design a hospital for the British Army in the Crimea. He replied the same day that his 'best time and exertions would be, without any limitations, entirely at the service of the Government'. Although the order came, formally, from Sidney Herbert, it really emanated from Ben Hawes' office. Had it actually come from Herbert, Florence Nightingale would have been involved but Isambard dealt exclusively with Hawes. Isambard's hospital was intended to show the unforgivably bossy woman, 'interfering' in the realms of men, what could be achieved without her. She in turn never mentioned Brunel's hospital.

Isambard had had some experience with sanitary requirements having designed 'model' cottages for the working classes but it is reasonable to suppose that, as the task was the larger one of designing a really modern hospital, Brunel used Florence Nightingale's principles on lighting, ventilation, and hygiene. He had always been adept at adapting other people's ideas and Hawes was, after all, only too well aware of Nightingale's requirements, having been frequently lectured by her on what constituted a good hospital.

It was a cunningly contrived demonstration for, only six days after officially receiving the request, he handed to the War Office Contracts Department detailed plans for a prefabricated, 1000-bed hospital and had signed up the necessary contractors to make the buildings. He must have had prior warning of the formal request. Officials at the Department, not privy to the plot, were thoroughly alarmed at such impetuosity and were foolish enough to write a remonstrance to Isambard. He replied with his own brand of virtuous pomposity:

Such a course may possibly be unusual in the execution of government work but it is only an amount of responsibility which men in my profession are accustomed to take. It is only by the prompt and independent actions of a *single individual* entrusted with such powers that expedition can be secured and vexatious and mischievous delays avoided.

That was indeed Isambard's management technique but, looking back at his career, it could not be said that his system had entirely avoided 'vexatious and mischievous delays'.

He described his design in March 1855:

The whole hospital will consist of a number of separate buildings each sufficiently large to admit of the most economical construction but otherwise small and compact enough to be placed on ground with a considerable slope without the necessity of placing the floor of any part below the level of the ground. These separate buildings have been made the same size and shape so that with an indefinite length of open corridor to connect the various parts they may be arranged in any form to suit the levels and shape of the ground.

Each standard wooden building was divided in two, longitudinally, by a central wall and housed thirteen beds per side. It was large enough to ensure a good air-space above and around each bed. Flush toilets, urinals and hand-basins were provided at one end of the room, while at the opposite end a hand-operated rotary air-pump forced air into the room through underfloor ducting, the air passing over a relatively large surface of water in order to humidify it. The rooms were lit by long, narrow windows placed under the eaves to prevent the harsh glare of sunlight. The roofs were timber covered in waterproof felt with a top covering of polished tin to reflect the heat of the sun.

The same huts were used to house surgeries and bathrooms and, with some brickwork to minimise fire risk, for kitchens and laundries as well. For men too weak to go to the bath hut, Isambard designed portable baths for use in the ward rooms. A standard drainage system of cisterns, water-pumps and pipes was also supplied together with several fire engines, a slaughterhouse and store yard. The prefabricated units and their stores were sent out as packages that could be carried by two men and the whole 1000-bed hospital was divided among five ships so each ship would land 200 beds complete with all equipment.

Isambard did not invent standardised, prefabricated wooden buildings; they had been around since 1830. Nor did he invent the principles for sanitary hospitals; Florence Nightingale had done that.

Isambard took the existing relevant ideas, added his own meticulous planning, rolled them together and kicked them into the future. He had more than a little assistance from a first-class engineer.

Isambard chose as Resident Engineer John Brunton, the son of William who had surveyed the 1832 Bristol to London railway and who had opposed Brunel's route. Brunton was working on the Wilts, Somerset & Weymouth line, at Dorchester, for the contractors Hutchinson & Ritson. Isambard telegraphed to Dorchester, requested Brunton to be in the Duke Street office at 6 a.m. the following morning – he gave no reason! The Brunellian 'request' was nothing short of an order in Brunton's mind, he at once obtained leave of absence from his employer, said good-bye to his wife and set out by stage-coach and rail for London.

Isambard was working and did not look up when Brunton entered the following morning. 'I knew his peculiarities', the latter wrote later, 'so I walked up to his desk and said shortly, "Mr Brunel. I received your telegram and here I am." "Ah," was his reply, "Here's a letter to Mr Hawes at the War Office, be there with it at ten o'clock." ' Brunton presented himself to Hawes and was offered the job of Engineer to the hospital but without sufficient authority to commandeer men and materials. He refused the appointment and returned to Isambard to tell him what had happened. Although Brunton had done exactly what Isambard would have done, he met an angry response: 'Brunton, you are a fool! I thought to do you a good turn.' Brunton thanked Brunel and returned to Dorchester with only ten guineas expenses for his trouble.

He had barely arrived home when a message arrived summoning him to the War Office again. This time he was allowed to write his own orders. He walked out of the War Office with these written orders, the rank of Major and, to quote Ben Hawes, 'with greater powers than any other officer in Her Majesty's army'.

Brunton went straight to 18 Duke Street, walked unceremoniously into Isambard's office and said shortly, 'Be good enough to read that, Mr Brunel.'

Isambard read Brunton's new rank, pay, ration allowances and commissariat powers and said, 'Well, Brunton, I did not think you could have got it.'

'Then pray do not think me such a *fool* as at our last interview,' retorted Brunton. After that bold rebuke, Isambard's attitude became what Brunton describes as 'confidential', which I take to mean ingratiating. Perhaps if people had stood up to him more he would have treated them better.

Brunton sited the hospital on the south coast of the Dardanelles, close to the village of Renkioi. It had a good supply of clean drinking water, it was sunny, sheltered, near the sea and *en route* from the war to England. The first ship unloaded on 7 May 1855. Brunton's construction gang of thirteen carpenters, one pipe layer, three plumbers and a blacksmith plus some local labour set to work and two months later 300 beds were ready for patients. But it was October before bureaucracy managed to transfer any men there from the foul conditions of Scutari and the other hell-holes. The full 1000 beds were in use by Christmas 1855.

Peace came in January 1856 but in its short life the hospital treated 1500 men; of those only fifty died – 3 per cent fatality compared to 42 per cent at Scutari. Isambard received £2265 15s 11d for 'Your professional services and payments made by you for bonuses in connection with the construction of the hospital at Renkioi'. He was very modest about his achievement and called it 'just a sober exercise of common sense'. Its complete success was, without a doubt, his best reward. His sincerity on this score cannot be doubted. At the Paris Exhibition, 1855, he had been awarded the Légion d'honneur, supposedly for his hospital. He could not prevent the award being made – but he disapproved of medals and titles and it is known that he never applied to the Home Office for permission to use the decoration in England.

26

Brunel – Brusque and Fretful

Russell's financial situation, strained after the September 1853 fire, was made infinitely worse when his financial support, Charles Geach, died in October 1854. Then, in May 1855, Russell's floating cupola was gutted by fire the night before it was to be launched. Russell had spent £45,000 on developing the vessel, but it was not fully insured and he lost money so it is unlikely that he 'arranged' the fire as has been hinted, although his competitors in the armaments industry may have been glad to hear the news.

Russell had erected special buildings and installed special machinery for the construction of the 'Great Ship' and its engines – which were scaled-up versions of his successful design for the SS *Adelaide* and SS *Victoria*. All four cylinders for the paddle-wheels' engines – 6 ft 2 in. bore by 15 ft stroke and each weighing 34 tons – were cast by Russell's men. The four cylinders were arranged in pairs, driving an overhead crankshaft. As Emmerson points out, whereas the screw-propeller engine from James Watt & Co. had been virtually redesigned by Isambard, he had very little to do with the Russell engine which performed perfectly.

The erection of thousands of tons of iron to construct the hull of the 'Great Ship' went on using equipment which would not have been out of place in the Middle Ages. Russell suggested that a travelling crane with a 60-ton lift would speed the work and save money, and he offered to build one for £2951 but Isambard rejected this sensible idea as 'very frightening'. Heavy plates for the riverward side of the ship had to be trundled round on barrows. Men climbed to the decks, 60 ft above the ground, on wooden towers. Hundreds of thousands of red-hot rivets were thrown by relays of boys, past scores of workmen, to the riveter who worked with a 'closer-up' to hand-hammer the hot metal into place.

So far as possible Russell standardised the plates, angle and bar-iron in the ship and his efficiency kept the work moving systematically forward. He gains no credit from Rolt for this, although Isambard's contribution – saving 40 tons of iron throughout the 8600-ton hull – is well documented. Russell knew his job and had a fine management team under him. Left to himself, he would not perhaps have built the ship as perfectly as he did with Isambard's suggestions, but it would have cost far less and it would have been in the water two years earlier.

As Russell was building the ship, Isambard had little contribution to make but to nag, worrying about the rate of progress on the hull while wasting Russell's time by pestering him for photographs and for indicator cards to show the performance of the engines' cylinders. Emmerson quotes Russell's reply on 9 May 1855 to Isambard's charge that progress was slow. It was, he said, the consequence of a delay in the supply of iron plates which had since arrived. As to the indicator cards, he had used the finest instruments to obtain them 'and as these appear not to be satisfactory I have arranged for the Woolwich collection of Indicators . . . to be used and when I have done that I shall have exhausted all the resources I am acquainted with.'

Isambard replied instantly with a thoroughly bad-tempered note: 'I do not want better indicators than usual . . . those made on this occasion and to which I object were absurd – like the attempts of a 2-year old at writing – and I take credit to myself that I did not resent the insult of showing them to me as indicator cards.' Can it be possible that a great marine engineer would have sent indicators that could be described in this way? The rudeness of the note suggests that Isambard was in pain when he wrote it.

In April 1855 the question of the launch was resurrected when a shipbuilder called Bull, from Buffalo, New York, wrote to Isambard to reassure him of the feasibility of a sideways launch. Bull had carried out hundreds, sliding the hulls on timber cradles down well-greased timber ramps. But Bull was advocating a *free* launch and Isambard had always wanted to make a *controlled* launch. He had intended to fit the ship's cradles with iron strips, like a sledge, and to lower the ship over ways fitted with iron rollers to the water's edge. This seems a good idea except that he then abandoned the rollers – on grounds of expense – while still adhering to the controlled launch.

Russell agreed to a free, broadside, launch but was opposed to a controlled launch. A veteran in these matters, he judged that the friction between the ship's wooden cradles and the wooden launching ways, however well greased, would itself act as a control. Indeed, he was sure that hydraulic rams would be required to start the thing moving – an idea Isambard also dismissed as too expensive, although, come the day, he would have to use whole batteries of rams.

Isambard had also dismissed Russell's dry-dock option as too expensive – and, in the arrogance of his inexperience, he dismissed as 'madness' the advice of two highly experienced men regarding the well-tried free launch, while advocating the unknown technique of a controlled launch – for which Russell would have to pay. Even Rolt admits the injustice of making Russell pay extra for a policy with which he disagreed, yet, a few lines further on, he accuses Russell of 'a policy of non-co-operation'. Isambard, of course, could not be 'unco-operative' since he was the Engineer in charge.

Isambard's double standards are infuriatingly well illustrated here. He had desperately wanted to make the atmospheric railway work. Careful calculations by acknowledged scientists showed that the system was expensive and impractical, so he dismissed calculations and appealed to 'experience'. The system would have to be built before its utility could be judged. Now in the case of launching the 'Great Ship', he dismissed two lifetimes of practical experience and turned instead to careful calculation.

While he dismissed Russell's experience he was at the same time demanding from him precise technical data, so that he, Isambard, could make the calculations necessary to ensure the success of the launch. The calculations for and the technique of launching are the preserve of the naval architect and shipbuilder. Isambard was neither, Russell was both – and by the terms of the contract was responsible for the launch – yet Isambard pushed him aside and detailed his, Isambard's, assistant, Jacomb, who had no more experience than he had himself, to make separate calculations from the supplied data as a check against the accuracy of Isambard's mathematics. This is what Isambard called 'not trusting to chance'.

On 21 August 1855, Russell gave Isambard a month-by-month

schedule for completion of the ship by March 1856, provided that Isambard gave permission for work to start on the stern, which had not yet been built as Isambard had not yet settled on a design for it, though he was fretting about the launch. On 27 September 1855 Russell wrote a long and patiently worded letter of protest regarding his lack of payment from Isambard and, among other information, giving the weight of the ship, for which he had been asked. Isambard did not answer any of Russell's protests but took refuge in a short, bad-tempered note, quoted by Emmerson:

> How the devil can you say you satisfied yourself as to the weight of the ship when the figures your clerk gave you are 1000 tons less than I make it or than you made it a few months ago – *for shame* – if you are satisfied then I am sorry to give you trouble but I think you will thank me for it. I wish you were my obedient servant, I should begin with a little flogging.

Without exception, in response to Isambard's hectoring demands, Russell's replies are restrained, optimistic and helpful, in his attempt to do his best under almost impossible circumstances.

It may well be that the weight of the ship varied by the month because Isambard frequently altered the construction. Late in September 1855 Isambard began to re-design the paddle-boxes and changed his mind once again on the relative height of the screw, which again altered the design of the lower stern and stern post. He gave fresh instructions to Russell on 5 October to which Russell patiently replied: 'I have examined your memorandum of immediate wants and shall work hard to supply them before your return.' On the 12th, Martin's Bank pressed Russell for £12,000 of his £15,000 overdraft and Isambard reluctantly let Russell have £10,000 but refused more until Russell had supplied the data necessary to arrange the launch.

Russell himself was responsible for the launch by the terms of the contract. He was perfectly confident of his abilities as a naval architect to arrive with the necessary data when the time came and was not keen to supply it ahead of time. Yet Isambard pressed him for it again on 30 November and again on 2 December 1855 with another arrogant note: 'I peremptorily require the plan of the cradle and ways . . . I have made up my mind as to how they may be made but as the pecuniary responsibility rests with you, I should wish to give your plan preference if I can.'

Russell gave all the data required for the launch, on 9 December, together with the designs for the ship's wooden cradles and launchways. Having clamoured for this information for months Isambard did nothing with it. Russell, having fulfilled all Isambard's conditions, asked to be paid, whereupon Isambard capriciously invented a new excuse for withholding part of the cash.

Two hundred tons of iron had been erected in the hull during a period which, by Isambard's reckoning, ought to have seen 230 tons erected. This was fine as a theory worked out for contract purposes in a warm office but the reality of November and December 1855 was one of bitter cold, rain, sleet and snow. Isambard had always paid, when he paid, at the rate of £6 a ton – £1200 in this case – but because the target of 230 tons had been missed by 30 tons, one-eighth of the total, he deducted one-eighth from the sum due. This was a departure from the written contract but as the contract also made Isambard's whim the law, Russell had no redress.

In January 1856 Isambard became convinced that 2500 tons of iron plate was missing. On the 9th Isambard wrote to Russell a letter at once solicitous yet slyly insinuating of wrong-doing – an 'own up like a man before I report you' kind of letter. Inquiry by Isambard's assistant, Jacomb, showed that an *estimated* 800 tons were missing, which could have been due to bad stock-keeping by the storeman, bad estimating in the bitter weather by Jacomb, Isambard's own miscalculations or his frequent changes of design which used up extra materials and caused the men to lose track of stock. Isambard reported the loss of 800 tons of iron to the ESN Co. Directors on 15 January based on his 'assumptions' of what was erected in the ship and his 'estimates' of what lay in the yard. He 'did not think the iron had been used for other purposes', yet he insisted the iron was missing.

The significance of this innuendo was that Isambard wanted to establish that Russell was negligent: 'he no longer appears to attend to my entreaties ... and I see no other means of obtaining proper attention to the terms of the Contract than by refusing to advance any more money'. Russell had not been paid that which he was owed and besides this he required £37,673 in excess of his original tender to cover extra expenditure caused by soaring inflation (which had already put many shipbuilders out of business) and, very substantially, by Isambard's changes of mind and lack of decisiveness. Without funds he would not be able to continue to employ a workforce to build the ship.

Russell had done his best to comply with Isambard's wishes but Isambard wanted to get rid of him because he was jealous of the part he was playing in the construction of the 'Great Ship'. Russell was willing to join a new agreement with Brunel, proposed by the ESN Co.'s solicitor, and if Brunel had wanted him he only had to say the word. Instead, at the end of January, he issued a formal notice of Russell's inability to proceed with the contract and on 4 February 1856, the Scott Russell Shipbuilding and Engineering Co. ceased trading.

Without the security of the 'Great Ship' contract, Russell was no longer creditworthy; Martin's Bank refused further credit and took possession of his premises. Russell's business was not actually declared bankrupt, neither was his private fortune involved. Some of his creditors were appointed Inspectors to supervise his continuation in ship building so that he could complete his Admiralty contracts and thus earn the money to pay his creditors.

At the ESN Co. shareholders' meeting on 5 February 1856, shareholders' anxieties were soothed with a wonderfully optimistic, thoroughly Brunellian Report, giving visions of future profits and diverting anger (over the delays to the ship and the loss of its most capable builder) from Isambard, who had pushed the victim over the edge, on to the victim – Russell. John Fowler – later to collaborate with Benjamin Baker in the design of the Forth Bridge – was engaged to advise the Company and he recommended that Russell be allowed to make a new contract with the ESN Co. for the completion of the ship.

Russell estimated that £9775 would be needed to complete the hull but Isambard decided that £3250 was the correct price. Emmerson has shown that his arithmetic was at fault. He allowed £6 a ton to erect the iron – a three-year-old price which did not take into account inflation – and there was, even by his own admission, 1100 tons in the yard waiting to be erected – so that the job would cost £6600 even on Isambard's out-of-date price. Russell's estimate of £9775 was probably correct, taking into account inflation.

If Isambard thought he would scare off Russell, and offer the job to some less illustrious engineer who would not appear as an equal in the construction of the 'Great Ship', he was mistaken. Russell was so keen to carry on as the ship's builder that he said he would leave the matter of costs to be settled by arbitration and would start at once to complete the ship. Seeing that Russell was not going to be put off, Isambard accepted him but only as an assistant on his private staff. Russell refused this as beneath his dignity. Isambard would have thought the same if the positions had been reversed.

Isambard tried to recruit Hepworth and Dickson as his assistants. They were experienced men and each expected an appropriate salary. This was no more than the free play of market forces but Isambard was outraged at what he called blackmail. After more haggling it was agreed that Russell should after all return as 'ship-builder and engine-maker to the Great Ship'. Rolt is incorrect when he states that Russell 'had nothing further to do with the "Great Ship" from the time of his failure until she was launched'.

Rolt also refers unjustly to Russell's financial recovery as 'miraculous' and 'a mystery', implying fraud. In fact the re-arrangement of his affairs was an ordinary business transaction which took a full year to complete. A measure of the high regard in which he was held by the engineering community is that in April 1856 he was appointed honorary secretary of the Sir Francis Pettit-Smith testimonial fund, an appeal for contributions for the inventor of the screw propeller who was in financial straits. Russell donated £100, Brunel half that amount.

27

The Great Dictator

Work resumed on the 'Great Ship' on 23 May 1856 with Russell charged by the Directors to 'undertake to organise the recommencement of the Works and to superintend the completion of the iron hull and her paddle engines' for a launch in Spring 1857. Russell, subject always to Brunel's over-riding authority as Engineer, was in charge of construction with Hepworth and Dickson as his assistants and Yates as Manager of the Yard. Early in June Isambard was taken ill but Russell kept him well informed through written reports. These made clear that rapid progress was taking place – which alarmed Isambard. How could there be rapid progress if he was not supervising? They must be skimping the job. Dragging himself from his sick-bed he discovered, to his great annoyance, that work was being tackled from plans which were – in his opinion – insufficiently detailed and which, in any case, he had not previously approved.

Russell had approved them and his highly experienced foremen were interpreting them as they always did under Russell's delegated style of management. But Isambard called this 'disorganised' and forbade any further work to proceed until he had approved it. As he was frequently unobtainable through illness or because he was in Devon or West Wales, or just as a result of the weight of decisions to be taken, this order would have caused delay, so the experienced workforce ignored him as far as possible in the interests of getting the job finished.

Brunel had hired Russell and his skilled workforce and then did not trust them to do their work. They had always worked out the small details of construction which were not shown on the working drawings, but Isambard wanted personally to see and approve a drawing for every job and even wanted to dictate the sequence in which jobs were to be tackled. Anything less was, to him, 'disorganised'. He simply could not understand Russell's delegation of authority. He saw the work galloping on without recourse to him and saw in these normal craftsmen's practices 'a conspiracy to deprive me of all proper authority', a plot to steal his glory! There is a cruel irony in that it is this period of happy progress under the democratic Russell which Rolt credits to Isambard's dictatorial management.

Without doubt, Isambard's obsession with his status and his belief that no one but he could do anything was a great stumbling block to the progress of the ship, for when he was removed from the scene the work progressed by leaps and bounds. In June 1856 he ordered the height of decks, which he had previously approved and which were already riveted into place, to be increased. By 28 August the decks had been cut out and re-positioned and Russell was pressing him to make up his mind on the arrangements for the masts, rigging, cabins and cabin fittings so that he could get on with the work.

And all the while Isambard was worried about the 'peculiar state of things in the works' – although no shipbuilder would have found them 'peculiar'. He condemned 'the total absence of control', something of an exaggeration, and complained to Yates that all this was done with intent to flout his authority. Yates replied about 15 September 1856: 'I court the most rigid inquiry into my behaviour by the Directors and I am quite willing to abide by the result.' Isambard also wrote to Russell, demanding that he submit himself to his strict instructions and to renounce his independence of action.

Russell's reply was the nearest he ever came to being sharp with Isambard:

> I have endeavoured to the best of my judgement to discharge the duties entrusted to me by the Directors with energy, fidelity and singleness of purpose and even where I have differed from you in opinion I have endeavoured to act courteously, considerately and with deference towards you. That these endeavours have not earned your approbation I am sorry and must await any further instructions which my employers may choose to give.

At a Committee of Works meeting on 19 September 1856, Russell proposed a diplomatic holiday for himself. The Directors sympathised with Russell's 'heavy trials' and hoped that he would benefit from his holiday but resolved that, in future, no works should be undertaken without Isambard's express approval as 'Engineer-in-Chief'. With polite but slight thanks for all his efforts, the Directors dropped Russell. Isambard was at last master in what he considered to be his own house. He had got rid of the man he saw as his rival for the glory of the 'Great Ship'.

He at once established his complete control with typically Brunellian words, demanding 'entire and undivided authority over everybody in the yard . . . and over the ordering of work and materials required'. He restricted individual initiative and responsibility in the vast undertaking and thereby introduced the very 'vexatious and mischievous delays' he hoped to avoid. It is a Brunellian paradox that while he loathed civil servants as men dedicated to the restriction of private initiative and responsibility he spent his life doing just that within the various works he directed. He even went so far as to adopt a missionary attitude towards Dickson and Hepworth saying that they were 'grossly over-paid' (£25 a week), and asserted that this 'could only produce a very bad moral effect on them'. One can only wonder what was the moral effect on Isambard of his own salary, which, from the GWR alone, was not less than 10 guineas a day.

The Directors had ordered Yates and Isambard, together, to reorganise the Millwall yard. As Manager of the yard Yates had expected to be consulted but Isambard saw Yates as his nearest rival for authority and at once began to place him in a subordinate position. Instead of consulting with him, Isambard merely presented him with his orders. These were that he would manage all accounting, stores, purchases, wages and hiring and obey Isambard's written orders. This arrangement was duly approved by the Directors but even then Isambard could not keep to his own brief. He had to control everyone and run all departments as if he was the employer instead of an employee like Yates.

Emmerson quotes this response from Yates to an unknown letter from Isambard:

I feel strongly that, from your having failed in your attempt at a quarrel with Mr Russell, you appear determined to pick one with me. I will not be provoked, neither will I swerve from the faithful discharge of my duties to the Directors, whose servant I am and to whom alone I hold myself amenable . . . you have repeatedly put me down when I ventured to advise the Directors . . . as something beneath their notice . . . a mere secretary . . . my right to advise the Board is perfectly equal to your own . . . and whenever it has been my duty to advise . . . I have done so in a respectful manner, without assuming the form of *Dictation* which . . . has too frequently been the case with yourself. I have no desire to quarrel with you . . . but I will not be constantly subject to your *misrepresentation* or be trampled on by you or any man.

Isambard found the work languishing while he was rapidly exhausting himself in trying to run everything. On 7 October, he wrote what can only be described as a 'whingeing' letter to the Directors in which he complained of his hardship in having to direct 1200 men: 'You are misinformed as to the amount of labour and the extent to which every detail of the minutest description devolves upon me,' as if he had never devoted his entire life to achieving precisely this situation.

In this atmosphere the work went forward slowly, owing to the necessity of every order having to be given by Isambard, every drawing approved by him. He attempted to fill the gap left by Russell by asking Gooch to assist him in supervising Dickson, Hepworth and the rest but Gooch detected resentment engendered in these marine engineers at having to take orders from a civil engineer and declined the offer. He did not want to become a resented locomotive engineer. The situation was then one that had become typical: Isambard, soldiering on, with undoubted courage and determination to see the job through in spite of his increasingly painful illness. The tragedy was that most of Isambard's troubles were of his own making.

Isambard's removal of Russell as builder of the 'Great Ship' was done without any of the foresight with which Isambard was reputedly so well endowed. Russell's mortgage-holder, Martin's Bank, had their eye on the 'Great Ship' as well as the yard already in their hands, and it is likely that they were manoeuvring to acquire them both for a song. Now Isambard's actions against Russell had placed the ESN Co. at the mercy of Martin's Bank which was charging the ESN Co. £2500 a month to occupy Russell's shipyard.

Isambard's great friend, Robert Stephenson, by then also a sick man, had been well primed by Brunel on his difficulties with sullen engineers such as Dickson. After Stephenson's first visit to the yard he wrote to Isambard: 'I dislike his (Dickson's) face immensely. I felt it an imperative duty to treat all his suggestions irreverently.' Dickson was caught between Isambard's customary arrogance and the occasional visits of the prejudiced Stephenson and it is a wonder that he was able to do any work at all.

Russell, Brunel and Napier (who invented the device) had previously used feed-water heaters around ships' funnels. This device increased the thermal efficiency of the engines by using waste heat to raise the feed-water temperature and thus save coal in heating water, and it also shielded the passenger accommodation from the great heat radiating from the furnace flue. It was a very good idea in theory but was insufficiently refined in practice and was potentially dangerous. Russell, Blake (for James Watt & Co.) and Napier himself had counselled Isambard against using these heaters in the 'Great Ship' but after the departure of Russell, Isambard had no one remotely able to restrain him and he ordered the water-jackets to be fitted around the two forward flues.

The water-heaters took the form of a closed casing of a half-inch boiler plate forming a 6-in. annulus around the hottest part of the funnel from the boiler to the deck, 40 ft above. To give sufficient 'head' of water in the heater so as to overcome the steam pressure in the boiler, a $1\frac{1}{4}$-in. standpipe from the top of the heater rose 30 ft up the outside of the funnel to a 180-degree bend which took it back down to the engine room where it was open to atmosphere. There was a half-inch vent-hole on the 'U' bend to prevent a siphoning effect and to give a vent to atmosphere for any steam that might collect during normal operations.

A 'donkey engine' pumped the boiler feed-water, cold, into the heater through a pipe at the base of the casing and heated water passed into the boiler through a connection at the top. The danger lay in the fact that the heater could be by-passed and cold water could be pumped direct to the boiler. If the heater was forgotten and further cold water not added the water within could boil away leaving the funnel, invisible within the casing, to become very hot, even red-hot, so that when cold water was introduced there would be an explosive generation of steam on the overheated metal.

On the 'Great Ship', matters were made more dangerous by the introduction of a stop-cock in the stand-pipe just above the top of the heater. The cock was nothing more than a temporary expedient, put in by Dickson, and approved by Isambard, to close the exit from the heater to permit the casing to be given a hydraulic pressure test. After this test the cock ought, perhaps, to have been removed but Dickson thought it would be useful as a way of shutting-off the stand-pipe should it be fractured and start pouring water into the accommodation and in this he was supported by the Company's engine-room engineer, McLennan, who obtained Isambard's consent.

Isambard changed his mind, yet again, about the system of launching. He had done nothing with Russell's plans for ten months and now decided that well-greased 'wood on wood', even with the wide bearing area designed by Russell, would 'bind' and the surest way would be to lay rows of iron rails down the ramp and to fit the underside of the ship's wooden cradles with iron strips. He asked a friend, the mathematician William Froude, to carry out experiments; the results seemed to show that Isambard's system was feasible – so, naturally enough, he approved of the experiments and went ahead with his own, gigantic experiment on a new launching technique.

Brunel had never carried out a launch. One also wonders in fact how Froude simulated, reliably, a deadweight of 12,000 tons. Russell's experiments had shown that 'iron on iron' would 'bite' after a little movement had scraped off the grease although he did not inform Isambard of his experiment. Would Isambard have listened to Russell's gloomy prognostications? Thomas Treadwell took the contract to build the new system on 19 January 1857 and the launch was planned for August.

Public interest was so great that on 18 April 1857 *The Times* carried a leading article on the ship, referring to Russell as 'the builder'. This description was no longer correct and Russell at once wrote a letter to the Editor, which was published on 20 April 1857:

Your mention of my name exclusively in connection with that ship may be interpreted injuriously to the rights of others. In justice to their rights I wish to communicate the following. I designed her lines and constructed the iron hull and am responsible for her merits or defects as a piece of naval architecture. It is however to the Company's Engineer, Mr I.K. Brunel, that the original conception is due of building a steam ship large enough to carry coals sufficient for full steaming on the longest voyage. The idea of using two engines and two propellers [Russell meant paddle-wheel and screw] was his. It was also his idea to introduce a cellular construction. It will be seen that these main characteristics which distinguish this from other ships are Mr Brunel's ideas.

In June 1857 Isambard still had not completed the stern, stern post, propeller or propeller-shaft of the 'Great Ship' but promised the Directors that he would have the work done by the end of July so that the ship could be launched in August. However by August Treadwell had not completed the launching ways. The ship was finally ready for launching by 31 October 1857 and Isambard wanted time to rehearse and to make trials but his hand was forced because Martin's Bank was charging so heavily for the use of the yard. Thus, without the careful planning he would have liked, Isambard set the launch date for 3 November 1857.

To start the ship moving, Isambard attached chains from amidships running out to four 80-ton hand-winches on barges moored in the river. At bow and stern chains went around pulleys on moored barges and back to steam-winches on the riverbank. He had also positioned at bow and stern a hydraulic ram. Isambard intended that once these arrangements had got the ship moving, he would control the descent by two, braked drums, 20 ft long and 9 ft diameter, wound around with chain which was attached to the cradles. Each drum could be restrained, as it revolved, by a hand-operated hand-brake.

Isambard, looking like 'a respectable carpenter's foreman' to quote a newspaper reporter, was worried sick by the awful uncertainties of the launch, having had no time to rehearse procedures, and he watched with anger and despair as the yard filled up with 3000 excited spectators, admitted at a charge by the Directors. He had asked for privacy and had not even invited Robert Stephenson. Outside the yard, the pubs were having a field-day. The streets were full of happy drunks and the discordant sound of brass instruments blown by inebriated bandsmen wafted above the milling crowd in the shipyard.

In the midst of this nerve-racking chaos Yates appeared before him, bearing a short list of names for the ship and asked him to choose one. He snapped back that they could call the ship 'Tom Thumb' for all he cared. The aptly named daughter of the Chairman of the ESN Co., Miss Hope, cracked a bottle of champagne on the hull and said she christened the ship *Leviathan* though the Company formally registered her as the SS *Great Eastern*.

At about 12.25 p.m. Isambard took his place on the signal platform high above the chaotic mob in a state of mind which can only be guessed at. The checking chains were slacked off by the manual winches and the wedges holding the cradles were driven out. For several minutes nothing happened, then, the forward cradle shot forward 6 ft. Isambard ordered the after-winch to be started and the after-cradle shot forward 15 ft. The movement took up chain attached to the after-brake drum and turned it. The men working this drum had not removed the winch handle which spun around with tremendous force, throwing several men into the air. One had his legs smashed and died later; all were injured. There was pandemonium in the yard and Isambard suspended operations.

28

Failing Fast

After the débâcle of the first launch attempt, it was a matter of sheer brute force to heave and shove the ship down the 1 in 12 slope to the water's edge as the iron-shod cradles bit into the iron bridge-rails over which they were supposed to slide. The dry-dock and the later, excellent, 'rollers' idea, both of which Isambard had discarded on grounds of cost, would have been cheap at twice the price. Isambard was deeply depressed and on 9 November 1857 wrote to a Director of the ESN Co., Mr S. Baker, trying to clear himself of any responsibility for the chaos:

> Our finances are indeed in a gloomy state and I feel that I have been somewhat cruelly treated. The enormous expenses must be thrown on me whereas 50% or 60% of them are the result of an attempt to carry on such a concern without an experienced Manager of Works.

Rolt accused Russell of 'making money vanish into thin air', implying embezzlement, yet Isambard, referring to the year when Russell was entirely absent admitted to Baker that:

> I have for weeks seen our money running away faster and faster each day with less and less result but it will not be fair to saddle me with the enormous cost of the work. As you know I have nothing whatever to do with employing men, settlement of wages or any expenditure whatever.

Is this the same Isambard who demanded 'entire and undivided authority over everybody in the yard'?

Isambard always worked best in desperate situations. Thirty years earlier, beneath the Thames, he had by day and night flung all his resources, mental and physical, into the fray. Now he gave his all to drive his 'Great Ship' down to the water. But he was not only thirty years older but a very sick man. Throughout the dank murk of November, the short dark days and freezing weather of December 1857 and January 1858, a few men, directed by one short, slight, utterly determined figure, forced the huge, black bulk down to the water's edge.

They did it with twenty-one hydraulic rams, finally mustered from the then little-known Birmingham firm of Richard Tangye ('We launched the *Great Eastern* and they launched us'). On 30 January, Isambard at last had the ship in the water, held down on her cradles by water ballast and awaiting a high spring tide to float her off. He and his second son Henry lived on board, Isambard barely sleeping, keeping a minute-by-minute watch on the tides and the weather, receiving by electric telegraph – that 'toy' as Isambard had once described it – information on the tides and the weather around the country.

At 3.30 a.m. on 31 January, Isambard perceived an improvement in the weather coinciding with the last of the spring tides. He ordered the water ballast pumped out. As dawn broke bright and fair after the storms the ship was empty and lifting slightly on the water as an exceptionally strong tide began to flow. The men who operated the hydraulic rams, barge-borne steam-winches and tugs were not booked on till 11 a.m. but Isambard ordered them out at once. As soon as they were at their posts the final shoves were given – and at 1.42 p.m. on 31 January 1858, the SS *Great Eastern* floated on the river.

There can be no doubt that the launch, from an engineering point of view, was a disaster, but like all the best British disasters it was conducted in a thoroughly heroic manner, with enormous courage and determination. Isambard believed in the frontal assault and when hundredweights did not suffice he used tons. But that was very often after he had refused to listen to advice. Russell later wrote:

Had the surface on which she was carried been simply the ordinary plank surface, well lubricated, the launch of the *Great Eastern* would have been no different to any other launch. The area of the ways covered by the two cradles was nearly 20,000 sq. ft and that was more than suffi- cient to conduct the weight gently into the water but it was the destiny of the *Great Eastern* to be the victim of experiments which had nothing to do with her original design or her ultimate purpose.

The cost of launching had been £120,000, almost half Russell's original tender to build the whole ship and six times Isambard's estimated cost of building Russell's 'too expensive' dry-dock. Nearly £750,000 had been spent on the hull and the unfinished machinery it contained, and £95,000 was owing for materials. The debit would have been greater but Isambard had worked for nothing since the ESN Co. had taken over as the contractors building the ship, and had paid his assistants out of his own pocket. The greatest cost to Isambard was the accelerated decline of his health. He had never enjoyed a robust constitution and now he had used up all his reserves. 'I am regularly floored by a concatenation of evils,' he wrote.

The ESN Co. Directors, several of them opposed to Brunel's continuing as Engineer, began to plan the completion of the ship and again consulted John Fowler as to a course of action. Fowler recommended that 'an opportunity be afforded Mr J.S. Russell to associate himself with some practical and substantial men to arrange a general plan for the completion of the ship'. Isambard expressed himself perfectly ready to aid such a plan and promised his 'loyal and zealous support, it being clearly understood that the obliteration of all illfeeling was to be a positive condition'. Fowler reassured Isambard that he would not interfere with his pre-eminent position as Engineer to the ESN Co., and Isambard asked him to put this in writing.

In March 1858 the ESN Co. set about raising £200,000 to pay debts and complete the ship, while in May Isambard was ordered to go to Vichy for a complete rest – or what passed for a 'rest' for him – touring the Swiss Alps and working on plans for his East Bengal Railway at the various hotels at which he and his family stayed. When he returned in September he found that no progress had been made owing to lack of funds. Some of the Directors wanted to sell the ship, while another party, led by Magnus, wanted to form a new company to buy the ship from the ESN. Magnus won the argument, the 'Great Ship Company' was formed, and it bought the ship for £160,000 on 25 November 1858. Brunel was appointed Engineer for the new Company.

Isambard's health had not improved after his European tour. It was at this time that Bright's disease was diagnosed (or possibly misdiagnosed). But whatever his illness in fact was, his doctor Sir

Benjamin Brodie ordered him to Egypt for the winter.

Isambard was very disappointed at having to leave but he did as he was told, and before he left submitted his specification of what was required to complete the ship, making some economies including the abandonment of a gyroscopic compass he had invented. Russell submitted a counter-specification which discarded even more decoration and 'mere frippery' than Isambard's. Russell undertook to complete the ship for £125,000, in six months from signing the contract, with a bonus to him of £1000 for each week ahead of the deadline and a penalty of £10,000 a day for every week overdue.

Wigram and Lucas made a bid based on Isambard's specification but Russell's specification allowed a lower price and late in January 1859 Russell's estimate was accepted. Russell took on the work of completing the paddle engines and the remaining structural work while subcontracting all other work – masts, rigging, furnishings. Work commenced on 15 February 1859 with a deadline for an Atlantic trial run in mid-July.

Isambard left England in mid-December 1858, taking with him Mary, his second son Henry, Dr Parkes the Superintendent of Renkioi hospital, and a great deal of luggage. He left behind, with the ship, then lying at Deptford, his assistants Jacomb and Brereton who sent plentiful reports to their chief. It should be recalled that this was the indefatigable Brereton who had also had charge of the erection of the Royal Albert Bridge.

Although Isambard was the sick man of the party, he gave himself tasks of observation and calculation. When the ship was plunging through a winter storm in the Mediterranean, he remained on deck in the flying spray, wedged into a corner, noting the number of turns of the paddle wheels, the strength of the wind and the time interval between waves. Meanwhile down below, his family and his doctor suffered agonies of sea-sickness. The Brunels spent Christmas in Cairo and had Christmas dinner with Robert Stephenson, also incurably sick.

On 30 December 1858 they set out up the Nile in an iron boat and reached Thebes on 21 January 1859. There Isambard and Henry took to donkeys to reach the famous ruins. From Aswan on 2 February they began to ascend the cataracts in a wooden boat hauled by thirty-five labourers. That inelegant and uncomfortable mode of travel cannot have been to Mary's liking but Isambard and Henry were in their element. Isambard was surprised at the efficiency of the men in hauling the boat up 'ramps' of water thundering between granite boulders. They asked for no advice from him and appeared to be 'disorganised', despite which they performed excellently. Brunel wrote:

> Until I had seen it and calculated the power required I should imprudently have said it could not be effected. . . . Between rocks (barely) wide enough to let our boat pass the men standing on the rocks, shouting, plunging into the water, swimming across the top or bottom of the fall, getting under the boat to push it off the rocks, all with an immense expenditure of noise, apparent confusion and want of plan – yet, on the whole, properly and successfully.

The party returned via Rome and arrived at Duke Street in May 1859, a few days after the opening, by Prince Albert, of the Royal Albert Bridge, on 2 May. From the designing of the first small exploratory tube, to the construction of a foundation 87 ft below high water, by way of the raising of the trusses and the final opening, the entire work – 2200 ft long – had cost only £225,000. Stephenson's Britannia Bridge across the Menai Strait, 600 ft shorter, cost £601,865 without the extreme difficulties with foundation work. Isambard was taken to see his masterpiece but was unable to stand and had to lie on a couch, placed on a carriage truck, which was pulled slowly across the bridge by a locomotive. Like many episodes in Isambard's life, this too has an air of heroic tragedy.

Isambard found the SS *Great Eastern* in an advanced state of preparation, which undermines Rolt's accusations that Russell was inefficient and that his estimates were fraudulently low to land the contract. As on the Nile cataracts, Isambard was unable to distinguish between organised chaos – and disorganisation. By definition, any work which was not subject to his rigid control was disorganised so he spent his remaining strength trying to control Russell and thereby bring some 'organisation' to what appeared to him to be pandemonium.

He visited the ship whenever he could get off his sick-bed, in spite of the pain he was suffering, and despite also his doctor's warnings and the entreaties of his family. He struggled round the ship, determined to be seen to be in charge, supervising all departments, undoubtedly to the annoyance of the engineers who had managed perfectly well without him for the five months he had been wholly absent.

Russell and his chief assistants were skilled organisers and, left to themselves, they had made rapid headway in spite of the *Great Eastern*'s being moored on the river so that every item, from the 40-ton crank-shaft for the paddle-wheel engines to the carpets for the saloons, had to be ferried out on barges and then winched aboard by the ship's derricks. On board, men of a dozen trades thronged the decks and passageways, hammering, installing and fitting. As if this was not enough, they had among them crowds of visitors who had paid to come aboard. Isambard strongly disapproved but the Directors ignored him. There was dissent between the Directors and understandable animosity and suspicion between Russell's marine engineers and Isambard's assistants, the civil engineers Jacomb and Brereton.

Although the fitting-out work had progressed largely without benefit of Isambard's advice, it was completed closely to the contracted time. In the small hours of 25 July 1859, a little behind schedule, Dickson gave the paddle-wheel engines their first few turns. He did so without asking Isambard's permission and with only his own men present. As he had helped to design the engines and had supervised their erection, there seems no reason why he should not have given them a spin. They were still the responsibility of the builder, Russell, whose employee Dickson was.

To Isambard this action was mutiny. The marine engineer, Blake, who had designed the propeller engines, submitted to Isambard's domination and kept him well informed of his doings but Russell and his men were not prepared to bow down to a man who knew less about marine engineering than they did. It is significant that Isambard had been obliged to make several alterations to Blake's engine and had, thereby, established his superiority over him. But he had not been able to make any improvement to Russell's paddle-wheel engines except for a modification to the valve gear; and the Russell camp refused to be intimidated.

On 5 August Russell gave a banquet on board the ship. Isambard was too ill to be present, but the distinguished guests, who included a large section of both Houses of Parliament and such engineering luminaries as Sir John Rennie and Joseph Whitworth, were given a demonstration of the engines. These were acknowledged to work perfectly. The correspondent of *The Times* at the banquet, reporting on 8 August, quoted the Chairman as saying that, other than Russell, 'no other man in the Kingdom could have fitted the vessel out in the same time and there were not a few who believed the task was too much even for his energies'. Toasts were drunk to 'Mr Brunel and Mr Scott Russell, the engineer and builder of the ship'. Russell replied 'regretting the absence of Mr Brunel, explaining his own share in the construction of the great ship and bearing high testimony to the share of his colleague as the originator of the great idea'.

In that report Russell had said no more than the truth, but it could not have pleased Isambard. He did not have colleagues in his great projects – he was in sole charge – and the fact that Russell had indeed been the designer and builder of the ship and had from January to September 1859 been in sole command of the works while he himself was abroad would only have made Isambard's jealousy the greater. Nowhere in his copious writings does he mention his debt to anyone in bringing to reality his conception of the 'Great Ship'.

No other details of Russell's speech were printed by *The Times*. Rolt does not quote anything from that brief report but asserts instead that Russell gave himself great credit for the ship in a long and very peculiarly worded speech which Rolt states was widely published in the press. *The Times*, traditionally hostile to Brunel, makes no mention of it.

On 20 August the Chairman of the Great Ship Company announced that the ship's engines 'worked well' and that 'it was expected that in a few days the ship would be handed over by Russell to the Company'. This was important in view of what happened later. The date of the maiden voyage, to Weymouth and Holyhead, was fixed for 3 September. Isambard was looking forward to sailing with her and had chosen his cabin. Pandemonium reigned as the deadline approached and innumerable small jobs had still to be completed – the decks to be caulked, kitchens to be fitted, cabins to be painted – as always in any ship's last-minute fitting-out.

On the 2nd the saloons were piled with bedding and furniture while smiths were still closing-up the last few rivets when Isambard came aboard to take his place for the voyage. He watched the final dock trial of the engines and had no complaints. At noon he was on deck posing before a funnel for the photographer: a little, bent figure, as thin and frail as a dry leaf, leaning on a stick. Seconds after the photograph was taken he collapsed from a heart attack, and was carried home, paralysed but still conscious. That was the last he saw of his 'Great Ship'.

29

Nemesis

Russell believed that, with Isambard's final inspection and approval, he had relinquished to the Company his responsibility for the hull and the paddle engines, and recommended to the Company a full set of officers and men to work the ship. The company refused his recommendation but they did take on to their payroll and therefore under their orders four engineers from Russell's staff.

Due to difficulties with the Board of Trade sailing was delayed until dawn on 7 September 1859 when with steam up the SS *Great Eastern* cast off her moorings and was towed down river for her trial trip. She was an unhappy ship. The Board of Directors of the owning Company were split into two warring camps, with Magnus, one of the Company's financiers, on one side, bitterly criticising the Chairman's handling of affairs and also Russell, while the Chairman swore that Magnus had made his life hell and that no one but Russell could have completed the ship in a mere six months. Her Engineer, Brunel, was fatally ill and more or less at loggerheads with Russell. Dickson was on board, as a passenger, but rode in the engine room to give advice to McLennan, though the men were rivals. This broken state of relationships was reflected in the lack of management method on board. The ship was under the command of her Captain, Harrison, and McLennan was in charge of the engines, but beyond that there was no clearly defined set of responsibilities for the ship's officers towards the equipment.

On the bridge Captain Harrison was guided by the River Pilot, Atkinson, with Russell alongside. The last was, technically, a passenger and ought not to have been on the bridge but he had been deeply concerned with the ship since its inception and was assisting Harrison by relaying the Captain's orders to the engineers in charge not only of the paddle-wheel engines which he had designed but also the James Watt & Co screw engines. As they were towed down river the leading tug swerved sharply to avoid sailing ships in mid-stream, causing the hawser to part. Had it not been for Russell's quick-witted and expert instructions to the engine room the great ship would have run aground.

She moored off Purfleet for the night and was serenaded with bands playing 'Rule, Britannia!' and 'See the Conquering Hero Comes'. Next day, 8 September, she sailed under her own steam for the Nore light where she dropped anchor at noon while her compass was adjusted. The following morning, her anchor was raised by eighty men, including Russell, a Director, and three noblemen.

One can only feel sad that Isambard was not there to help. On his sick-bed he was thinking of his ship continuously and on that morning he wrote to the GWR Directors asking that the workers in the Swindon factory be given free passes and a day off, with special trains, to go to Weymouth to see his ship. This was the last letter he ever wrote. Swindon works' oral tradition asserts that small pieces of machinery for the SS *Great Eastern* were manufactured there, including the ship's siren. Neither documentary evidence nor oral tradition exists to show that any men were given the day off.

The great ship made her way swiftly down Channel at 13 knots, through heavy seas and under grey, lowering skies. Towards 6 p.m. the cloud lifted, the seas abated and all the passengers in the Grand Saloon went on deck to enjoy the late summer twilight at sea, the coastal lights and a breath of air. A few minutes later, off Dungeness, they were terrified by an explosion from within the ship. The noise was described by witnesses as 'the mingled roar and crash of a battery of artillery and a line of musketry'; it was accompanied by a vast cloud of steam and smoke. The forward funnel shot up like a rocket 30 ft into the air, together with assorted bits of ironmongery and plumbing, and fell back on to the ship like shrapnel.

The confusion on deck took some time to die down, fed as it was by the sight of stokers rushing on to the deck, boiled alive, and jumping over the side in a demented attempt to escape their agony. When calm was restored it was discovered that the feed-water heater around the forward funnel had exploded, damaging the Grand

Saloon and causing the furnace of the forward boiler to blow back. Several stokers were injured by fire and scalding steam, and five were dead. Although noisily spectacular, the explosion had done only minor damage to the ship itself. The vessel was never in any danger and held its course for Weymouth where it arrived next day, 10 September.

Isambard's health had shown signs of improvement since his heart attack. Resting must have helped him, but it is unlikely that he was on the happy road to recovery, since during the time he lay at 18 Duke Street waiting to hear how his great ship had fared he spent the time getting his affairs in order and correcting the draft inventories of his beloved Watcombe property, which was to be sold. This suggests that he knew that the end was near and was preparing to sell-up in order to repay the bank the money borrowed for Watcombe.

Rolt has implied that the accident to the SS *Great Eastern* killed him, and that if he had not been told until he was stronger he would have been better able to cope with the disappointment. That, though, supposes that he was growing stronger. In fact his illness had been of many years' duration and was terminal. One shock more or less could not have affected the outcome. As it was, he lingered on for five days and on the afternoon of Thursday 15 September he called his family around him, called their names and spoke to them all. As the twilight deepened he grew weaker and at half past ten that night he died, peacefully and without pain.

Epilogue

Isambard was buried in Kensal Green Cemetery on 20 September 1859, in the presence of a large number of friends, relations and members of the engineering profession. The route to the cemetery was lined with thousands of railwaymen and others gathered to pay their last respects to a singular man. At a meeting in November, under the Presidency of the Earl of Shelbourne, it was decided to erect a monument to commemorate his achievements and to show the very high esteem in which these achievements and his memory were held by his friends and, indeed, by the nation.

The legend I.K. BRUNEL 1859 was placed over each arch of the Royal Albert Bridge, his greatest triumph, and in 1860 a group was formed within the Institution of Civil Engineers for the purpose of putting a suspension bridge across the Avon gorge at Clifton 'as a monument to their late friend and colleague Isambard Kingdom Brunel'. Curiously enough, those who had most actively opposed Brunel and the broad gauge – Mark Huish of the L&NWR, George Bidder and John Hawkshaw – were at the forefront of the movement. Hawkshaw was at that time engaged in the demolition of Isambard's Hungerford suspension footbridge to make way for a railway bridge into Charing Cross station, and was able to buy cheaply the scrap chains off that bridge for use at Clifton. But these were not strong enough to support the bridge as designed by Isambard so the roadway was narrowed by five feet. The suspension towers were reduced in height, made to taper inwards at the top and were built without the planned decorations. The bridge is a much-reduced version of Isambard's design, although the magnificent span and the siting is as he intended. It was opened with much ceremony on 8 December 1864, a very beautiful bridge and a fitting memorial to an extraordinary man.

Isambard's 'extensive ambitions' drove the railway from Paddington to Penzance, Milford Haven and Wolverhampton. His eye for the land and his daring genius as a bridge-builder are such that we stand in awe of the Maidenhead or Royal Albert bridges to this day. One could say dozens of his bridges, large and small, his viaducts and all his cuttings and embankments are in use, carrying trains at speeds even he did not anticipate – although one of his drivers, John Almond, did ask for permission, in May 1847, to drive from Paddington to Bristol in the hour. Without him the routes, with the possible exception of Newton Abbot to Plymouth, would not be capable of the high speeds they now permit.

His SS *Great Western* was the pioneer transatlantic liner, making regular fortnightly crossings between Bristol (and later Liverpool) and New York from April 1838 until December 1846 when she was displaced by larger vessels. His enormous concepts in the SS *Great Britain* and SS *Great Eastern* forced engine designers to the limits of knowledge to comply with his requirements, not only in engine design but also in the manufacture of tools to build these engines. He was the inventor of the cellular hull, a principle of the utmost importance to ship building.

He was indeed a great man, an exceptional man, though he did not, by himself, 'build the railway' but received vital assistance from untold thousands of other men – whose efforts he rarely if ever acknowledged. It is astonishing to think that his seemingly superhuman labours and the intense mental energy he focused came from an unhappy mind, a mind plagued with 'blue devils' and so supremely lacking in self-confidence that he believed he had to slave incessantly or be destroyed by the hobgoblin of 'idleness'. It was no accident that his private signet was a horseman's spur with a sharp, six-pointed rowel crowned with the motto *En Avant* – 'Get going'.

His perfect taste, his insistence on only the best workmanship, his obsession with his status and his frequent changes of mind and grievous mistakes cost his shareholders dear (their life savings very often) while he himself did not achieve great wealth and indeed paid for his dreams by his death at the early age of fifty-three. But he did not dream in vain. He took up his challenges as an honourable knight-errant should, he pursued his dragons with the utmost tenacity and executed them with reckless bravery. Never a man to allow his dreams to remain nebulous, Isambard Kingdom Brunel had the courage, tenacity and skill to translate his aspirations into the practical achievements which stand as his lasting memorial.

Further Reading

For full coverage of Brunel's life and works the following are, I suggest, required reading: *The Birth of the Great Western: Extracts from the Diary of George Henry Gibbs*, ed. Professor Jack Simmons (Adams & Dart). Gibbs was a Director of the GWR and Isambard's staunch supporter. His criticisms are therefore the more valuable. On Isambard's civil engineering I recommend the excellent *Works of Isambard Kingdom Brunel*, ed. Sir Alfred Pugsley (Institution of Civil Engineers, University of Bristol). On the subject of his marine engineering I would suggest *Brunel's 'Great Western'* by Dennis Griffiths (Patrick Stevens), Professor George Emmerson's *John Scott Russell* (John Murray), and *The SS 'Great Eastern'* (David & Charles). Also of great importance is *The History of the Great Western Railway*, Vol. 1, by E.T. McDermott, reprinted by Ian Allan. This is the GWR's official history and gives a great deal of evidence on Brunel and his work for various companies. As a balancing view to this, my book, on I.K. Brunel, L.T.C. Rolt's *Isambard Kingdom Brunel* is also required reading.

INDEX

Index